Oops Upside Your Head

The Life and Times of a Nightclub Manager in The Great Days of Disco

P.J. Shevlin

Copyright © 2017 P. J. Shevlin

All rights reserved, including the right to reproduce this book, or portions thereof in any form. No part of this text may be reproduced, transmitted, downloaded, decompiled, reverse engineered, or stored, in any form or introduced into any information storage and retrieval system, in any form or by any means, whether electronic or mechanical without the express written permission of the author.

The views expressed in this work are solely those of the author and do not necessarily reflect the views of the publisher, and the publisher hereby disclaims any responsibility for them.

ISBN: 978-0-244-94020-1

PublishNation
www.publishnation.co.uk

*For Jacqueline,
without whose patience, encouragement
and constant support,
this story would never have been told.*

Foreword

Well, what else could I have done?

Sure, I had aspirations to be a journalist or perhaps even to go into law. But there were no doors opening for me and I was far too easily dissuaded. Perhaps I should have persisted and God knows I have spent a lifetime condemning myself for not doing just that. Fate, however, has a habit of intervening and when that happens there's really no point in fighting it.

That's what happened to me. The advert for 'NIGHTCLUB MANAGERS WANTED' screamed at me from the pages of 'The Stage' and signalled the start of a non-stop roller coaster ride. There were some sublime highs and some truly gut-wrenching lows; but it wasn't too bad a hand to be dealt.

I found myself embarking upon a journey that saw me zig-zagging across the country in pursuit of what, I was never sure. A wise man once said; 'Happiness is not having what you want, it's wanting what you have'. I can truly say that was exactly the case for me except that it used to seem like a bar of soap that kept slipping from my grasp.

No matter though, for mine was being part of a way of life that represented fun and good times for an awful lot of people. It was a scene that provided sublime memories and wonderful soundtracks in life for the thousands who I knew as 'my' customers.

I was fortunate enough to meet many aspiring artistes along the way who went on to find fame and success and I remember fondly those who didn't quite make it in the same way.

Of course, the tales you will read of all happened a very, very long time ago. Whilst every word is based on actual events, the recollection of them is derived from a view back through the murky, foggy mists of time. A time which itself was distorted by a haze of smoke and alcohol often accompanied by the deafening soundtrack of that era. No doubt fellow travellers from that period will have totally different recollections and they are no less valid even if they are contradictory.

It all happened for me at a time of great awakening in the culture that was Britain's nightlife experience. I witnessed the decline of the mass market ballrooms and their resident bands and saw them being surpassed by the booming success of the discotheques which proved accessible to all and allowed people to embrace new music and dance scenes beyond that being dictated by the British pop charts.

Vinyl was the format you listened to your music on and that too looked like becoming a relic of the age until a new embrace for it in the 21st century.

Tastes change of course and the impact of modern technology has not nearly been harnessed well enough by the nightlife industry.

Many would argue that the relaxation of the licensing laws signalled the death knell for nightclubs as they started to lose the competition with pubs for late night drinkers and dancers. The pubs themselves are taking a hammering these days with many potential patrons choosing to source their drinks from supermarkets and stay at home listening to their downloaded music. Many of the owners of the old nightclubs have found it more prudent to just give up on the chase and allow developers to extract some value from their premises.

Who knows what it will all mean for the next generation? Maybe there will be the sort of revival which has seen Northern Soul flourish again in recent years. Once the most 'underground' of scenes, it has used the internet to spread the word and 'keep the faith' amongst both its old devotees and a whole new demographic which appreciates the integrity of appreciating the music and atmosphere in a communal setting the way it used to be.

Let's hope so anyhow. To live and work in clubland during the halcyon days of disco was something to be very grateful for. And I am.

Chapter 1

'Young Hearts Run Free'

'Get that down you boy!' said Chris Collins slamming down a flat pint of Stone's Bitter, 'cos it might be a while before you get another off me'.

I gave a rueful nod and started sipping my third pint of a keg bitter that can only be described as 'ordinary' at best. We found ourselves together for our very last session at 'The Observatory' public house in Hanley just across from Northwood Court, the residential tower block for students of The North Staffordshire Polytechnic. It was nearly three years on from the very first time I had enjoyed a pint with Chris in the very same pub. On that occasion we were all excited, albeit very apprehensive new students away from home for the first time. It hadn't taken us long to get into the social whirl with the Scousers, the Geordies, the Brummies and the Taffs. The stereotypes of which we had only encountered through watching The Comedians on TV or seeing the odd interview on Match of The Day. It was also our first encounter with 'public school' types, one's impression of which had largely been formed through reading Billy Bunter style comic strips or the Just William books of Richmal Crompton. 'What a wheeze!'.

In truth, the 'public schoolers' were far more apprehensive about us and the guys from the regions were equally fascinated by my 'Ketrin' drawl. I soon realised what a small, inconsequential town I hailed from when people constantly referred to the racecourse and the army barracks there.

'Nooooo, that's Catterick' I'd say, 'I'm from Kett-er-ing!'

That invariably drew blank looks made worse when they asked what Kettering was famous for.....err, they make Weetabix there', I'd quietly offer.

It was different with the locals though - the Stokies – they all knew Kettering. Of course, hadn't Kettering Town Football Club sold them the great John Ritchie?? Indeed they had, for all of £2,000 a decade earlier and now Mr Ritchie was back for his second spell at Stoke City which was great for me. I even had a connection with the great man having for five years played football every day in the playground with his brother Bob at Kettering Grammar School, and who, I assured them was actually a much better footballer.

    I did come to love Stoke, I loved the warmth of the people and I indulged myself in their ways, the local football and the 'Soul'. People choose their seats of learning for all sorts of reasons and surely the course should be the main one. Well the North Staffs Poly did offer a course I wanted to do, but the real catalyst for me ending up in the city was the magazine, Blues and Soul. Every fortnight, I had immersed myself in reading of the music coming out of Black America. Their columnist, Dave Godin, had a quite magical turn of phrase when analysing what amounted to 'soul', what it was, who was doing it and crucially where to find it. I had already been acquainted with local soul luminaries in and around Kettering and the scenes established in venues there like the North Park and The Tin Hat were as good as any I was ever to encounter. I wanted to be at the heartbeat though and Blues and Soul told me that was in Hose Street, Tunstall, Stoke-on-Trent; the home of The Golden Torch Allnighters! It was indeed SOUL-on-Trent!

    Now though, sitting here with Chris, things were totally different. We had just completed our last day at college and soon we would be homeward bound to face what? We had no idea. We had said our goodbyes to all knowing we were unlikely to cross paths with many of them again despite the best intentions and promises of all. Both of us had embarked on a law degree course and switched to business studies at the first opportunity. Why? Well how many barristers do you know of who can point to a polytechnic as their alma mater? We had all been shocked when the 110 students on the course were told at the start of our first term that the college only expected 10 to 20 to come out the other end! Why didn't they tell us that at the interviews? Our degree courses were actually 'external' degrees awarded by the University of London; no less valid for that but it meant that nigh on half the course had to be researched and self-taught by the students themselves. To this day I feel we were misled if not conned by the college who were intent on just getting the numbers on board and I know many who started with me took years to get over the sense of failure they were consumed with. That is apart from one bright spark who came to visit us in the second year. Immaculately groomed and driving a smart company car. He had landed a job in the buying department of C & A, the Dutch fashion retail chain, and had already earned a couple of promotions. Knowing how high the benchmark was for the C & A graduate entry scheme, I asked how on earth he had managed to get hired.

'I lied' he said. He might have found it more difficult these days but rarely if ever were job hunters asked to provide paper proof of their academic achievements back in the '70s and this chancer knew that when he claimed he had passed with an upper 2nd degree. Fair play to him for his chutzpah at least.

Neither Chris nor I had got anything lined up, though I'd planned to spend a summer working with my father building roads and bridges somewhere. The money was always very good and the craic would be fantastic. I knew too that the experience would stand me in good stead whatever Fate had in store for me. Journalism had been my original career goal but I had been too easily put off by a couple of rejections and I guess my esteem was just too low to persevere with it. Instead, I had set a course for retail management. I surely ticked all the boxes and figured I'd have the social skills at least to make a fist of it. Looking back, I obviously didn't set out to change the world. I just wanted to be settled in a structured career that promised respectability and reasonable rewards. How boring was I? I've spent the decades since then encouraging young people to just 'go for it'. It's better to have tried and failed than never to have tried at all. Unfortunately, back then, the 'safe' option seemed to be the way to go and whatever my instincts were, I thought that I had to be 'sensible'. However, Fate was to intervene to great effect.

The entry into retail management wasn't that easy either. It was the chosen career path for thousands of others as well it seemed. C & A, British Home Stores, Beatties, WH Smith and a few others all interviewed me before the best of the lot, Marks & Spencer, gave me the affirmative and sent me along to their Hanley store, where I would be working if the store manager approved of me. He didn't! It had seemed like a shoe-in, but the boss man declared he didn't fancy college boys in his store and wouldn't have one foisted upon him….and that was that, in and out in twenty minutes.

A letter then came through from International Stores, once one of the pillars of English retailing. In truth, I didn't fancy it one bit so I knew I would probably get it. So it was, that the day after passing my driving test, I borrowed my father's Ford Cortina Mk 1 and drove to

Birmingham to meet them. I remember being awed by the wondrous engineering feat that was Spaghetti Junction which I drove through on the way there.

I knew I had to take the job if offered but what future did it promise? I would learn to stack shelves and rotate stock no doubt and at the interview I was told that an added treat would be learning to bone pigs and become a master butcher! Being a graduate, I could expect to make rapid progress within the company and they'd be disappointed if I didn't have my own store within two years. The prospect didn't excite me one iota but at least I would be gainfully employed.

I was to start at their branch in Kettering and within a few weeks would be asked to attend their management college in Brentwood for a two-week residential course. The store in Kettering was a real eye-opener being something of a throwback to a bygone age. Not surprising really when many of their staff had worked there for several decades but they were all quite wonderful characters in their own way and made me feel very welcome. The store manager himself was in his late 60s, a gnarled, wiry, thin figure with heavily lined features who puffed Woodbines incessantly. He was full of surprises though, not least when he introduced me to his wife - who was just 23 years old - and their 6 week old baby! He revelled in the amazement my look betrayed saying I was going to love it here as there were perks to the job, nudge, nudge.

One soon presented itself to me. Amidst the Daphnes, Doreens and Dollys, there emerged one rather engaging young stunner who tagged onto me. I thought it was probably because she had found someone to talk to of a similar age. It all started when one of the Doreens asked if I could fetch some Jacobs Cream Crackers from the back store. Taking an age to find them, Doreen sent in the stunner to help me.

'Want a hand?' she asked, 'it'll cost you!'

Before I could quite comprehend what on earth she was inferring, she yanked my head forward to hers and locked me into a vice like snog with her.

'You don't mind, do you?' she asked.

'As long as we get the cream crackers' I answered.

Soon 'cream crackers' became the code for a sojourn out the back. It sure broke the monotony at least.

Kettering is a town where news travels fast and there are no hiding places. It was bad enough when friends would drop in and laugh at my stripy apron but it was simply excruciating when former teachers would shop there. 'Did you finish the course?' they'd ask as if to say was I really serving a Community Service Order! If I saw them coming, I'd turn to the stunner and plead for those cream crackers.

Respite came with the management training course and so I set off for Brentwood in my brand new car, LVH 639F, a turquoise Mk II Ford Cortina that my dad had bought for me for £100. Young, free and single….with wheels, nothing's going to stop me now.

In many ways that management course was the catalyst to my moving on sooner rather than later. There were about 15 or 16 of us on that course and we enjoyed the course and each other's company immensely. Nearly all were in the same position as me; new graduates who had been relieved to take the offer of employment from International Stores but by the end of the fortnight we all seemed to be of the same mindset that there had to be more to working life than being a small town grocer. There was no doubt that once indoctrinated, the company was capable of inspiring great loyalty and their conviction in developing fast track advancement for graduates was laudable and much appreciated by me. In fact, my short experience with them probably developed my self-esteem in more ways than anything I'd experienced in life up to that point. At last I had the belief that I was capable of much, much more and that I might as well make sure that there would be fun in my quest.

First though, I was obliged to make a move within International Stores. On completion of the course they promoted me to Assistant Manager and dispatched me to their Oakham store which was just 21 miles away. It meant a nice jaunt through some glorious countryside every day, a journey which allowed me to consider how I might escape from the drab routine which I feared would engulf me.

I was pinging off applications everywhere at this time and seriously considered I might have to take refuge in banking, teaching or even the civil service but calling into the Manor House Reading Rooms in Kettering, I found my escape route! It was contained in the situations vacant pages of 'The Stage', the weekly paper for the arts and entertainment industry.

'Graduates Wanted for Management Positions In The Entertainment Industry'.

'Perfect', I thought and knocked off a letter of inquiry to them immediately.

A week later, the letter landed on the doormat. From the top of the stairs, I could make out the green print and the famous gong logo of The Rank Organisation. My mother had never seen me move so fast that early in the morning but surely this was it! I wasn't disappointed; it was an invitation to meet Rank Leisure's Regional Director, Alan Goldman, at The Sundown Discotheque in Charing Cross Road, London. It was hard to concentrate on the pig boning and bacon slicing that day because next week I was going to be heading for London and The West End!

Just the journey was an adventure in itself. I dressed in an immaculate, white button-down Ben Sherman shirt set off with a sober brown knitted tie which I always thought the epitome of coolness. I wore my new brown tweed suit (remember it was the 70s, everything was brown then) and the ensemble was set off with my heavy, shiny, but far too tight, brown Oxford brogue shoes. At least I didn't wear platform soles but photographs exist to show I was guilty of that fashion faux-pas too. I also carried a regulation briefcase which only contained a copy of The Daily Mirror.

It was a boiling hot day as I set off on the train to St. Pancras Station and I was bathed in beads of sweat by the time we reached Wellingborough. That tweed suit suddenly didn't seem such a good idea. I'd only been to London a couple of times before that and I still found the underground system a fascinating novelty, but I imagined myself as a young guy going places who would soon become very relaxed in The Big City. It crossed my mind that if I messed up, I would still be slicing bacon in Oakham for the foreseeable future, but it was but a fleeting thought because I was quite sure I had a date with destiny.

Back in the 70s, if you needed to research a company you really did have to put the legwork in and I made sure I would be as prepared as it was possible to be. Rank Leisure were the giants of the entertainment industry at the time with only Mecca giving them a run for their money. They dominated cinema theatres with their Odeon chain, they had scores of bingo halls and bowling alleys and they had their nightclub division which was the focus of my attention. Up and down the country in every large town were the famous Top Rank Suites, multi-purpose entertainment venues which would stage concerts, dinner dances, exhibitions, conferences, discos etc. In recent years they had been building up their smaller nightclub operations which were cheaper to run but generated far more revenue. Bring it on...I couldn't wait.

Mr Goldman was a very, pleasant, affable gentleman; sharp suited and precise with an easy, quite charismatic presence. He had been given a brief to oversee the development of a large part of Rank's estate. They were obviously growing at a rate of knots and at the time were converting many of their large single screen cinemas to discotheque operations. They needed able personnel to undergo fast track training quickly and they needed them to be prepared to move to wherever in the country the company needed them. It was a pretty straightforward interview really, he read my CV, such as it was, and I found myself nodding 'yes' to every question.

Mr Goldman then leaned over, shook my hand and said he'd like to offer me a position. Could I therefore attend a 6 week training course in Brighton? You bet I could!!!! I was quite ecstatic as I climbed up the steps from The Sundown and turned into Tottenham Court Road. 'Oh, glory be', I thought. I couldn't wait to tell my folks. Before heading back to St. Pancras, I stopped off at Westminster Cathedral to offer a little prayer of thanksgiving, a practise I still try to repeat whenever I pass that place.

Chapter 2

'Play That Funky Music'

It was strange working out my notice with International Stores. My colleagues there weren't surprised that I should leave but they were amazed at the nature of the job I'd taken and the fact that I had no idea where I was going to be living in a couple of months time. In the 70s young people were still not particularly socially mobile. The instinct for most of my contemporaries was to seek a job close to home where the family and friends network was strong and support was always readily available. There was a lot to be said for that but somehow when I catch up with former schoolfriends, I wonder if some of them feel a tinge of regret for having never wandered far from home. Many of them took on board exactly what some of our teachers had recommended and duly took up positions in banks, building societies and the Civil Service….and have stayed there for their entire working lives.

As I worked out the four weeks' notice, I did occasionally wonder if I would be able to fend for myself. Cooking, washing etc., I really hadn't got a Scooby doo but figured there were always Pot Noodles and launderettes to fall back on and I'd somehow managed to remain intact after three years at college. There was no doubt I was stepping into a great unknown. Brighton was to be my home for the next six weeks and after that I was obliged to go wherever The Rank Organisation chose to send me.

I arrived in Brighton at the start of the summer of 1976, a summer which was to go down as one of the hottest of the century and one in which rivers and reservoirs were to run dry. Every day for six weeks though, I, along with half a dozen more aspirants, was cooped up in a classroom learning everything that one needed to know about being a nightclub manager. We learned the value of public relations and promotion, the need for controlling food and liquor stocks, how to deal with the great British public whatever their state of sobriety and how to manage staff……before they managed you.

Our tutor for the six weeks was Colin Fox who epitomised just what an 'old school' entertainments manager really was like. There was not a scenario which Mr Fox had not previously encountered at some stage in his long and seemingly illustrious career. The course was based in Brighton's Top Rank Suite, a vacuous 2,000 capacity venue which morphed into a different guise every night. A ballroom dancing venue one night, a concert arena the next. Banqueting events for up to 600 patrons would be held regularly through the winter season and at the end of the night one may have to prepare for a trades exhibition, a darts tournament or a roller skating disco the next day. I loved it all because it offered sheer excitement and challenge. You knew if you could crack this, you could crack anything. It could be extremely hard work and as I was to find out on numerous occasions, one's personal safety was certainly at risk. But it was usually a lot of fun and a highly sociable way to earn a living especially once I learned that one item of clothing completely changed how people perceived you and how you perceived yourself. It was a symbol of authority to some and best of all; it was evidently the ultimate aphrodisiac for many female patrons. Oh, the power of the dicky bow!

I absorbed it all willingly despite the long, long nights and the interminable problems being presented by staff and customers alike. Brighton too, was just a cracking place to be. To have even have heard of a homosexual man in Kettering, Stoke or Oakham was a talking point in itself. In Brighton, it didn't warrant comment. There were thousands of gay people in this town and it was just no big deal. I loved the tolerance and acceptance of minorities I found in the town and wondered how long it would take for the rest of the country to 'catch up', if indeed it ever would.

Compared to where else I had lived up to this point in time, I found that Brighton was a town that never slept. The 24-hour economy is a more common feature in many British towns and cities now but it was very much the exception in the Britain of the 1970s. Working until after 3am was the norm but many club workers, taxi drivers and a whole menagerie of various waifs and strays deemed it necessary to make their way to establishments such as the wonderful Market Diner in Circus Street to down one of their famous Gutbuster breakfasts before going home to retire. Surely fried eggs, bacon, sausage, tomatoes, chips, black pudding, mushrooms, beans and fried bread can't be good for you at 4.00am in the morning, but in those six weeks it began to become a staple feature of my diet.

The sea too was quite a novelty for me but on my first visit to it, I was quite startled to find there was no sand on Brighton beach, just pebbles which of course were baking hot to stand upon.

I often used to reflect on the risqué nature of the place which seemed to appeal as much to the Prince Regent a couple of hundred years previously as it did to so many still enjoying 'dirty weekender' trysts. I often wondered why the latter didn't choose somewhere far more anonymous like Bexhill or Littlehampton….but then again??

Time flies when you're enjoying it and the six week induction finally ended with The Day of Reckoning. Would we all be retained by the company and if so, where were we to be dispatched?

I'm not sure what logic was applied in determining our destinations but I was slightly surprised to be sent to the extreme backwater of Plymouth. 'So be it', I thought. I knew the city had a certain history which I would find fascinating and second division football with Plymouth Argyle would surely be a consolation.

My first thought on arriving in Plymouth was that it really was a long way from anywhere. The second realisation was that, to my ears at least, the people spoke a completely different language! It didn't take too long though to tune into the West Country burr of the locals with all its strange and unexpected inflections. My home for the next few weeks was to be The Deva Guest House which was very near to the site of Sir Francis Drake's bowling activities on Plymouth Hoe. The Deva was run by Harry Pook who happened to be the resident bandleader at Plymouth Top Rank Suite to where I was bound the following morning.

The Top Rank Suite was sited at the start of Plymouth's, then infamous, Union Street which stretched from the edge of the city centre right down to the city's famous naval base and docks area in Devonport. It had at one point been a grand boulevard housing the officer set and middle classes but it had degenerated in time to house the city's red light district amidst a virtual cesspit of seedy nightclubs, bars and fast food joints. Bombing raids in the Second World War had left a legacy of derelict waste sites so Union Street was akin to a mouthful of rotten teeth with a host of glaring gaps.

Yet one, if minded, could look beyond the dismal facades and get a glimpse of the street's former glories. There were some real architectural gems and I marvelled at the spectacular Victorian elegance of The Palace Theatre with its wonderful mosaic commemorating the Spanish Armada's foray into Plymouth Sound. In its heyday, the theatre had been a stage for Lilly Langtry, Gertie Gitana, Charlie Chaplin, Harry Houdini and everyone who was anyone it seems. By the time I came across it, it housed only ghosts although there was a brief renaissance for it during my time in Plymouth. Three decades later, I was to visit the now derelict property with a friend from Brighton and encouraged him to take a punt on the place. He succeeded in re-establishing it as The Dance Academy and it became one of the UK's hottest dance clubs for a period.

The locals often referred to the Top Rank Suite as 'The Magic Stick' as it had been known during its former incarnation as The Majestic Ballroom. It was an establishment that many were obviously endeared to as they recalled its former grandeur, the marvellous sprung dancefloor and the excellent dance bands that once resided there. By the 1970s, times had changed and The Top Rank had become all things to all people. The resident band remained but there was little call for strict tempo ballroom dancing and now they were forced to deliver their versions of current pop hits. 'Disco' was the name of the game now and it used to be quite galling to see the crowd visibly groan as the DJ handed over to Harry Pook and his reluctant, ageing ensemble who would struggle to 'entertain' the punters with their soulless versions of 'The Best Disco In Town' – hardly – and other top pop chart hits of the day!

I made sure I reported in good time for my first day at Plymouth Top Rank Suite. On entering the building, I inhaled my first whiffs of the distinctive furniture polish and carpet shampoo used throughout the Rank estate. It was an aroma designed to smother the scent of tobacco, spilled alcohol and occasional dollops of vomit; but its effectiveness was limited. Brenda, the secretary, was on hand to welcome me and immediately put the kettle on. Brenda was to prove to be a rock for me, the whole operation seemed to revolve around the woman, who, with her fiery red hair and steadfast manner, reminded me of the indomitable Barbara Castle. Barbara who?, some readers may ask....well she was the firebrand in Harold Wilson's Labour Governments of the 1960s and early 70s who introduced the breathalyser test and paved the way for equal pay for women. Brenda in the office was no meek subordinate to male dominance either but she was deserving of respect and I made sure she was always aware of my appreciation.

Whilst we awaited the arrival of the General Manager, Brenda took me on a quick reconnaissance trip of the venue and introduced me to the few full-time members of staff, who, she told me, I needed to be able to rely upon. It didn't take me too long to realise the wisdom of her words.

The venue consisted of a large ballroom with two large bars at either end of the room. A large stage, capable of accommodating a 20-piece orchestra was sited centrally and in front of it was an excellent, sprung maple dancefloor which was rarely appreciated by the revellers who lurched over it during the disco sessions.

This room could accommodate 1,000 patrons and above it was the Disco One 5-0, which could hold, yes, 150 patrons. It was rarely used, just the odd wedding function I was told, but I figured I could do something with it.

There was a full time cellarman who didn't seem too chatty and a Welsh engineer who was the complete opposite. Bill the handyman emerged to greet me from his puggyhole under the stairs where he seemed to be permanently resident; alighting only to change the odd lightbulb or unblock a toilet.

Eventually, the GM arrived. Denis was his name and though I've rarely met a man less suited to the job he held, I was pleased to find a very personable character who would prove a pleasure to work with. He looked so familiar but it was clear our paths could not have crossed; yet there was something about him which kind of haunted me.

Denis quickly made it clear to me he was unhappy in his role. He didn't like Plymouth, he didn't like nightlife, he didn't like handling staff, he clearly did not get on with his boss, the regional director, and his wife would have preferred him sweeping roads rather than continue with this job. I felt very sorry for the guy but said I would do all I could to lighten his load in any way I could. In a very short space of time it was clear that Denis saw me as something of a salvation for him. After only a couple of weeks he took me aside and asked if I'd work the nights and he'd handle everything by day….I could stay in bed all day if I wanted to!

The arrangement was great for both of us. I assumed a position of 'responsibility' very quickly whilst Denis was content to take on the admin burdens knowing that he could enjoy his home life without fear of getting the occasional physical battering at work every now and then. Unfortunately, I was soon to find that fear was not without foundation. The threat to one's physical wellbeing was very real in this job...and the magic dicky bow had a far different effect for the tanked up low life who got their kicks out of putting the boot in as long as they were part of a sufficiently large enough mob.

The club's door staff soon put me right on what to expect but looking at them I wondered what sort of protection I could expect from them. Strategy and psychology were the answers and the ability to think quickly and laterally on one's feet.

Two of the guys were well in their 60s and dockers by day, but they should have been writing self-help manuals. The first Saturday night I stood on that front door in Union Street, I was positively 'bricking it'- you know what I mean - and nervous to the point that my bodily functions may have operated quite involuntarily. Controlling entry to the venue meant having to carefully filter a constant flow of people, instantly applying value judgments as to their worthiness of entering the venue. Very tricky, but the dockers had elevated the process to a fine art.

The smart minority were whisked inside in an instant whilst others took some deeper analysis. The criteria was to assess their age, standard of dress, state of sobriety and their apparent associates. The last of these was always the most difficult as groups of guys would split up beforehand to try to secure entry by coming in either individually or coercing a young lady to let them pretend they were their boyfriend or brother. Once inside their glee would be unbridled if they had all managed to get in; but often we had sussed their presence and would deliberately let one or two in before stopping the rest. It was a slightly sadistic ruse on our part to see the frustration this often caused and if we weren't careful it could sometimes escalate into something troublesome if they reacted. More often than not though, the right balance was achieved and it was always very good for the morale of the door staff as they worked well as a team to achieve the desired balance.

Something as simple as asking someone their age often sparked accidental mirth. The first time someone was turned away on account of their age, they would generally just accept it but after that they needed to have a plan if they were to enter Fortress Top Rank. This often involved borrowing someone else's ID or driving license and committing the detail to memory. Easy surely, but it never was. You'd notice the apprehension etched on their faces as they approached the entrance and then that sudden intake of breath as they hoped to escape interrogation. Sometimes we'd even let them get past us, before asking if they had proof of age. The said documents would then be produced and checked to see if the birth date tallied with the age they quoted – often it didn't as people would be too flummoxed to make that simple calculation...but the killer question which usually tripped them up was 'What's your star sign?' Everyone knows their own star sign but rarely do they know those in the rest of the calendar.

Sometimes, if our guys were feeling particularly sadistic, they might admit a good looking young girl in without any questions whilst turning away her boyfriend. That was often a bit much for me and I'd have to remind the guys that we did actually need as many people as possible to be allowed entrance. In the long term though, it does pay to have a very strict door policy for the good, both of the venue itself and the rest of the patrons. Time and again I was to find that a lax door policy might return short term gain but it meant trouble was inevitable and your worthwhile punters just do not want to know once a poor reputation has been established.

Alongside the two dockers there was a very motley crew making up the rest of the 'bouncer' personnel. A butcher from Totnes proved very handy in scrapes but he found the job was just perfect for meeting young ladies and getting to know them, and he sure got to know an awful lot of them. We also made sure we had several off duty Royal Marines working for us too. Besides being especially well equipped to deal with most troublesome elements we encountered, these lads proved particularly effective when dealing with the huge numbers of navy personnel roaming the strip. Confronting a squad of matelots shortly after they'd disembarked can be quite daunting when you knew they were intent on 'going on the lash' in a serious way. A matelot who got into trouble whilst ashore could expect to be severely reprimanded and punished back on ship if caught, so we used to exercise the most effective deterrent of all. We merely asked them to surrender their identity cards on entry to the club and pick them up at the end of the night. If they were involved in any incident the cards were withheld and returned to their ship's command. Simple really!

Trouble though, always occurs when least expected and is often instigated by the most innocuous looking characters. It became my observation too over many years that one had to be particularly alert during September and in periods when a full moon came into view. I was in full agreement with the ancient philosopher, Aristotle, who asserted that the full moon instigated acts of insanity in certain susceptible individuals during nights which would otherwise have been dark. They would become 'lunatics' and of course alcohol fuelled their power and helped them to abandon their inhibitions. Whilst an individual flaring up in a rage was usually instantly suppressed by the team, I soon found that one person was capable of inflicting considerable damage if given sufficient time and space. One September evening though, we encountered a guy who was well in control of himself but was still intent on inflicting considerable malicious and physical damage.

It had been a very quiet evening with no incidents of note bar a few people who had been turned away on account of being under age or not complying with dress standards – always a very arbitrary test. As the evening wore on, the door supervisor allowed a couple of the guys to go home early because it was so quiet. Across the road one guy was watching the movement of staff and decided to put his plan into action. It seems we had turned him away earlier but there was no scene or threats of retribution as was so often the case.

In an age without mobile phones or the like, he managed to assemble a small team of cohorts who one by one succeeded in slipping into the premises. They spread themselves to every corner of the vast room and one amongst them created a diversion calculated to get all our team (which now numbered only three plus me) into the same area. Suddenly the sound of broken glass was heard at the far end of the room where one individual was seen to be recklessly sweeping glasses off tables and lobbing them everywhere. The DJ was soon alerted and immediately reached for the 'trouble record'. On hearing the opening riffs of Apricot Brandy's 'Rhinoceros', our door staff immediately sprang into action and taking their steer from the DJ headed to the lone 'lunatic' who was disturbing the peace.

The object of their mission ran towards a rear exit so drawing the team into a confined area where the rest of his associates were assembled and armed with chairlegs, heavy glass ashtrays etc., we soon found ourselves on the wrong end of a real pasting. It was to get worse though as another dozen or so of the gang were able to storm in having seen the door staff abandon their post on the front door. They just proceeded to let rip by smashing glasses and thumping innocent bystanders in other areas of the building.

The cashier, who had been left alone near the entrance, had the presence to lock herself in the ticket office and call the police. They soon arrived but on seeing what confronted them decided that an incident on private property was beyond their remit and promptly retreated! I've always thought their actions a dreadful dereliction of duty when the safety of so many members of the public and our staff were in real danger but I knew that post-mortem would have to take place another day.

Eventually with the house lights on and the arrival of bouncers from other clubs nearby the troublemakers dissipated and we were left to contemplate the injuries sustained and the considerable destruction that had resulted. We had been humiliated and were fortunate that really serious injury had been avoided. Yet, somehow the night proved to be a catalyst in establishing a wonderful team spirit down there.

After checking the wellbeing of all concerned I decided to clear the building of the remaining members of the public and to arrange a drink for the staff, all of whom were pretty shell-shocked by the experience.

We knew that news of the incident would spread like wildfire and we could expect both our business to be hit hard and our attackers to strike again. At the time, we knew that we couldn't expect part time staff to put themselves in the line of such danger and a few of them quite understandably did quit. I felt like it myself, but by the end of that terrible evening there was a real resolve that we would take control of this situation and come out stronger for it.

The next morning Denis was horrified when he found out about the previous night's events and seemed guilty for not having been there but I didn't mind, we just needed to form a strategy...and quickly. We resolved not to tell Head Office, if we did it would mean unwelcome scrutiny. Plymouth often felt so far away from the rest of civilization to me but on occasions like this, that could be a good thing. There was no point in talking to the police either. To do so might have led to problems when the renewal of our license was due and we knew that we couldn't count on their support anyhow. All incidents logged with the police were likely to be picked up by the local press. Rumours would become facts once in print and the power of the local press's printed word was considerable in those days. We always craved publicity from them...but not of that nature.

During the course of that day, rumours were rife throughout the city and many were being picked up by our own part time staff in their neighbourhoods and in their workplaces. We established that the attack was the work of 'The Swilly Mob', a notorious element from the part of the city they derived their name from. The ringleader we learned was a guy going by the moniker of 'Pretty Pete' and we learned that they planned a further attack on the same night a week later but with a considerably bigger army in attendance.

So, without engaging a new team of bouncers and without the police to help us, how were we going to repel a further attack when dozens more were lining up to take a pop at us? The answer lay in coming up with a strategy which was to become something of a template for other nightclubs in urban areas across the country.

Plymouth's nightlife was essentially concentrated in the Union Street area and all the other bars and clubs faced the same threats as well as the taxi drivers and fast food joints; the latter concerns being particularly vulnerable.

We quickly linked up with all the other venues to exchange the intelligence we had gathered and to find out if this gang and 'Pretty Pete' were known to their personnel. They may have acted like London gangsters such as the Krays, but Plymouth was too small a town to hide in anonymously and we were confident of identifying many of the likely protagonists.

The bars and clubs all agreed that should a major incident 'kick off' then we would all go into lockdown mode in our own venues whilst security resources were channelled to where the major incident was. Taxi drivers too and the burger boys would also wade in as best they could. Our strength would be in our unity and by the time our plans were in place there was a feeling of 'bring it on'.

Our Marines had not been on duty that night and they resolved to 'make up for this' in every way possible. The military establishment did not generally approve of their personnel working on the doors of nightclubs but in practise it suited the Military Police who patrolled Union Street because they helped to keep the lid on high spirits amongst the naval ratings. The young ratings too were especially vulnerable to attacks by local yobs when they found themselves detached from their mates. The MPs were quietly advised of our Swilly problem and made it clear they too would be on hand.

All we could do now was to wait to see what transpired but we really did feel that we were as ready as we could be when The Big Night finally came around. At the start of the evening, I assembled all the staff for the usual Staff Parade but I didn't quibble about the state of their uniforms that evening. I warned them of the possibility of trouble that night and advised what was expected of them should there be any re-occurrence. As soon as they became aware of an incident, the bar shutters were to be brought down and the bar staff and glass collectors were to retreat to the kitchens. The DJ was not to play his trouble record that night – its effect had now become counterproductive by alerting troublemakers as well as our personnel. The door staff were deployed strategically around the building but others had been drafted in in plain clothes.

The front door was not to be abandoned at any stage although we expected to go into lockdown mode again should trouble erupt. In such event the punters would be evacuated from the building through side exits.

The cashier would be our link to our external forces and she was on standby to connect to the nearest venues to release their personnel before a chain reaction brought the rest along.

Surely, I thought The Swilly Mob would have got wind of our preparations and would come calling on another day when our guard might be lowered? It seemed though that they had been so buoyed up by their success the previous week that they were just determined to finish the job. We hadn't been open long before we noticed small groups gathering outside the neighbouring Two Trees pub. They were ostensibly independent of each other but frequent exchanges were seen between the groups. Others would saunter by before returning from whence they came and a few were even brazen enough to taunt us directly.

I had made a point of just positioning two of the lads on the front door, the two elderly dockers in fact who seemed to be positively enjoying the banter and anticipating what may lie ahead.

I noticed Fred (No 1 docker) greet a very smart couple upon entry before turning and winking to me. Perhaps I was a little slow on the uptake again but then I realised he was drawing my attention to Pretty Pete himself. He was certainly an imposing figure alright. Extremely well built and with a smart, charismatic presence not unlike the character played by Sting in Quadrophenia; indeed, that is how he probably saw himself. I was amazed that he had brought along a lady and figured that perhaps violence may not have been on his agenda tonight. However, on following him into the main dance area, he and the lady went their separate ways. I advised Fred and pointed out Pretty Pete to the lads inside.

From our vantage point on the front door we could see more groups of young men congregating at The Two Trees. Many of them seemed to be looking over to us, perhaps they were assessing our state of readiness or maybe it was just my paranoia. There was no doubting the apprehension that I and my charges were feeling but we were actually well fired up and almost willing anyone who was up for it to come and do their worst.

The number of punters arriving that night was surprisingly well up on our normal attendance and they all seemed to be arriving in waves. We tried to apply the normal processing drill and stuck to our routine diligently but we were well aware that some of our adversaries were already inside and mingling with the crowd. I decided to take a quick recce inside to gauge the atmosphere and the state of readiness of all our staff; they all seemed to be on a high state of alert and all of them had Pretty Pete in their sights. He stood quite alone seemingly lost in the general atmosphere and casually inspecting the talent on show that night. No one seemed to approach him and outwardly at least he showed no signs of being part of a network of conspiracy.

Returning to the front door, I noticed the numbers congregating outside The Two Trees had multiplied considerably. If they were all linked to The Swilly Mob then there was a danger that we could be overwhelmed by their sheer force of numbers if they were to deploy the same kind of pincer manoeuvre they had practised the week before. Just then a small convoy of Military Police vehicles trundled down Union Street and parked a few yards down the road, just behind the taxi rank where a dozen or so drivers were gathered smoking and chatting. On the other side of the road, I could see the doormen from The Roxy standing at their entrance exchanging banter with their opposite numbers from Boobs Disco. One of the Boobs' crew caught sight of me and gave me a wink before jerking his thumb behind him. I was delighted to see the formidable figure of 'Tiny' loom into view, all 7 foot of him. A real man mountain in every respect, he was just like the wrestler, Giant Haystacks, who used to appear on ITV's wrestling programme every Saturday afternoon in those days. Tiny bounced at the strip club at the far end of the Union Street drag near The Palace Theatre. They just *never* had trouble there. I was delighted to see him and was confident then that we had sufficient manpower and muscle power to confront anything that lay ahead.

It was coming up to midnight and the dockers and I were beginning to wonder if the night would actually pass off peacefully. Inside the ballroom, the atmosphere was quite welcoming. DJ, Jon B, was in the groove but I thought I must tell him to stop playing that rotten Euro Disco trash he persisted with. It grated on me like chalk on a greasy blackboard, the man had no soul! Unfortunately, the punters seemed to love it. 'Funky Town' was the big tune of the day and it seemed to get constantly played. As if to just annoy me, Jon B nodded down to me, gave a wicked grin then played the damn thing yet again. It was an attack on my senses and ordinarily I would have bolted to the office to get away from it but amidst the cacophony of tuneless, female shrieking vocals there was another high-pitched sound effect followed by screams which were definitely not on that record.

At the far end of the room it had finally kicked off. Two morons were brazenly smashing glasses causing pandemonium all around them. The bouncers stood stock still as I had instructed them. Seconds later, more glasses were smashed on the opposite side of the dancefloor where three dickheads were goading the door staff who they assumed were too scared. In the middle of the room, perched at the edge of the dancefloor, stood Pretty Pete; still looking as innocent as Mother Teresa. I gave the nod and our plain clothes attendants smothered him in seconds. He had no time to react and the guys ran him backwards through the room to a rear fire exit using his head on the bars of the fire doors to blast the exit open.

The glass smashers instantly gave chase to assist their leader and we soon had them where we wanted. With our bouncers now coming up behind them, they were corralled in an exit passage well away from the general public and out of sight of any auxiliaries they might have had in the audience.

Word had got to the front door where the dockers had gone into lockdown mode. This alerted the Two Trees posse which now numbered perhaps 50 or 60 or so and they started to storm our front door. It was then the cavalry arrived…..a dozen Military Police alighted from their vehicles and ambled across the door swinging their truncheons almost nonchalantly. A whole platoon of dicky-bowed reserves arrived simultaneously from the other clubs....though I think Tiny on his own would have sufficed. There may have been one or two heads cracked at that stage but having effectively outflanked the mob, a dawning reality soon spread amongst them that there was to be no fun for them on this occasion. They gradually dissolved, some back into The Two Trees but more took advantage of the taxis perhaps unaware that their drivers had been on standby to take action against them moments earlier.

Back inside the club the music was still throbbing away, even if Jon B's choices had not improved. The knot of glass throwers, numbering a dozen or so, was still corralled in the rear passage whilst we wondered what to do with them. Yards away, their hitherto leader stood cowering wondering if the bouncers might inflict the sort of gratuitous violence on him that he had been so happy to order upon others. When one of the door staff called me 'boss', it encouraged one of the knot in an act of bravado perhaps, to run at me lashing out with his fists. I had little time to react but found myself acting instinctively when I tightened my neck and launched a head butt on him which happened to land sweetly and send him flying. It probably hurt me as much as him for I'm no fighting man. I was mildly shocked by what I had achieved. My bouncers were well impressed though, so I guess it earned me some kudos at least.

The mood afterwards was quite euphoric, everything had worked perfectly and I felt like Napoleon! Not only had a dangerous and troublesome issue been resolved but measures were in place to act in collaboration to tackle serious violence on the strip and it was soon evident that the public began to see The Top Rank as a safe, secure and respectable place to come for a night out.

The next few months proved to be some of the most rewarding times I ever had in the nightclub world as Denis and I discussed how we might develop the business at a venue which in truth, had been on its knees for a considerable time.

During the course of developing plans, Denis began to open up about his own background and eventually made the startling revelation which explained why I felt I had known him from the start. Denis's wife had been a model and one day when picking her up from a photo-shoot he was asked if he could help with a campaign that her advertising agency were proposing to pitch to The Health Education Council. Denis readily agreed and found himself posing for a few shots.

Just as the session was coming to an end they asked him to put on his pullover and stick a cushion under it. It seemed a joke and it was, but the image captured was to make a nation laugh. The shot was used to launch the unforgettable Pregnant Man campaign in 1969. It became an advertising classic and its message really hit home.

Looking at the diary ahead I noticed that we had a dinner dance booked into the venue in a couple of weeks' time. Given that the existing schedule was for three disco sessions a week and an 'Over 25's Night (aka the 'grab a granny' night), I wondered just how we would handle such a night. Denis warned me that such a night was bound to prove very stressful but, if done right they would be the most satisfying of all. He explained the format of these occasions, how the food was ordered, how the catering staff was requisitioned, the role of the band and the DJ and the instructions for the house engineer. All in all, a very precise operation but if everyone carried out their role correctly, there was no reason why we couldn't have a very successful night and in terms of revenue these private functions were the saviour of the business.

Denis though, made it clear that the key man in all this was undoubtedly the Head Chef and he tasked me with liaising with him the next morning. That was fine by me but I asked how I could contact this gentleman. Denis told me that Brenda, our secretary, would give me all his details, but I must have failed to see Denis smirking!

When I asked Brenda the next morning for Chef's details, a smile broke across her face as she revealed;

'The Head Chef is Bill'.

'What?' I spluttered, 'Bill the handyman?'

I couldn't believe that our beloved handyman dwelling below the stairs in his dirty, oily overalls was the man entrusted to deliver a sumptuous banquet to 350 of the great and the good members of The Plymouth Round Table. But like a butterfly's metamorphosis from the caterpillar, Bill arrived on the day in immaculate chef's whites. Truly, seeing was believing, but the man who took all day to replace a toilet seat was quite comfortable in marshalling a kitchen crew to produce a splendid banquet with Baked Alaska proving to be his signature dish.

Soon after the Regional Director descended upon us for an unannounced site visit. A big, ignorant bellicose figure in all honesty, he obviously enjoyed the power of his authority. I'm sure he had ability but he disguised it with his bullying nature and his treatment of Denis was appalling and quite unnecessary. On that first visit, much of his behaviour seemed designed to make some sort of impression upon me, but bullies have never impressed me. By way of introduction he grunted at us at all before running his finger along a dado rail and showing us all the dust that had gathered upon it. He had different standards for himself of course because he never bothered washing that finger before scoffing the cake put out for him.

For the rest of the day he ploughed through paper returns demeaning Denis for the poor performance of the venue which was compounded by poor stock returns, poor wage control, poor standards of the premises etc.

Poor Denis. I'm not exactly sure how things came to a head but shortly afterwards Denis announced he was leaving to work for a local authority's leisure services somewhere in East Anglia. I was so pleased for him, for judging by his relief it was clear that he could now resume his life in a relatively civilised environment compared to the hell hole that Plymouth had become for him.

The next incumbent in the General Manager's role was a rather pompous character called Ralph who I thought would find the whole Union Street environment totally alien to him. He did indeed, but Ralph was no shrinking violet and though he gave the impression that he had landed amidst an alien culture, he soon displayed the kind of mettle needed to get results in this place and to ensure that he himself would be propelled up the greasy promotion pole within The Rank Organisation.

Many of the staff were pretty cynical at the outset but he was a systems man and if he had a system that worked, then it would be deployed to great effect. I had a lot of respect for Ralph's drive and his determination to master and improve every aspect of the operation. He wasn't afraid to get his hands dirty and whether that involved lugging kegs around or helping to turf drunken matelots out; he was never found wanting. He was a firm believer in setting an example and if necessary making an example. That became necessary when we became aware of stock shortages on the bar and came to the conclusion that a fairly efficient scam was being perpetrated against us.

Ralph became so incensed that he took it as a personal affront against himself. The scale of the shortages became so large that we felt it necessary to get the police involved but we had nothing to go on, nor were there any likely suspects in mind. As the shortages only came to light in the wake of our weekly stocktakes, we didn't know whether we were being ripped off by staff, thieves or dodgy draymen!

The bars were arranged in such a manner that it was well-nigh impossible to conduct observations on them ourselves although we regularly crashed the tills in an attempt to foil attempts at under-ringing which was a favoured technique of the practised scammers. We engaged the police on an 'unofficial' arrangement. Fred Taylor, our catering manager, was an ex-cop himself and still kept in touch with many of his old colleagues. We figured if we could get them to do the observing, we could at least have the staff monitored unknowingly. We marked a dozen £5 notes for the use of the cops but only expected them to fund a few drinks for the boys in blue at our expense. To our utter surprise, the villain was identified within minutes. The method used was one of the simplest – and most effective – I have ever come across. When the thief's identity was revealed, it came as a massive shock to staff and management alike.

A couple of months previously we had taken on a character who wandered in looking for a part time evening job with us. Outwardly, he cut a very unlikely figure being grossly obese and wearing clothes that hadn't been trendy 30 years earlier. Nevertheless, he convinced Fred that he was up to the job and when he added that he was a carer for a wife who depended upon an iron lung for survival, well Fred thought he deserved a break. Charlie, as he was known, certainly threw himself wholeheartedly into the role. He had a great sense of fun and quickly connected with the rest of the staff who found him great company. They also had great sympathy for a man they thought had a mighty burden to bear.

There were 5 off duty policemen who came in for drinks on us that evening. They arrived early and positioned themselves at the end of one of the two long bars, which were each were around 15 yards long and had three till points spaced evenly apart along the back bar. There were about 8 bar staff on duty that night and in an era before CCTV and the like; I thought it was going to be well-nigh impossible to trap the perpetrator, if indeed there was one there at all. The cops though felt differently. They surmised that whoever it was had developed a routine and they were likely to get bolder and greedier as their confidence grew.

Barely 15 minutes into the session, one of the police followed me into the Gents to say;

'I think we've got our man'.

'Who, how?' I asked.

It seems Charlie had served the police their first order and had engaged in his usual jolly banter with the cops which they noticed never seem to stop. One of them noticed though, that he chose to use a till at the very far end of the bar. Telling his colleagues that, they arranged to have an officer in sight of that till when their second order was placed. Charlie was seen to ring in a sum that was only a fraction of the order.

The practise was repeated again and again whilst the increasingly well oiled officers tried to work out how Charlie was actually pocketing the money. As far as they could see the cash was actually going into the till, so I made arrangements with Fred to 'crash' the till at some stage. Assuming Charlie was 'under ringing', the till would surely be in surplus and we'd catch our man before he had the chance to pocket the differential when cashing up at the end of the session.

But our Charlie was wise to that and instead had prepared a methodology unlike any other I had ever come across…which was almost quite brilliant for its simplicity.

Fred duly crashed the said till and asked Charlie to accompany him to the kitchen where it would be counted before him. The police then came through to tell Charlie of their suspicions and to ask if he was prepared to admit to any theft. Charlie insisted he had done no wrong and challenged Fred to reconcile the till. It was of course spot on which Charlie took as a vindication but then one policeman asked Charlie to drop his trousers. I was astonished as were some of the passing barmaids when Charlie's huge rear end came into view. I still hadn't quite twigged what was happening and assumed that a full strip search was about to be undertaken. One policeman took the trousers from Charlie and revealed two secret pockets which had been stitched inside the rear of Charlie's trousers. Inside one of them was a £5 note which Charlie argued was there as an emergency.

He was then asked to take his shoes and socks off whereupon another £50 or so emerged. Charlie was in the habit of constantly pulling his trousers up, as many big men are obliged to often do, but he used this as the opportunity to transfer the 'under rings' whilst simultaneously laughing and chatting with staff and customers. During repeated toilet breaks he would take, he would move the cash from the concealed trouser pockets and into his socks.

It's sad to see a big man cry and only the stoniest heart would have no sympathy for a man in his situation. Inquiries revealed that in all probability, this was not an isolated offence on his part and ordinarily the guy deserved some severe retribution. Ralph was hopping mad with him at the time but we realised that Charlie's wife was the only real victim in all this. To get him out of our business was all we needed so we asked the police not to bother pressing charges.

I was beginning to realise that nightclub management was one long running soap saga packed with incidents which could be both highly comical and highly dangerous...often at the same time. There were also the highly mundane everyday routines and threaded through it all were the personal trials and tribulations of each and every member of staff and each and every customer who walked through the door. I'm sure the same can be said of any workplace in any walk of life but venues such as The Top Rank Suite were places where people sought escapism and perhaps experiences in such an environment were highlighted all the more.

The undercurrents used to worry me quite a lot not least because one developed a certain profile working in such an establishment and it was not always healthy. I soon became conscious of people in Plymouth evidently knowing me just because of where I worked. I liked to go and watch Plymouth Argyle occasionally but after the Swilly episode, it became a little uncomfortable going into pubs before the match and even choosing where to stand within the ground. If you wanted to go for a quiet drink, it was better to do so either away from the city centre or to choose one of the smarter establishments in town. Venturing down Union Street, one had to be particularly wary and wearing a dicky bow anywhere was just asking for trouble.

Gradually though one develops a certain awareness and your instincts keep you out of trouble but you always knew to expect the unexpected.

One Tuesday evening, I was reluctantly getting myself ready for work to prepare for the Jets' Disco sessions. I would have preferred to slump in front of the telly all night but I figured that once the doors were open I'd be able to take refuge in the office and catch up with the Evening Telegraphs that my mother used to send weekly from Kettering. We couldn't expect more than a hundred or so customers and I generally employed a skeleton staff of a couple of doormen, three bar staff and the DJ. The journey into work was only a 20 minute walk and as I passed The Duke of Cornwall Hotel, the Top Rank Suite used to loom into view.

On this particular evening I expected nothing out of the ordinary; but as I cast my eyes down towards Union Street I saw literally hundreds of people milling about there and they all seemed to be intent on getting into the Suite!

As I got nearer, the crowds seemed to swell even more but I just couldn't figure what was happening….and then I heard the American accents.

I quickly got into the Suite and asked the staff to get ready to open as soon as possible whilst I desperately hit the phones trying to get more staff into help us. Within minutes of the doors opening we had reached our capacity…and our three bar staff were completely overrun.

It turned out that the USS J F Kennedy had docked into town for emergency repairs and that evening 5,000 of America's finest were let loose on the streets. They had been at sea for weeks…and their ships were 'dry'. These guys needed a drink and they wanted to party.

The only problem for them was that on a Tuesday evening in Plymouth very few of the local girls came out to play. Jon 'B' did his best to entertain them but to the unknowing the place resembled one huge gay bar. I did notice though that many of the guys were focused on the cartoons that we used to run as a backdrop to the disco sessions. I decided it would be amusing to have a little fun at Jon 'B's expense. I joined Lloyd, our amiable Welsh engineer, in his booth to ask if he could accommodate me. 'You bet', he said before cutting the sound on Jon B's music. The whole room stood transfixed whilst Jon gesticulated thinking there'd been a power failure. For effect, I got Lloyd to wait ten seconds before we unleashed, at maximum volume, the soundtrack to Woody Woodpecker!!!

That evening still ranks as one of the most surreal I ever encountered. To see nearly one thousand US Navy personnel delighting in and cheering the antics of Tom and Jerry, Road Runner and the rest is quite beyond comprehension. The fact that they were to remain in town for a further three weeks meant too, that our business was in line for a much needed and very welcome boost.

Of course, the presence of 'The Yanks' in town was a great boost for the wider economy in Plymouth too....and indeed well beyond that as we were to find out in the next few days.

On the day of their arrival, we had but half a bottle of tequila in stock. The next day we took in 30 cases and that was repeated every week during their visit.

When 5,000 fit young men roll into town, there are others who gauge what comforts they may be seeking. The fact that they had lacked female company was an obvious one. The very next day Plymouth's Holiday Inn reported 'No Vacancies' in their establishment and it remained like that for the next three weeks. The good time girls were on their way and I marvelled at their speed of response and attention to details. Each room was booked out to two girls and with two double bedrooms in each the girls could virtually guarantee a 24-hour service. They in turn 'sub-let' their rooms to others who came down to Plymouth just for a day; the 'have It Awayday' girls as they referred to themselves!

All too soon though the Yanks were on their way and life in the Top Rank Suite soon returned to normality....so what could we do next?

Chapter 3

'You To Me Are Everything'

The nightclub manager's way of life could hardly be recommended as a sure path to health, wealth and eternal happiness but along the way it offered extreme highs and lows and the chance to observe people at their very best and their very worst.

Union Street in Plymouth was a byword for decadence and craven behaviour in the eyes of many 'respectable' inhabitants of the city and sure enough every week there was ample evidence there to support their assessment. Violence, drunkenness, prostitution and lewd behaviour; they were all plain to see and the never-ending cycle of it all led to an air of hopelessness being associated with the area. Yet, it was still the destination if you wanted to party in Plymouth and, providing one exercised a little care, a good time could be almost guaranteed.

Standing on a nightclub door, it is of course one's job to sift the tide of human traffic and in an instant, form judgments as to the suitability or otherwise of individuals to be welcomed as patrons to your establishment. People would present themselves in varying states of sobriety and one soon learned to appreciate the effects of alcohol. The wealthy, the learned, the professional; all could be reduced to a state of human wreckage incapable of standing up or speaking lucidly simply because they failed to respect the boundaries which drink, and sometimes drugs, demanded of them. Most of the time it was almost funny, but too often the sight of teenagers going just a little too far gave grave cause for concern should one be considering their welfare. I found it disturbing back then when one realised the cycle some were getting into but in the years since, binge drinking seems to have become the norm and one wonders at the lack of shame and the extent of public depravity evident on the streets in our towns and cities these days.

Despite my reflections now, I was probably leading a hedonistic way of life as much as anyone else. I can't say I didn't enjoy the attention I was getting from female patrons even if it just came by virtue of the job I was doing. I like to think I was discriminating in the choice of those I wanted to get to know a little better. Maybe it was the Catholic guilt inherent in me which ensured I didn't abuse the power of the dickey bow, because it certainly did present opportunities.

I always sought to foster good working relationships with staff and although I was often warned that it was better to put a certain distance between yourself and them, that was not my style and I thought that engaging with people would bring out the best in them and if one was honest, then one would earn their respect. That policy worked for me 99% of the time but it works against you when people think you can be exploited - or when Romance presents itself.

I fought to stop myself getting involved with any of the female staff but it's difficult when a person is aware of their own allure and seeks to do mischief with it. There was one particular barmaid who fell into that category. With a wonderful figure and very striking looks, I may have gone off in pursuit in different circumstances but I knew her to be influential amongst her colleagues and decided that it was just too dangerous for me to get involved. Although I had kept a very wide berth, she was a girl not used to being rebuffed and she soon proved she was determined to cause a bit of devilment….and in the process was not bothered about who got caught up in the slipstream of her actions.

There was one young impressionable member of staff who had recently joined us and who had already impressed me with her helpfulness and general attitude. Some would have regarded her as plain maybe, but she was quiet, very pleasant and kept herself to herself. Noticing that she did not easily socialise with the other staff, I often made a point of encouraging her and thanking her for her efforts. She deserved it.

Danger Woman though was watching and hatched a plan to embarrass me and humiliate this young girl.

One evening a party for the staff and management had been arranged some distance from where I lived. I was invited and offered a room for the evening which I was happy to accept. The party was no great shakes even though all the staff had been in attendance and Jon 'B' had been brought in to spin his magic….never a guarantee for a great evening if he was going to serve up some more trashy Euro disco. Soon though, the crowd thinned out and I sat up sharing a few drinks with the boys before heading to bed.

I was absolutely jiggered and couldn't wait to crash down for the night so got undressed in a flash and hopped into bed……only to find there was already a naked occupant under the blanket! I was astonished to find that it was the new girl, hitherto so quiet and demure by nature….was she now suddenly a vamp?

Friends I have related the story too, say I should have just enjoyed her company but I saw a girl frozen with fear, not knowing what to say or do. I knew there had to be a third party involved and sure enough it transpired that Danger Woman had put her up to it. Young Miss Innocent had been told that I was very sweet on her and that if she was to get on with me, then she should make a gift of herself. Ok, it might have seemed faintly amusing; but the girl had been cruelly manipulated by a devious individual who could well have placed her in a dangerous position, all for some sadistic kick. Even though no harm was done that night, I really was worried about how she had been affected by the experience.

I knew I had to call her a taxi and send her home but she needed a lot of reassuring before it came. She said she felt humiliated and I wasn't sure if that was because of the joke played on her or because she perceived a rejection on my part. It was a real conundrum, I thought I was doing the right thing by getting her home but maybe her feelings would have been spared more if I had spent the night with her. I imagined Danger Woman would be having a great laugh about it all and, if she found out more details, she'd exploit the situation even more. Fortunately, I was able to impress this on the girl and together we vowed not to say anything to anybody. 'Let them wonder' I told her and answer any questions with an enigmatic smile. She did it so well I started to call her my Mona Lisa!

Girls had always been the great uncertainty in my life before taking up this vocation. I'd had two lengthy relationships which I'd ended for fear of getting 'too serious'. In hindsight, I had been unfair to them both, but I just hadn't been mature enough to handle commitment. Others came and went, usually very fleetingly, but always there had been fear and trepidation – probably for them as much as myself. I couldn't previously have been accused of being hedonistic in any way nor did I envy others who certainly were. A few months as a nightclub manager meant an inevitable change of attitude and one's self confidence improved immeasurably.

I used to point out to the other doormen that if more than a thousand girls a week were coming into the establishment then the law of averages dictated your success rate must be considerably higher than Mr Average's. What I hadn't banked upon was just how many of them would be on a mission and how many made sure that you knew their intentions. It's all very flattering at first…and hard to resist; but gradually you do become more and more discriminating. I always preferred the quiet ones, maybe the ones I'd have been happy to show to my own mother. I hadn't banked on their mothers though singling me out as a target but that was to happen a few times over the years….and I never, ever saw it coming.

During the late summer of '76 not long after I had been in Plymouth, the venue was staging a heat of a teen magazine's 'Face of '77' competition. Glamorous young ladies descended on the venue from all over the south west of the country including one terrific beauty from Bristol who arrived with her mother at 3 o'clock in the afternoon.

I made them tea and told them what the format was before directing them to the guest house they were staying at. The pair returned for the competition that night and the daughter succeeded in being chosen to go through to the national finals. At the end of the evening the pair came over to say goodbye and thanked me for helping them earlier. I wished them well and thought that was it; before her mother returned ten minutes later. She had noticed that The Real Thing were playing at the venue the following week and said that her daughter was very keen to see them. I said that would be fine and I'd get them a couple of tickets but Mother said only one ticket was needed as the daughter would be coming on her own so would I be kind enough to look out for her? 'No problem', I said, just tell her to let me know when she was arriving.

I thought no more of it and not having had a phone call since their visit, I assumed I wouldn't ever be seeing the girl again. It came as a real surprise then when the daughter sauntered into the venue halfway through The Real Thing's soundcheck a few hours before the gig.

'Who's this then?' Ralph mischievously asked me.

I was almost dumbstruck at the surprise she'd sprung upon me, but managed to murmur 'Hello Rachel' though I wasn't entirely sure that really was her name.

'I'm fine', she said and stood there looking quite stunning as all there just gawped in awe.

I introduced her to those present and then brought her over to the boys who I assumed to be the real focus of her attention. It was the first time I'd also encountered The Real Thing though I was to work with them many times in the years that followed. Chris and Eddie Amoo along with Dave Smith were the perfect gentlemen, as I have always found them since, and they, along with the late Ray Lake who was with them that day, welcomed the star struck Rachel and soon set her at ease. It was all very exciting for them too at the time for having spent years paying their dues they were now enjoying huge success on the back of their No 1 hit, *'You To Me Are Everything'*. Their follow up was also doing well and America beckoned, for they'd managed to crack the Billboard charts too.

I'm sure at that time that the boys were beginning to get used to adoring fans but I thought it nice that they afforded her the time and attention they did that day. Or maybe, like me, they just found her extremely attractive.

Eventually the band finished their soundcheck and we all prepared to go home for a few hours rest before the show that evening. I asked Rachel if she was staying at the same guest house and promptly got my second shock from her when she said;

'No, I'm staying with you!.....Mum said it would be alright'.

Well that was that then, except I had no idea how I was going to accommodate her in the flat I shared with two others. I shared my room with Gerry, the bars manager and a nurse from Derriford Hospital slept in the other room. Both were there when we arrived at the flat but the nurse saved the day when she said Rachel could have her room as she was spending the weekend away.

The show went off superbly that night, it was the first proper concert we'd staged since I'd been in Plymouth and it encouraged us to try and engage a few more bands. The Real Thing were excellent and I wished them well as they set off for Exeter to meet up with David Essex who was playing at the University there that night. Rachel? Well, she was as high as a kite it seemed and demanded to know where we were off to next.

I always had to be wary when socialising in Plymouth, there was always some dickhead who would recognise you and lob a few words of abuse if not worse. On this occasion though, I figured I might be safer with female company and I felt obliged to give Rachel a nice time to report back to her mother.

Mind you, there weren't too many salubrious joints you could take a girl too at that time in Plymouth and we ended up in Boobs, a small drinking club just up the road which was popular with Plymouth's night time workers just wanting to wind down a bit. I nodded to the bouncer who stood aside to let us in. I used to like his company as he had a great fund of stories to tell which no one else listened to. Perhaps that was because he claimed to walk in the same circles as The Kray Twins. I believed him though because he was a rather sad character who'd spent too many of his 50 years locked up because of the company he had kept. Outwardly a little fearsome looking, he was actually frightened of the course his life had taken. He came down to Plymouth to escape the spiral of violence he had been caught up in but because of his record, he felt virtually unemployable and so had to resort to offering his muscle for hire.

I said I'd leave him a drink behind the bar then took Rachel upstairs to a quiet little nook which was just alongside the piranha fish the owner kept in an aquarium there. Now, if you've not seen them before, piranha fish can generate a nice relaxing aura when they're quietly swimming around but watch them when they're being fed! The owner liked to lob them a mouse occasionally….dead or alive it didn't really matter. They were also an amazingly effective deterrent to unruly customers when the bouncers offered to introduce their right arm to the fish!

Rachel found it all 'pretty cool' but I figured her mother would rather I didn't expose her to too much of the seedy side of life in Plymouth.

Back to the flat then where I put on the kettle for my usual ritual of tea and hot buttered toast before bed and at that point I showed Rachel to her room and said goodnight. Now at last, I could relax and read *The Guardian* for half an hour….it's funny the rituals one develops, but they're so comfortable don't you think and so aggravating when you're denied them. I was to be denied them that night too…but I didn't complain.

I always make a point of reading the obituaries, it never ceases to amaze me how sworn enemies call a truce when asked to pass comment on the dead. I'm not sure if I was engrossed in such morbid fascination when Rachel came up behind me, whispered my name and touched me lightly on the shoulder. I thought she was after toothpaste perhaps and turned to offer help. I was confronted by my third Shock of The Day from her. She stood there so sweet and beguiling wearing just a smile and a hint of Estee Lauder Youth Dew. She put her fingers to her lips and just reached for my hand and then my head. She kissed me softly then firmer and harder and harder until my lungs were fit to burst. Putting *The Guardian* aside and turning off the light, she led me silently to her room. Oh well, I could read it in the morning.

Chapter 4

'You Just Don't Know'

The Real Thing show was something of a watershed event in life for me at The Top Rank Suite in Plymouth (and not just for Rachel's intervention). We found that a whole new audience was prepared to check out the place and if the offering was right they would set aside preconceived notions of what they expected to find at the venue and in Union Street. Ralph and I badgered Rank's head office to get the venue included on tour schedules for bands that were working the circuit. Previously Plymouth would be bypassed because if it wasn't too remote, it was too provincial or there was the 'wrong' market there. The Real Thing proved not only was that not the case but that a local market craved such attractions.

When head office still seemed to ignore us, we decided to take matters into our own hands by creating sessions ourselves and hiring bands directly to play. Thus, we introduced a Heavy Rock Night and a Rock'n'Roll Night. Both these sessions were largely anathema to me but we were catering for markets we knew existed and which simply were not being serviced.

I did rather enjoy the Rock'n'Roll Nights which succeeded because Plymouth really was in something of a time warp. We hired a local DJ who I knew had a good following in the city's pubs. He had a great vinyl collection, he wore the drapes and Teddy Boy suits complete with brothel creeper shoes and sported a magnificent brylcreemed quiff atop his Duck's Arse hairstyle. A host of rock and roll revival bands were lined up including Crazy Cavern and The Rhythm Rockers, Rocket 88, Rocky Sharpe and The Razors (who were later to enjoy success as The Darts) and one Shakin' Stevens and The Sunsets. Shaky, of course, was to go onto huge success but he and his band were happy to come down from South Wales that night for a mere £50.

The best of all these rock'n'roll outfits actually hailed from my own neck of the woods, Northamptonshire. Freddie Fingers Lee and his band would trek 300 miles in a cramped transit van which contained all their equipment including a piano....and a mattress which occasionally came into use when one of them 'got lucky'.

Freddie was the most modest and unassuming character you could meet in the world of rock and roll but the man had done everything and worked with all the legends including The Beatles, Fats Domino, Chuck Berry and his own hero, Gene Vincent. When he took the stage, he would proceed to rip the place up playing the piano with his feet and anything that came to hand. We brought him down several times to Plymouth and whilst the shows were always brilliant it was his off-stage antics that are remembered longest.

Freddie lost an eye when he was three years old, apparently the result of a stray dart thrown by his father. He made light of his disability though and had endless fun with his glass eye. A favourite trick was to drop it into someone's pint whilst distracting them. Yuk!! He became such a friend of the staff and management at the Suite that one assistant manager invited him to his wedding sometime after I had moved on. At the wedding Freddie took his eye out, not for effect but because it was irritating him. He meant to put it in his pocket but his arm was nudged and somehow the eye shot out of his grasp before rolling up the aisle coming to a stop between the bride and groom. The happy couple and the vicar gazed in disbelief before Freddie stepped forward, picked it up and popped it back into his gaping eye socket!

Music always takes you back to a time and a place and the tunes that evoked that particular era for me were Heinz's *'Just Like Eddie'* and Freddie Bell and The Belmonts *'Giddy Up A Ding Dong'*. The latter tune was written as far back as 1953 and the publicity for it had urged 'If these sides don't move you, see a doctor – you're dead!'.

Those rock and roll nights in Plymouth were raucous occasions. The crowd knew exactly what to expect and quite spontaneously duly turned up in all the 1950's gear. Whilst the rock and roll nights were quite clearly defined, the same could not be said of the heavy rock nights.

You just never knew what to expect; from headbanging heavy metal one week to introspective psychedelic musings another week. It was often such torture for me personally that I found myself longing for some of Jon B's trashy Euro disco. To be fair, in amongst the dross, some fairly agreeable outfits emerged. Frankie Miller played one week and Deaf School and Babe Ruth were two of the better acts who came down. As attendances continued to improve, we found that at last we were being included on 'the circuit' for some fairly 'hot' bands.

There was talk of Tom Petty and The Heartbreakers coming and The Ramones which would have lifted us to another level but the biggest disappointment was when the American band Television pulled out in order to secure a bigger date. They were one of the punk pioneers of course and we were told they'd be using one Debbie Harry on lead vocal. She was to break it big in the UK just a few months later but already her reputation had preceded her.

Instead the record company (EMI) asked us to take a band they were pushing like crazy. The fact that they had a proper tour bus and were staying in a hotel suggested that someone meant business with them. Our £50 fee to them wasn't going to go very far.

In truth, they were awful and the crowd booed them mercilessly but they were undeterred and a couple of months later their backers got their dividend when The Tom Robinson Band had a massive hit with *'2-4-6-8 Motorway'*. You just never know what Fate has in mind for people. Years later I was quite unmoved when I met Wham as a struggling outfit for whose services, I paid the princely sum of £10. There was also another promising young Irish band I had who went down pretty well; but I didn't expect U2 to enjoy quite as much success as they have since managed.

However, the proverbial messy stuff was about to hit the fan when Rank's head office ordered us to cancel another act that we had booked. Punk was now taking off big time and though I pretty much hated all of it, we were happy to ride the wave and enjoy the business. Looking back punk was really all hype and much of it was pretty well stage managed too. Never more so than with that ensemble of limited talent who called themselves The Sex Pistols. They couldn't sing, they couldn't play but they could shock and their publicists were happy to let them carry on whilst the tabloids indulged them. Their record sales soared and they played to sell out audiences.

To be anti-Establishment may be a great idea for certain rock bands but there is a line that must not be crossed and The Sex Pistols managed that on December 1st 1976, when they were interviewed by Bill Grundy on the tea time London regional news programme *'Today'*. If The Sex Pistols had escaped many people's radar up to that point, things would rapidly change in the next 24 hours. In a few short minutes Grundy's career was virtually destroyed when the Pistols took exception to his questions and responded by mocking him and swearing gratuitously. The F word uttered live at teatime caused a media hurricane and the tabloids in particular went to town. *The Daily Mirror's* headline the following morning; 'The Filth and The Fury' became itself a rallying cry for the new punk generation with the phrase becoming emblazoned on thousands of t-shirts and used as the title for Julien Temple's documentary on the band.

The band were about to go on a national tour which included visiting us in Plymouth. We were already expecting a good response to them but the uproar they caused was gold dust for the band and their manager, Malcolm McLaren. It had all happened by accident too as they had been a late replacement for Queen on that particular programme. We couldn't wait, but Headquarters had other ideas and immediately banned the band from all Rank venues. It was understandable I guess, a company like Rank, originally founded to propagate the word of God, did not need such an association but we knew we were gifting our local competitors and sure enough the gig was moved to Woods in Plymouth. Woods went onto establish themselves as a very credible rock venue in the city on the back of that one gig.

The heavy rock nights were not something I generally enjoyed having to work and they made me yearn for some of the proper soul music which was such a staple diet of the clubs in Kettering, Stoke-On-Trent and across the Midlands and The North. It was no better on my nights off, for nowhere in Plymouth was Soul Music to be found. It seemed if a record wasn't in the charts, then the local DJs didn't deem it playable.

In a town of nigh on a quarter of a million people, I just couldn't accept the majority of potential club goers had such narrow tastes. All the time I was seeing naval personnel coming into the club and noted that many of them had northern accents. I decided to take a punt and asked Ralph if he minded me taking over the Disco One-50, our upstairs function room. He thought the very notion of a Northern Soul night working in Plymouth was a fantasy, but, as he would often say, 'what do I know, I've only been in this business 30 years?!'

In the pre-internet age, there was of course no social media network one could engage to spread the word and the age of texting etc., was still many years away. The advertising budget consisted of a single £10 advert in the Plymouth Evening Herald and a single handwritten poster on the outside of the premises. Far more powerful in those days it seems was 'the grapevine' or word of mouth. I'd stand on the front door and on hearing the regional dialects I'd just ask people where they were from. If it was Manchester, I'd ask if they knew of The Twisted Wheel....of course they did....then I'd just say 'you'll be up for the Northern Soul next week then?' The reaction would be instant with a pledge to get all their mates in. Wigan Casino was at its peak at that time and clubs like 'The Wheel', 'The Torch' in Stoke-on-Trent, 'Catacombs' in Wolverhampton were revered amongst the Soul fraternity. For many 'the Soul' was the most thing they missed on leaving home and joining the forces - I wanted to put that right.

I didn't say as much to Ralph, but I just felt there was a buzz going about which you could sense even more when I asked the 'divvi DJs' to announce it to the regular punters. People would start to ask who was DJing that night and I'd tell him a guy called Brillo was coming down from 'up north'. They'd nod approvingly but had no idea who the guy was......just as well too.

The big night finally arrived and I went in early to set up the gear and prepare the floats for all the bars as one of the dreaded Heavy Rock nights was to take place downstairs that night. I landed in the car park at exactly the same time as Ralph who was positively beaming.

'What's up?' I asked.

'Look!' and I turned to see over a hundred punters queuing to get in. 'The band must have worked hard to promote it', he said.

'Oh yeah', I replied but I'd already noticed the Spencers, sports bags, badges and attire of many in the queue. 'Ye Gods' I thought....and felt a panic attack looming.

I quickly helped Ralph get the place set up and he muttered something about me going upstairs to play with myself.

'OK boss, see you later'.

I asked old Roy, the elder statesman doorman to let the crowd in just as soon as he heard the first record being played upstairs. I checked the bar staff upstairs to see if they were ready to go.

'We are', Sandy said, 'but there's no DJ here yet'.

'He's just arrived!' I told them before watching them collapse with laughter as I placed the needle on Chubby Checker's *'You Just Don't Know'*! They knew now that Brillo was yours truly!

Downstairs Roy heard his cue and watched as a legion of hitherto Soul starved punters stormed in, paid their cash and belted past the Rock stage and on upstairs to their Soul heaven. The staff stood aghast as I welcomed them all through a mighty cloud of talcum powder.

'Brothers and Sisters, we're here to Keep The Faith!' I proudly announced.

I was so proud of those Northern Soul sessions at the Disco One-50 and I do get a great kick to see it often referred to in articles by people who were there to witness them. Soon minibuses would leave Plymouth to travel the 285 odd miles to Wigan, sadly I couldn't join them because of the need to work weekends. Their devotion was fanatical and soon I, their teacher, was learning from my students as they brought along the latest in-demand sounds every week. It was a very special period, for me and for them.

Chapter 5

'Don't Leave Me This Way'

By now Life was chugging along very nicely in Plymouth. The entertainment game was definitely for me as I always figured it would be but I enjoyed all the nuances that went with it. I enjoyed dealing with the issues thrown up by staff and patrons notwithstanding the inevitable bit of 'grief' one occasionally encountered. I enjoyed the minutiae of promotions, stock control etc., and now I was ready for the next step.

The company sent me up to Brighton to undertake a Deputy Manager's course and having passed it comfortably, I was told to expect a promotion imminently. A pay rise was always welcome of course but I was equally excited too, at the prospect of relocating to another town or city with a whole set of new challenges and a different way of doing things.

Back in Plymouth, Ralph made it clear that he would like me to stay on a little longer but I felt I'd stagnate there and miss the opportunity of advancement. I'm not sure what I was aiming for but I liked the company and was keen to make waves within it.

However, Fate as ever, would intervene and it chose to visit on one very quiet Tuesday evening when we were staging our regular Jet's Disco session. I had been working on some papers in the office and thought I'd take a wander around the unit before finishing them off. When I arrived at the front door, Andy, one of our Royal Marine doormen was looking particularly pleased with himself.

'I've got a date boss', he blurted out before I even had a chance to ask him the question, 'and she's gorgeous!!'.

I had to laugh; Andy was probably the most agreeable guy on our payroll, so I was genuinely pleased that he had met someone he felt so good about. He just wanted to tell me all the details there and then; 'next Wednesday, so please don't book me for working boss'.

'No worries', I probably said adding that I hoped it went well for him.

Back in the office a little while later I thought I'd get the paperwork wrapped up when there was a furtive knock on the door and a young girl, not quite 18, popped her head through the door.

'Excuse me sir', she said, 'is it possible to book your function room for a party?' I beckoned her in but she said, 'I'll just get my friend'.

The two of them came in and we duly put the date in the diary for the young lady's 18th birthday party in a few weeks' time. All the time the business was being conducted her friend sat in complete silence but I couldn't help being fascinated by her appearance. She was so slender with features that seemed carved out of porcelain set off by pronounced cheekbones and a certain dewy-eyed look. I was moved to the point of distraction but was intent on just completing the business in hand so why then did I say;

'Would you like a drink girls?'.

The birthday girl was delighted, the other less so but no matter, I ordered two Ponys for them and expected to just indulge in small talk for a few minutes but by now I was feeling quite disarmed in the presence of her friend. She had a certain aura about her which both unnerved me and left me truly spellbound. This was silly now and my uneasiness seemed to worsen when the birthday girl excused herself to go to the ladies. Left alone with the friend, my brain was a complete mush but I found myself asking her name.

'Carrie' she said.

'Oh, that's nice', but now my brain was completely addled. I felt my face warming up like a radiator and I just couldn't get any words out. I just had to, I told myself, I must ask her. I knew the friend would be back soon, so, taking a deep breath I somehow uttered; 'Would you, would you, would you care to go, go, go out for a drink one night' I stuttered and waited for the ground to open up and consume me.

'I can't' she said but she must have seen how deflated I was, 'I'd love to but I'm afraid I've agreed to see someone else who asked me earlier'.

'Ohhhh', I said, 'I understand' and prepared to accept the situation but no you don't get too many of these chances in life so I just blurted out; 'See us both, but see me first'. Carrie seemed stunned at that point but whilst I awaited her response her friend bounded back exhorting Carrie to come dancing with her.

I nodded and sloped back to the office. I was hugely disappointed and I realised that it was probably Carrie who Andy had referred to earlier. There was certainly no other vision of loveliness on the premises that night that fitted the glowing description Andy had given of his prospective date. Ah, good luck to him I thought.

I wasn't in the mood to leave the office for the rest of the night. The music was palpably awful as usual and I sat there contemplating the likelihood that my time in Plymouth would probably be drawing to an end soon and nights like this would be consigned to the dustbin of memories. An hour or so later, I took the till readings on the door then the bars and prepared to cash up quickly with a view to having an earlier night than usual…..and then there was another knock on the office door. It was Carrie.

She stepped inside and shyly asked if I meant it when I asked her to go for a drink with her.

'Yes, of course' I answered in a state of semi-shock perhaps.

'Well, I'd like that too', she said, 'but I'll have to cancel with Andy now, you must think I'm awful'.

'No, no, I don't' I found myself saying, 'but please don't cancel Andy tonight'. I figured Andy would be hugely disappointed and really cheesed off if he found I'd stepped in. I suggested to Carrie that we go out for a drink and that if I passed the test, she could call Andy afterwards. I took her number and she scurried out before her friend would find us and twig what was going on! I was so happy, I felt this was someone really special and so it proved, though the script ahead didn't quite go the way either of us might have envisaged or planned for.

I couldn't wait for Tuesday evening to roll around, the night of The Big Date. I couldn't stop checking my appearance every time I passed a mirror. I agonised over what to wear and wondered if I should splash some of the old Brut over me in the way that Kevin Keegan and Henry Cooper were constantly imploring every male in the kingdom to do so at the time. 'I'll be different', I thought and opted for Hai Karate before pushing the boat out and investing in a small bottle of Aramis from Boots, because that was really 'top drawer' according to Helen in Boots who advised me.

On Monday evening, I phoned Carrie to check we were still 'on' for the next evening but when she paused, I feared she'd had second thoughts…but no, it was a goer!

'Yes, ok' she said, 'shall we meet in town'.

'Oh no' I suddenly found myself saying 'I'll pick you up'. I put it down to my state of euphoria for it was a pretty stupid thing to say when I didn't even own a car at the time!

It caused a state of panic for me then as I wondered how the hell I was going to get hold of a car within the next 24 hours. If I couldn't get one it would be taxis there and back to her far flung village. Fortunately, Gerry, the bars manager, granted me the loan of his Austin A40. I hoped she'd be impressed.

Carrie proved to be delightful, everything I hoped and imagined she'd be and once I'd conquered my nerves we had a really nice evening. The highlight was probably her saying that she would ring and cancel the date with Andy that had been scheduled for the night after. She didn't even mock me when it was time to take her home and the car failed to start. Gerry had warned that it often proved temperamental in that respect but I was not to worry, I'd find the remedy in the glove compartment. The remedy was a starting handle! I thought they'd disappeared in the 1920's but apparently not. I took it anyhow and pretended I knew what I was doing. I muttered a couple of Hail Mary's, found a hole in the grill which it appeared to fit and duly started cranking. Voila! It spluttered into life and we were away! I felt very smug now.

The courtship with Carrie proceeded nicely and I was truly very happy at this period. I would talk to my family and friends back home a couple of times a week and assured them I was loving the job and had now met someone who seemed a bit special. But then I was presented with a dilemma.

The improved performance of Plymouth Top Rank Suite under Ralph and I had not gone unnoticed and in the wake of the successful course I had undertaken I shouldn't have been surprised when the Regional Director arranged to see me with a view to promoting me which would mean a relocation.

All I could think about was Carrie for I didn't want to leave her behind. Should I quit the job, find something else and stay there? I figured that would amount to putting pressure on her and I didn't think that was fair. Her family seemed to like me, but of course she was so young and they were so protective of her. I knew we had to take it one step at a time and if I did move on then maybe that would be a proper test of our relationship. That's the way things were heading and we were both resigned to the fact that I would be taking up the Deputy Manager's role that I was now being offered in Redhill. It was one of Rank's flagship operations and it would undoubtedly be very good for my profile as it was on the doorstep of their headquarters in Godstone, Surrey.

That didn't alleviate the angst I was feeling though as our relationship deepened and I came to regard this lady as being very special. Our time together was usually confined to meeting for lunch when we could, an evening in a pub or cinema and taking time out at her parents' house. I was wary of taking it further in a deep and intimate way for fear of 'spoiling things' but eventually our feelings led to that and it seemed right and proper. I was hoping we were in it together for the long haul and depending on how we each reacted when I moved away, I hoped things would progress accordingly. If we were meant for each other then they surely would.

Preoccupied as I was with Carrie, I was rather looking forward to the new role that beckoned in Redhill. The venue there was 'Busby's' and it had only launched a couple of years earlier as Rank Leisure's flagship discotheque. The name was inspired by the Busby Berkeley musicals of the 1930s and it was one of the first themed discotheques in Britain with its design and fittings alluding to The Rank Organisation's essential role in the development of the British film industry. There were props and paraphernalia from Pinewood Studios and blown up imagery derived from the great Hollywood movies. It was a dream move for anyone climbing the ladder in the company but, as I was to find, Busby's had certainly had a fair share of problems since opening and I was not in for an easy ride.

Life at Plymouth Top Rank Suite was nothing if not uneventful and in the last few months of my spell there we managed to pull off some unbelievable stunts….but I was also subjected to a staggering betrayal of trust.

In the pre-internet age, promoting your entertainment venue had to be done in 'the old-fashioned way'. You had to get noticed and talked about. Perception was everything but a year on from arriving in Plymouth, there was no doubt that it was not as negative as that which I had first found. Changing it was as slow and as difficult as turning around 'The Ark Royal' aircraft carrier which was docked at nearby Devonport but we had lanced a few boils along the way whilst staging events which forced many to reappraise our offering. Slowly but surely, we found that the sentimental attachment many people had for the old Majestic Ballroom was being reignited again and it was with that in mind that I floated an idea to Ralph which he backed enthusiastically.

I put it to Ralph that as we were the longest established public dancing venue in the city then it was not unreasonable to assume that more couples had found love at The Top Rank Suite, or 'the Maj', than at any other venue in the city. Surely, there was a good story for the media here and surely we could come up with a night to capitalise on it? A little brainstorming ensued which resulted in us proclaiming that on a certain date we would be welcoming our one millionth customer! OK, we were using a little poetic license here but we knew we could conjure up a narrative to guarantee us coverage and it was an ideal human interest story for the local paper to push.

We duly put out a press release which the Plymouth Herald feasted upon. In it we invited couples to get in touch who had married after meeting at the venue. We were inundated with stories and even had people claiming their very existence was as a result of their parents' chance encounter at our Ballroom of Romance! A local travel company was tapped up to offer a weekend in Paris and so we prepared to greet our millionth customer.

The press duly turned up in force along with several hundred curious locals who seemed intrigued by the fuss being generated. Ralph asked how I was going to determine the winner. I confidently told him that would be the easy part, we just had to pick a photogenic woman arriving after 10.30pm when we knew the place would be pretty full. I would whisk the lucky lady up onto the stage as the band struck up *'Congratulations'* and Jon 'B' would emerge with champagne popping. Ralph and I would then pose with the lady in front of a tumultuously applauding audience and the press would get their front page picture.

That's largely how it all transpired but not before I had been forced to sweat a bit thinking I might have blown it all completely. There had been a steady stream of people coming in all evening until about 10.20pm…but then nothing. One toothless guy sloped in just after 10.30pm wearing what looked like a patched up demob suit and the thought crossed my mind 'Should I?' but I reasoned that readers of The Herald or The Western Evening News should be spared the sight of his molars….and he probably wouldn't have been too welcome in Paris either.

10.35, 10.40 and people were getting impatient. Outside, Union Street was empty with just the fast food wrappings blowing up the street like tumbleweed. Then out of the gloom a taxi stopped by our front door and two couples got out. The two ladies turned out to be office staff from Rank Bush Murphy, the television manufacturers....and yes, one of them was reasonably photogenic. I waited with baited breath whilst they deliberated about coming in at all and then as soon as they paid their admission...we pounced. 'That's her!' I said as our lucky winner stood open-mouthed whilst poppers popped and streamers rained down on her. I held her beau as two of the doormen whisked her onto the stage as the crowd went mad and the champagne flowed. One very happy couple and one very relieved junior manager who could now start planning the next stunt; The Midsummer Christmas Party!

When a promotion plan works out well it is a mighty relief and that night was especially so as I knew there wouldn't be too many more in Plymouth for me. I couldn't wait to get back home and crash out for the night and urged Gerry the bars manager, and by now my roommate, to make sure we closed up as quickly as we could that night.

My routine most nights was to get into bed and read *The Guardian* for a while before crashing out. Once asleep, wild horses couldn't disturb me. Gerry knew that and sadly set out to capitalise upon it.

I had a habit of taking my bunch of keys out of my pocket and placing them by the bedside lamp. That way I figured I would see them at the start and end of every day. On this particular night, Gerry waited until I had fallen into a deep sleep before reaching over and taking the keys.

Waiting outside our house near Plymouth's West Hoe was Davey Simmonds, a doorman we had taken on just recently. Davey, we later found out, was a one-man crime wave and on this particular night he was going about his usual suspect business. Ours was obviously a cash business and Davey had obviously done his sums when observing 700 patrons coming onto the premises that night and stumping up at least a tenner or so each between admission and bar bills. Knowing that Gerry shared with me he put it to him to that there was a tidy sum to be earned.....and why couldn't they get away with it?

It could have been the perfect crime for this Dynamic Duo but for one little detail missing from their calculations.

There was no need for them to break into the building as Gerry always had the back door keys and he knew how to disable the burglar alarm. My keys would allow them into the Manager's Office and the safe would be there for the taking.

The first part of their plan went smoothly enough, entry was gained and there had been no one to disturb them. Into the Manager's inner sanctum they then crept; before the door suddenly slammed behind them! The pair of them jumped out of their skins as they turned to find a baseball bat descending from a great height to smash into the desk beside them. 'F—K Off!' bellowed a figure from the shadows....and they didn't need to be asked twice.

I woke up as Gerry came back into the room and must have blearily muttered 'what's happening?'. Gerry was looking breathless and saying something about not being able to sleep. He put my keys back on the table saying something about them having been in the kitchen. I thought no more about it and went back to sleep.

When I arrived at work the next morning, the place was swarming with police and I soon learned that there had been an attempted robbery during the night. The police advised that there were no signs of forced entry and nothing appeared to have been taken. They put that down to the vigilance of our man on site.

'Eh?', I asked, 'who was that then?'

'T'was me!!' and I turned around to find that our hero was none other than our very own Bill, the handyman! Yes, the man who had rescued our dinner dance awhile back by morphing into a Master Chef had now emerged from his den of broken toilet seats and oily rags to display himself as a supreme and fearless fighter of crime.

The reality of course turned out to be a little different. Bill had been out for the night, got drunk to the point of paralysis and rather than go home to his lonely bedsit in Mannamead, he thought he'd crash down in the club figuring at least he'd get to work on time the next day. He'd been making himself some tea and toast when he heard the intrepid raiders creep in. He recognised them both straight away so grabbing the bat and covering himself with an old coat with a mop head atop he thought at least he'd give them a scare. He didn't want to spoil a good story though and I watched as he regaled the police and later the local press with his account which steadily got ever more colourful and dramatic as he warmed to his theme. He made sure that the perpetrators weren't revealed though and took delight at describing the villains as desperate men who would have stopped at nothing had he not been there!

When the fuss died down though, Bill sought me out and told me who it was. It put me in a difficult position of course for, were they to be publicly revealed, then I would be seen as the idiot who slept on whilst my keys were taken.

Back home that evening Gerry tried to behave normally whilst reading the newspaper coverage of the story.

'What do you think?' he asked.

'I think you have to find somewhere else to live and somewhere else to work' I replied and left it at that. He didn't turn up for work the next day and I never saw him again.

I was looking forward to seeing Carrie the next day in Debenham's café where we often rendezvoused. The days were counting down to my transfer and I was really feeling the pain of moving away from her. I was always excited at seeing her and hearing all her news but when she arrived she looked a little subdued and I found conversation with her very strained and very difficult. I thought at first, she was upset at the prospect of me moving on but her indifference to everything I was saying suggested that wasn't the case. She was so detached that I thought maybe she was going to call it a day on our relationship and I remember the emptiness I felt at the prospect of this or that she had indeed met someone else.

'Please Carrie' I eventually implored her, 'what's the matter?'

After what seemed an age she looked up at me and said, 'I think I'm pregnant'.

Chapter 6

'God Save The Queen'

'Oh, My Gawd!'

'Pregnant?' Are you sure?'

She wasn't but all the signs pointed to it. She hadn't told anyone and was dreading her parents finding out. I knew exactly how she felt for I had the same feeling of foreboding myself and began to imagine the hoo-hah likely when my folks found out.

We sat in silence as the gravity of our situation sank in and every question I put to her seemed to meet the response 'I don't know' and I had no answers either.

There wasn't a lot more to be said there and then so we left planning to meet again the next day. I thought I needed the news to sink in and eventually I would think of something rational. We would attend to the necessaries, face up to the situation and a few months down the road would be prepared and ready to welcome our beautiful baby into the world.

We met again the next day and that weekend I went over to her home. All the time everything was outwardly calm and normal but I was just dying to blurt the news out. It was proving impossible though with Carrie of the mindset that she just didn't want to talk about it for now. My move to Redhill was now only days away and I was beside myself with worry. I was ready to quit the job and stay there with her if we thought that was necessary but then I was shaken when Carrie announced that she was going to move to Torquay to take up a position at a hotel there for the summer, along with her sister.

I thought that she probably would be just better off without me around. I'd got her into this mess and she probably didn't want me dictating what she should do. At work, I was barely functioning and people were beginning to notice. Perhaps they thought I was gearing up for Redhill and merely going through the motions for now. Brenda the secretary was the first to suss me though.

'You can tell me', she said, when I found myself alone with her in the office one day.

'Is it Carrie?'

I looked at her and just couldn't hold back the tears. When I eventually pulled myself together I just felt an enormous release as I at last felt able to share the burden I was carrying. Brenda was the rock in our operation. Apart from totally taking care of the administration, she managed the diaries for both me and Ralph and was always able to offer a constructive and objective view on countless issues that arose in the business. Now, she was there to offer her support again in her own quiet and discreet way which always had the effect for me of helping me see things in a clearer perspective.

She warned that Carrie had to be given space and said she would look for support away from me. I had to expect to find her become a different girl entirely for this was a life changing experience and she would adjust accordingly. She reckoned that in a few months this girl would be a maturing woman with a different outlook on many things - me included. It was a sobering analysis but I knew it was the voice of experience. I just had to get on with life in a different town; she'd have space and, if and when she needed me, I'd have to reassure her that I'd be there.

It was so difficult saying goodbye to Carrie and her family knowing that they would soon be rocked by our news. I decided to head back home for a few days before taking up the Redhill post. It was great to see my folks of course but my secret was consuming me. I dreaded to think what their reaction would be. Disappointment? Shame? All of that and more no doubt. The thought of it all filled me with such dread that I felt myself in a constant cold sweat. I kidded myself that I couldn't tell them anything until Carrie had broken the news to her parents, but really, I was being a coward.

I finally landed up in Redhill, only to find no one to greet me. The club was shut and, not having enough money on me, I was resigned to kipping in the old banger, an orange Austin 1100 that I'd just bought myself. I thought I'd take a spin around the town and soon realised why many had labelled it Dead Hill. It seemed to me a pretty soulless commuter town with a town centre so typical of the worst excesses of 1960s planning policy. The only activity seemed to be around the railway station where hundreds of commuters would be disgorged after another day in the city. The only other sign of life seemed to be at The Wheatsheaf pub, so I thought I'd acquaint myself with it and have a pint at least.

Inside were a gang of a dozen or so Paddys who were working on a section of the M25 then being constructed a few miles away. I thought I'd have the craic with them as there was bound to be a Mayo man among them and I'd no doubt make some sort of connection. I was right, there was one amongst them; Luke from Castlebar. He was a huge article with jet black wavy hair atop the ruddy features so common in men from the west of Ireland. He proved to be a softly spoken, intelligent man who seemed to have an encyclopaedic knowledge of Britain's motorways which had provided a living for him for the previous 15 years or so. Luke seemed to engender respect from all around him and just a look from him would ensure no one got too loud or rowdy.

As expected Luke knew a number in my father's circle and we enjoyed a pleasant drink exploring common ground. One of the company came over and asked if he was up for giving a song, Luke declined for fear of taking liberties in an unfamiliar pub but the landlord assured him it would be fine. A hush descended on the gang as yer man looked down then took a deep breath before stunning the whole place into silence as he launched into *'The Foggy Dew'*. I was astounded. His voice was a deep, rich baritone that was so pure and emotional you felt your heart would seize. Spine tingling would be a gross understatement. There was spontaneous applause at the end and audible murmurings of appreciation from all around the bar. English and Irish had been drawn together by the power of a single human voice. There was to be no encore though, Luke knew how to make an impact and he knew how to withdraw gracefully with maximum respect.

At some point one of the gang asked me if I had far to go and I told him I'd be kipping in the car that night but it'd be no hardship. The boys wouldn't have that and they insisted I came back to the flophouse they were all renting....about 20 of them! It was not so Dead Hill after all!

I reported for duty the next morning at Busby's having had barely a wink of sleep but I'd had a great craic and a wonderful fry-up to set me up for the day.

There was a lovely new secretary, Betty, to greet me. A very kindly lady, Betty was in her 60s and had for years been manageress of the Odeon Cinema which had closed and been converted by Rank Leisure into the discotheque it now was. Betty took me on a tour of the premises which turned into a potted history lecture. The building, which was built on stilts over Redhill Brook in 1938, was apparently the local for J Arthur Rank himself who had lived just up the road in Reigate. There were echoes of its former glories in every corner especially when Betty took me upstairs to the former circle where the red velvet seating was still in place. We ventured up as far as the Projection Room where the original equipment from 1938 was still intact. Betty was almost tearful as she took me around and told me how she had worked there since 1953. She was of course heartbroken when the cinema closed, but was now coming to terms with the new role of the building. She had been resigned to a quiet life of retirement looking after her 90 year old mother but someone in Rank had been savvy enough to think of her when they realised a good administrator was required at the unit.

Downstairs it was a completely different story as the stalls had been removed to house a state of the art discotheque which had been garnering rave reviews since it opened the year before. The sound system was top spec as was the lighting rig. The DJ booth was perched high above the dancefloor providing a great vantage point over the gyrating masses which I expected to be greeting. Two large bars were positioned at either end of the room and there was also a restaurant capable of producing hot snacks and an a la carte menu. Classy or what?

The film theme was everywhere though with blown up images from some of the great Hollywood movies ranging from Charlie Chaplin's silent era through to John Wayne's *'Green Berets'*. Busby Berkeley's work was well represented and setting it all off were props and paraphernalia which had been salvaged from Rank's own Pinewood studios. Scaffolding was erected throughout the venue and with neon and Tivoli lighting effects the place instantly delivered the 'wow' factor to the unsuspecting patron as they stepped in. It was a superb concept and it was easy to see why people had been raving about the place.

The trouble is when a place is popular, everyone wants to come. When that happens, crowd control becomes paramount. At Plymouth, we used to be just happy to see a good crowd but here in Redhill, we somehow had to be far more discerning and indeed discriminating. Not on the grounds of race and religion but certainly as a means of maintaining a certain standard. Thus, we determined to have an older age profile who presented themselves smartly. It's not easy being an arbiter of fashion and good taste, nor at finding a way to reject a group of 18 year olds. One ended up deploying a whole series of techniques; 'Sorry sir, couples only now' to 'Are you a member?' The latter was always very difficult when we didn't actually have a Membership scheme but for the most part it was mighty effective, certainly more so than the many times we found ourselves in dispute with someone wearing jeans or similar. Then, people would be prepared to argue for what seemed hours to be allowed in, invariably claiming that because their jeans cost a certain amount, then that alone should warrant their right of entry.

It was all very wearisome but worth it when you looked out to a full house prepared to meet your standard.

Unlike Plymouth, Brighton and any sizeable town or city; Redhill did not have much in the way of alternative entertainment. Ours was the only show in town really and one had to travel to East Grinstead or Croydon before finding any other semblance of nightlife. Thus, if a large group of males were denied access after having travelled a fair distance (invariably from South London), then they would often take umbrage when they found their night was ruined and all too often this resulted in a physical encounter with the 'bouncers'.

The success or failure of the venue was dependent not on the standard of the décor, not on the quality of the music, not even on the atmosphere to be found in it…..but purely on the ability to effectively control the 'quality' of the customers attracted.

The controller of Busby's was the General Manager, one Steve McGarrigle, who was probably as outrageous a character as one could ever expect to encounter in the nightclub world!

No one knew where Steve hailed from and no one knows what happened to him after he left the industry two or three years later but his tenure in Redhill proved unforgettable to all who had dealings with him there. He was an enigma wrapped in a mystery, capable of acts of great kindness but equally able to be cruel, callous and sadistic. His mood could change from light hearted merriment to dark, brooding menace in an instance. That he was a very capable and intelligent man there was no doubt, but he had a masochistic urge to self-destruct and one felt it was only a matter of time before the bosses at a staid company like Rank Leisure lost patience with him.

The staff would talk constantly about him but no one dared to cross the man. To do so invited a devastating putdown or worse a slap across the face and even, it was feared, the stubbing out of his cigarette on your arm! That last reaction was usually saved for unruly customers and was carried out without a word being said. It was usually followed by a twitch of the nostrils and the raising of an eyebrow as if to say, 'What are you going to do about it?' In an era, long before the common usage of CCTVs he knew he was on safe ground, particularly as he made a point of entertaining the local police practically every session.

Steve happened to be a gay man and he made sure the world was aware of it. Remember this was the 1970s when camp TV characters such as Larry Grayson and John Inman still had the ability to shock and any suggestion that a person had homosexual tendencies would invariable give rise to nudge, nudge, wink, wink gestures if not an outright 'Oooohh Ducky' in the manner of Dick Emery.

Steve would freely talk about his philandering and I received a crash course education in the ways of life for many gay men in that era. We had all heard of such practices as 'cottaging' and 'cruising' but Steve sounded as if he was the main ringmaster of it all. He did like to shock and revelled in the impact of his quite outrageous behaviour. Seducing straight men was his favourite challenge and I found his 'hit rate' quite astonishing. Whatever the circumstances, no matter the location; Steve's 'gaydar' was permanently switched on.

My first meeting with Steve established the pattern for our working relationship. He told me he hated his job, hated the Operations Director and only liked 'posing' in the club. He told me he wanted me to do everything really which also meant covering for him when he preferred to spend a night in London or wander around the town. I didn't mind at all really, Steve said he'd let me get on with it and he'd make sure I was 'looked after'.

This was beginning to look like an interesting assignment for sure and as I settled in at the lodgings that had been arranged for me, I wondered what Destiny had lined up for me. The papers and television had non-stop coverage of the Queen's Silver Jubilee celebrations taking place that week and I had a chuckle when I saw that my old friends, The Sex Pistols, were continuing to outrage the establishment by topping the pop charts on Jubilee Day with their alternative *'God Save The Queen'*!

I was surprised to find that managing a nightclub in a town like Redhill actually conferred minor celebrity status on one. That explained why I was invited to such as judging the children's' Jubilee Fancy Dress competition which was duly reported by the Surrey Mirror who always seemed happy to cover me opening an envelope!

The whole vibe in Redhill was so much different to that which I had left behind in Plymouth. The difference in the attitude of people was enormous and by comparison Plymouth folk seemed like distant country cousins. That was no bad thing though for they were distinctly friendlier than the Surrey set who seemed more mindful of money, money, money. Maybe it was because the capital was so near and so many worked there; but I couldn't understand the greater urgency of the people around me now. Everyone seemed to have a value judgement whether in terms of status, mode of dress, music listened to., etc. After a while one adjusts of course but that summer of '77 was the time when I crossed a huge cultural divide.

The staff at Busby's reflected these changes perfectly. Whereas in Plymouth they were mostly happy to have the job and tended to stick at it for a long time, here they expected you to be grateful they even turned up. The job was a temporary, transient exercise for many of them – a means to an end maybe – to be passed up if something better could be found.

For the door staff, to a man, it gave them pole position to assess the female talent. 'Pulling' was THE perk on offer here. Physical altercations with the public were to be avoided at all costs. Now I would say the same thing in that respect, but the way some of them avoided it was a complete non-starter in my eyes.

Perhaps it was because Redhill was your archetypal 'one horse town' that our door staff were always keen to avoid altercations with characters they had known for years in the area. After a while the 'faces' sussed they were not going to be stopped or challenged .....and so they used to just walk straight in without paying or being challenged. I asked Steve if he was aware of what was going on and he just suggested I turn a blind eye. Letting a few locals in was a small price for keeping the peace and anyhow weren't they spending at the bar?

I was distinctly uncomfortable with it all and felt that the lunatics really were starting to run the asylum. It was patently obvious that all the doorstaff were bent in harmony and if one was censured then you would have to censure them all. Steve had thought it prudent to leave it to them and would not even stand on the front door for fear of being compromised in some way. If all the door staff behaved in this way and the General Manager was complicit then it was impossible, I thought, to be able to do anything about it. But then we received some visitors who got me thinking.

I took a call from one of the managers at the Top Rank Suite in Cardiff who asked if one of his ex-staff could be allowed entry along with some friends. Apparently, this guy, called Joe, was studying in Croydon and would be bringing down some doormen from Streatham who worked at the Mecca ballroom there.

Joe and his mates duly arrived and proved to be great fun. They were all Thai nationals and I happened to ask if any of them were kick boxers. They all laughed then I recoiled as one of them leapt in the air and in a single movement kicked the glasses off his friend's head catching them behind his back. It was a great party piece alright but I realised this set them apart and I knew my ensemble of miserable, preening prima donnas were no match for them. I asked Joe that if I should need some help on the door, could he find me any guys.

'How many?' he asked me.

'How many can you get me?'

'I can get you an army - 20, 30, I just need a couple of days' notice'.

Eureka, I thought, but did I dare risk almost certain confrontation?

Every couple of nights I was still in touch with Carrie who by now was in her new job which meant it was impossible for me to visit her. Still nothing had been said to her parents and she was still not inclined to talk about it. My stomach would curdle with fear the more I thought about our quandary and the uproar which was bound to come; but I knew that poor Carrie must have been suffering mightily ….and there didn't seem a thing I could do about it.

Setting my concerns aside, I was beginning to really enjoy Busby's. We were still getting rave reviews, even from the London press and it was becoming something of a place to be seen in. I enjoyed some surreal nights with the snooker player Alex Higgins when he dropped in and the actor Tom Baker who was filming *'Dr Who'* nearby. The atmosphere was pretty electric for the most part and with the release of *'Saturday Night Fever'* around that time, suddenly everyone wanted to check out 'the disco'.

One of my standout memories from that time was entertaining the actor, singer and broadcaster Al Matthews who arrived for a PA appearance at the club. As the club's reputation grew we were getting a number of record companies and management agencies keen to foist their acts onto us. Most were a bit on the dodgy side but Al had scored with '*Fool*' the year before and I knew he'd be a pull.

He was every inch the 'pro' as I'd expected but he proved to be a charming and fascinating character all round. Over dinner the subject of Vietnam came up as I knew Al had spent some time out there. He'd actually covered himself in glory being promoted as the very first black Marine Sergeant and picking up numerous military awards including two public hearts. The experience was still raw for him though and from happily singing Ella Fitzgerald songs one moment, he broke into tears as he recalled of some of the terrible sights he'd witnessed.

My time in Redhill also coincided with some of the worst excesses of the IRA bombing campaigns on mainland Britain. My father had been telling me how it was becoming a problem for him at work as the police routinely called on construction sites where Irishmen were known to be working. That was understandable enough perhaps but even going into a shop for him and my mother had now become an uneasy experience when their accents gave rise to mutterings. There was a heightened sense of alertness in Redhill as memories were still fresh from the 1974 pub bombings in nearby Guildford. We would instigate random baggage checks to assure customers of a state of readiness but I doubted their effectiveness. You could always count on one idiot though to exploit a situation and for a time we endured a spate of telephoned bomb hoaxes.

On occasions, we could even see the perpetrators in the act. We would turn people away from the door for whatever reason and they thought it clever to just walk across the road and make their threat from a public phone box outside the railway station. The first time we received one, Steve and I did consider evacuating the premises but being convinced it was a hoax thought better of it. Thereafter we ignored them every time. Looking back, we were making ourselves hostages to fortune and some would accuse us of putting people's lives at risk. It's an easy call when you don't have to make it but maybe we were just chancers?

The nightclub industry is a great refuge for the drifter looking for occasional work and a chance to drop out of the regular rat race.

Redhill was no exception in that regard and we had two or three characters who fell into that category. Usually it was an arrangement that suited all parties but occasionally the louche lifestyle and Temptation itself would prove an unhealthy mix. Plymouth had introduced some interesting methods of fiddling to me but Redhill added an extra dimension to my education.

It's always a disappointment when one's most attractive and appealing members of staff let you down badly and reveal themselves as common thieves. You don't want to believe your eyes and sometimes you look for a way out to let them off the hook. That happened twice at Busby's with Britta, our stunning Danish barmaid, and Bill, our charming cellarman from Ulster.

Our weekly stocktakes suggested that something was amiss on one particular bar, but I just couldn't put my finger on it as the tills were always correct and all the protocols were being adhered to. It was impossible to discreetly observe the bar staff because the layout of the club prevented one from doing just that. Again, I had to resort to asking for outside help and this time it was in the form of our hapless representative from Bass Charrington; Claude.

Claude wasn't really a drinker; neither would he ever have been a clubgoer. His social activities didn't veer from the Tuesday night bridge club he attended and his cricket obsession in the summer. He was the wrong man in the wrong job in so many ways but I hoped he'd be able to stand at the bar, order a few drinks and see if there was anything unusual in the service. In truth, I didn't expect him to deliver. He did like looking at Britta though, couldn't take his eyes off her in fact. He made sure she served him every time as he knocked back one Holsten Pils after another. She always had a bewitching smile for him and he noticed she was constantly popping glace cherries into her mouth. He mentioned this when I bumped into him in the gents. He hadn't seen anything untoward he said but 'wasn't she gorgeous, especially for the way she pops those cherries?'

I agreed with the first part of his observation but the cherries were news. Going past her bar a few minutes later, she smiled at me in her usual alluring manner and yes, I noticed too, that the cherry bowl was running low, but why were the used cocktail sticks being put in a small glass by the till? Have you ever had that sinking feeling when realisation dawns on you? I decided that I'd do a till crash and just knew my uncomfortable hunch was going to confirm my fears. As I pulled out the till drawer I scooped up the abandoned cocktail sticks. Britta noticed and looked at me solemnly.

I took the till into the office to reconcile it and found the shortfall I was expecting - £11. There were 11 cocktail sticks in the glass too. So, it was just a simple underring each time with a cocktail stick counter. I phoned down to the bar asking for Britta to come to the office.

'Sorry boss, she ain't feeling too good – she's had to go home'.

I never saw her again.....but she had the grace at least, to put £11 cash into the replacement till. I wondered if she had had that fatal, compulsive urge that compelled her not to resist temptation but concluded that she, like so many more I would meet in this game, was an opportunist who would steal if they thought they could get away with it. Very sad.

Compared to Britta, Bill's little scam was all the more galling because it meant we had to get rid of a capable individual doing an essential job for us. Because it would take some time to find a suitable replacement it also meant I had to do it myself in the interim.

Bill was your classic drifter character. He said he had had to get away from the troubles in Northern Ireland but he never spoke of them nor of anything else he had done in Life. A very private character, he had no friends at work or outside of it as far as we could see. He lodged in a small room above a pub on the way to Reigate and could be found most evenings drinking and smoking in the bar below but invariably he would be alone. He was very softly spoken and had a very, quiet, dry sense of humour. An odd guy for sure, but he seemed inoffensive and we were happy to have him around.

Stocktaking was conducted on a quarterly basis by a team of outside auditors and once their job was done and a satisfactory result achieved then we could relax for a further twelve weeks or so before preparing for them again.

Liquor stocktakes can be very volatile because of the nature of the goods and the value of the items, especially spirits. However, once the modus operandi is established any mistakes are usually remedied on subsequent audits. Bill knew this of course and could calculate how long he would have to cover his tracks. His method of dishonesty relied on a conspiracy. It wasn't an original technique, but if the right partners in crime could be found then it was almost fool proof provided complacency didn't set in and the perpetrator took reasonable care and precautions.

The auditors had visited this particular week and had recorded a satisfactory stock which we were pleased to hear of but had been expecting. The following night we were enjoying a particularly busy session when one of the bar staff called out to me saying a barrel needed changing. Bill was nowhere to be found so I thought it easier to go and do it myself.

In the cellar I started cursing Bill, because he had so much stock in there. I duly changed the keg but when removing the empty one I found the best before dates to be out of kilter. I changed the keg again fitting the hose to one with an earlier date. I thought I'd sample the goods myself and, telling the staff that a new keg was now fitted, I asked for a half pint of it.

'What have you done boss?'

'Eh?', I asked.

'This is all water boss….you're Jesus in reverse!!'.

I wondered for a second if I'd actually fitted a cleaning bottle and raced to the cellar before some poor customer imbibed himself on cleaning fluid, but no, it was clearly marked Carlsberg. Puzzled, I fitted another keg and asked for another pint to be drawn. Same again….water!!!

Fortunately, as the session was nearly over we managed to finish the night without needing to source more Carlsberg. I knew I'd have to find the answers the next morning.

What I was to uncover was a fiddle by Bill on an almost industrial scale. In tandem with the draymen, Bill was arranging for our stock to be sold to other pubs on their rounds and he was receiving half of the proceeds raised. He had covered his tracks by filling empty kegs with water and placing new, full kegs above them. Auditors can never be bothered to shift heavy 22 gallon kegs piled on top of each other and will invariably tick off stock items if they see their seals intact, as Bill had made sure they were.

The ramifications were horrendous as Bill and the draymen were all sacked as well as crooked managers of hostelries en-route who were buying the cheap beer. Given that the stock control was part of my remit, I feared retribution myself but thankfully the brewery concerned wanted to maintain a good relationship and agreed to reimburse the missing stock.

Greed, pure greed had ruined lives again and whilst those involved got their just desserts, I wondered how their families would be affected as a result of their actions.

Another misdemeanour tackled and Life went on; but more trouble was just ahead and this time Life very nearly didn't go on.

Chapter 7

'Darlin', Darlin' Baby'

Every night was pretty busy at Busby's and Life was pretty full on in every respect. Unlike Plymouth, one didn't feel so isolated there with London only 20 minutes away by train and Brighton just half an hour in the other direction.

On my nights off I'd often head to Scamps in Sutton where the jazz-funk scene was now getting well underway and sometimes I'd take in Martine's in East Grinstead and The Hunter's Moon in Copthorne. You had to see what everyone else was doing but these were heady days and providing you got the basics right, then your business was as guaranteed as it was possible to be. Gatwick Airport was on our doorstep and with Crawley and Horley having little too offer, we could be sure of a bonanza - if we could just manage to attract the air hostesses!

It wasn't too hard and got easier when on a whim I announced that air crews would be admitted free of charge on Wednesdays and Thursdays IF they turned up in their uniforms. Bingo!! It's always the simplest ideas that work but the sight of that fleet of Laker's Airways hostesses in their scarlet apparel sure did attract the bees to the honeypot. We did get into a little bit of trouble when we extended the same offering to the emergency services. The nurses didn't all have to come in stockings and suspenders in the way that they did but I guess that was the stuff of fantasy for some. It was a pity, but not unexpected, when the hospital authorities ruled it out of order for nurses to go socialising in their uniforms.

I was still living in lodgings at the time and finding it difficult to find somewhere suitable of my own to rent. Steve heard me placing an ad with The Surrey Mirror and asked would I consider sharing his flat. I first recoiled at the suggestion thinking I might be viewed as being of the same persuasion as him but he insisted that was never going to happen. It was a nice place and the rent would be a lot easier so over to Elvington Lodge in Reigate I now decamped.

In truth, Steve was a very decent man but he had some tremendous hang-ups and I came to appreciate the difficulties a gay man expected to face in everyday life in that period. He tired of telling people, including his own family, that the right girl had just not appeared yet. He especially hated having to invite lady friends to accompany him on certain social occasions when it was the 'done thing'. I guess it was his frequent bouts of depression that led to him taking more and more risks and indulging in totally outrageous behaviour on occasions. He was letting his guard drop too often and you just knew he would eventually go too far.

One night I noticed him talking to a guy at the bar and when Steve waved me away as I approached, I thought he had latched onto another prospect. Sometime later the two disappeared and I assumed Steve may have taken him down the road to The White Lion where he used to love to retreat. I thought no more of it and returned to the office to catch the TV news and do a little paperwork. I'd been there a good half hour when John Harrison, our chef, came into the office asking to use the management toilet.

By day, John worked at Rank Leisure's headquarters in Whyteleafe, just a few miles away. He had a pretty stressful job there by all accounts and he enjoyed the nights with us. Apart from earning a few extra shillings, he found it therapeutic to do a little cooking as he enjoyed it so much.

'Go right ahead John', I said as I beckoned him in. In an instant John yanked at the toilet door and opened it to find Steve and his hitherto drinking partner in what can only be described as an uncompromising position which left no room for ambiguous interpretation!

John took flight at a pace to belie his 19 stone frame whilst Steve launched into me with a volley of abuse, his face contorted in a purple rage. Pulling up his trousers he insisted he would never have crashed in if I was doing something in there with a woman. I think I would have dropped the latch first.

It was a measure of the man though that he was laughing about the incident half an hour later describing how the look on our faces was priceless. I've no doubt, but I also knew John wouldn't keep the incident to himself. Sure enough, a couple of days later I was being interrogated by the Operations Director who wanted to know every last juicy detail. I tried to play a straight bat but it makes no odds when your interrogator has already made up his mind about a situation he perceived as being nothing less than deviant. Within a week, Steve had been dispatched to Bristol and I found myself in total charge and was now the company's youngest manager.

Some regarded the appointment as being handed a poisoned chalice and I didn't welcome the close monitoring by Head Office and the Ops Director in particular. You are always going to get that though when you control somewhere so high profile as Busby's was at that time but you can only do your best and be true to yourself. The truth of it all was that it was a very lonely position. I had no support, not even a cellar manager now to clean the pipes and stock the bars. My doormen were next to useless being afraid to turn away those who might turn on them. All the time I was more than a little pre-occupied with the situation in Devon. Carrie had finally told her folks which was a relief in many ways because I knew they would rally around her but I was worried that that might cause me to be regarded as a pariah. But, hey, I was going to be a Father. Amidst all the worry, stress and sheer exhaustion I was experiencing; that was a prospect of sheer joy.

Steve's exit also meant my rent was doubled to an almost unmanageable level now, what else could go wrong I wondered? I didn't have long to wait for the answer to that one. One of the staff had asked if they could borrow my car for the afternoon to go on a short trip to Croydon, I reluctantly agreed on condition that they filled it up with petrol. I was annoyed when the car wasn't returned to me that day and was worried in case he had been involved in an accident with it. When he bounded in the next morning my relief turned to disbelief when I was told what had happened. The idiot had left it in a no parking zone in Croydon and returned to find the car had disappeared. Assuming it had been stolen he contacted the police who had been in touch that morning. The car had been impounded and as the tax had not been renewed, the pound had disposed of it!

'Where is it then?' I asked. I just knew the answer….it had been put through the crusher. It sounded like a Candid Camera hoax and I waited for him to smile and put me out of my misery….. but he wasn't joking.

The next few days saw my burden lightened somewhat. A new cellarman, Mark Humphries, was appointed who proved to be just the tonic I needed. He was a cheerful and hardworking chap with a great attitude who seemingly had not had too many breaks in life. Another drifter really, sometimes the whole show used to seem like a cowboy film, but he had a great attitude and with him in situ I had one less thing to worry about.

The Ops Director then announced that I was to receive the services of an Assistant Manager who had recently joined the company.

'Please make him feel welcome and don't demand too much of him?' I'd do my best I assured him and looked forward to meeting the new boy.

When Peter Langley turned up, he looked like a man totally devoid of confidence wondering what he had let himself in for. He was a big guy who looked much older than his years, probably the result of the obvious stress he seemed to be bearing. Peter had set his heart on becoming a comedian and entertainer but after a summer season in the holiday camps he decided that that was not his vocation though he was equally uncertain that his new career path would be any more fulfilling.

He needed somewhere to stay so I thought he might as well take Steve's old room which would help to stabilise my fragile finances. Even though I was now established as the manager in one of the company's showpiece operations, my wages were still only about £70 per week. Though it was a whole £1.30p over the national average at the time, it didn't seem great. It wasn't that much more than the cellarman's rate and certainly not as much as the new resident DJ I had appointed that week. There was the prospect of bonuses and good pay hikes down the line but I knew it was ill reward for a job that was taking a severe toll on my health and wellbeing. Until Peter and Mark arrived I had been obliged to work daily from 9am through until 3am when we had evening sessions. It was physically demanding of course but equally mentally exhausting given the endless staff issues and constant battling with the Ops Director and the Head Office regime.

A further worrying trend that was now becoming evident was the increasing level of trouble and violence being experienced. That's always a dangerous by product of becoming too successful but hitherto we had managed to keep the lid on it by the expediency of utilising our fictitious membership scheme and restricting admission to couples only when it got too crowded. Tanked up groups of males in a stag party or out on the lash were not going to buy that and emboldened by alcohol and the strength of their numbers they would occasionally take on the bouncers. It was bad enough when the violence erupted on the door but when it occurred inside the premises the results could be catastrophic and often quite dangerous. Bad news spreads quickly of course and I knew all the good work could be quickly undone if we were to develop a negative reputation as a place where one could expect to see trouble.

My door staff were just not up to the job and were not prepared to put themselves in the line of fire or to entertain any risk. So, if they weren't prepared to get physical and weren't averse to a little fiddling in the way of backhanders, what use were they to me? Knowing that is one thing but finding a remedy is another, it was a cancer that threatened to destroy our business…and probably my career as well.

During one quiet Wednesday night session, I decided to let Peter look after the shop on his own for a few hours whilst I drove up to the Tiffany's Ballroom in Streatham to explore the possibility of the Thai boys helping out. Joe gave me a great welcome and we retreated to a corner to discuss what help he may be able to give me. True to his earlier promise, he would indeed provide me with a full team with a further squad in reserve should we need to deploy them. The wages were agreed with an additional 50p per hour being paid to his crew PLUS a Big Mac meal!!! The latter condition threw me but it seemed the Thai boys were addicted to McDonald's and their first British restaurant had opened just down the road in Plumstead. I readily agreed on condition that they brought one for me as well. That was the moment in time when I put the kybosh on my own physical fitness, for ever since, I too have been far too partial to the offerings from The Golden Arches!

The boys were to make their debut at Busby's on Christmas Eve at a lunchtime session I was putting on for staff from the local offices and businesses who would be breaking up for Christmas. They would then hang around for the evening session when the normal crew would turn up….and be issued with their dismissal notices, although I did decide to retain a couple of them. Christmas was still a week or so away and I remember the pressure of the enormous risk I was taking at the time. I had placed my trust in the hands of the Thai boys, would they even turn up? How would the other guys react? Were the new team up to the job? I couldn't breathe a word, not to Peter, not to the Ops Director. I doubted anyone would support me if I had and failure would have meant the exit door for sure. I'm not sure how I functioned that week but it was probably the knowledge that within days I was due to be a Father.

On the morning of Christmas Eve, it seemed I suddenly realised what I'd let myself in for. I had not one but two disco sessions ahead or ten hours of mind numbingly average music to be subjected to at up to 110 decibels. The great days of disco were now well under way and whilst a lot of classics emerged there was an awful lot of dross too. That alone would be addling my mushy brains but I groaned at the thought of all the grief I was just bound to encounter that day. 'Happy Christmas Everybody?' It hardly seemed possible. I had to get out there though, put on the tux and be the front man. Heck, Rank were sure getting their £70 worth!

However, it was a reassuring sight to see Joe and the Thai Army turning up especially as they hadn't forgotten the promised Big Macs! They all looked immaculate and with their diligence and respectful manner I was sure the whole dynamic of our operation was about to change. From the very start the punters loved them. At first it was something of a novelty to have an assembly of quite exotic looking characters to greet them but more than that it was knowing that these guys could actually deal with any threatened hostility levelled against them or the venue.

When the regular door personnel turned up for work that evening, they were agitated to say the least when hearing that their services were no longer required. I'd outflanked them on this occasion but their mutterings confirmed my certain belief that there would be recriminations down the road.

I had been prepared for the reactions of the former door staff but what was less certain was the response from those they had failed to control. The undesirables who could be relied upon to cause a fight or disturbance, the spongers who expected to walk in for free and indeed the Redhill Establishment figures who expected free admission and free drinks....and still they were likely to cause ructions. If we were ever going to turn it round, it had to be now.

Most of them in fact did comply. They probably thought they'd had a very good run and they could see that we were at least prepared for them. There were still some though that I didn't want in at any cost and we endured a few uncomfortable moments when standing firm and turning them away. Again, I knew I was harbouring trouble. Was the job really worth all this stress? Not at all, but I just felt it had to be done.

The dividends began to be realised straightaway. Door revenue immediately increased as expected but the general atmosphere seemed to improve immeasurably. Once again it was a real fun place to go to and to work within and the word began to get out. Even the music seemed to be getting better. There was too much Boney M being played and it's hard to believe now that Paul McCartney's dirge, *'The Mull of Kintyre'* was the nation's number 1 tune and also got plenty of airings. It was the era though of Donna Summer's *'I Feel Love'* and Chic's defining disco classics. Not especially soulful to my ears but considerably better than the Eurotrash which seemed to be the norm in Plymouth for much of the time. Even the notoriously slow Wednesday sessions became worthwhile and I looked forward to maybe even getting a pat on the back from the hierarchy. In retrospect, I must have been getting carried away if I'd hoped for that!

At the end of the Christmas Eve session, I ordered a drink for all the staff and flopped down with them exhausted but relieved. Looking around I felt that at last I had the nucleus of a team who could be trusted and relied upon. It was a huge feeling of satisfaction and I felt at that stage I could enjoy the Christmas and look forward to a happier new year ahead.....as well as the imminent joys of fatherhood, much though that scared me to death!

On Christmas morning, I stirred myself to head for home and to meet with the family again. First though I put in a call to Carrie who assured me there was no sign of the baby arriving soon. She sounded anxious but content and that encouraged me greatly. She must have been so apprehensive but she had her family there alongside her and I knew that was as good as it could get in all the circumstances.

I always loved Christmas back home. Apart from catching up with the folks and my sister, I knew I would be taking in a match at The Poppies, my beloved Kettering Town Football Club. In the evening, I'd get down to The North Park Working Men's' Club for some proper Soul and Motown music. I had yet to find a club in all my travels where I would enjoy the music quite as much as I did there. Maybe it was the thumping sound system with the treble so full on that it made those Motown tambourines reach out and tickle your feet or maybe the low ceiling and layout of the place that just generated at-mos-phere the moment you walked in. I knew most of all though that it was the people themselves who were just so passionate about the sounds they were hearing. Most of us can relate to a time and place where everything just came together in the most perfect of ways but The North Park in Kettering was Soul Heaven to me. What I heard and experienced there instilled into me a lifelong passion that has never ceased to sustain me. Kettering was home, and as Bobby Womack will tell you; *'Home Is Where The Heart Is'*.

The journey back to Redhill was one of contemplation. I imagined what Life might have in store for me. Soon there would be another little person for us to consider and provide for, how was I going to do that? Despite my optimism for the future at Busby's, I knew trouble and strife would never be far away. Should I persevere or should I move on? Should I do something completely different? The more I thought about it, the more I knew I had no idea whatsoever.

The train pulled into Redhill station at around 8 o'clock that evening. The station was directly opposite Busby's and I imagined all the debris from Christmas Eve that would still be lying around in there. I thought to myself that I'd face it all in the morning but then found myself compelled to take a quick look in.

As I opened the front door, the phone started to ring and I hurriedly raced towards it thinking it was probably someone inquiring about New Year's Eve tickets. What I wasn't prepared for was the sound of Carrie's mother telling me I was now the father of an absolutely, beautiful baby daughter! I didn't know whether to laugh or cry. I thought of all those days and weeks of fear and anxiety, of all that Carrie had endured on her own….but now, she was here….our baby. I thanked her mother and sank to my knees in prayer. I was I felt, truly blessed.

Chapter 8

'Disco Inferno'

As I came out of Busby's that night, I locked the door behind me and felt the urge to share the news of the baby's arrival. I should have been in a state of euphoria but there was no one to tell. I couldn't phone home because, for now, her arrival would have to remain The Big Secret, until such time as the way forward could be determined. I felt very, very alone and quite utterly useless. I should have been there, beside Carrie. How had it come to this?

Crossing the road to take a taxi, I decided instead to veer into The Wheatsheaf where I'd enjoyed the craic with Luke and the other Paddys a few months before. This time the bar was all but deserted and I found myself staring into my pint of Harp lager. It would have to be my companion that night and I decided I would fill that glass a few times more. A shadowy figure then loomed in front of me and made their way over to the jukebox. I had thought I was all alone so his movement gave me a jolt; I wondered though what choice of music was now about to break the peace and assault my ears.

I was surprised to hear the clip clopping sound of the intro to The Four Seasons', *'Sherry',* fill the room. I've always liked Frankie Valli's falsetto voice and this, his first hit with The Four Seasons, has always resonated for me. Sherry? That'd be a nice name I thought. I'll have to mention that to Carrie.

The next few days were a bit of a blur, there was so much to think about but I knew everything was out of my hands. All I could do was to occupy myself with the business in hand but I was just going through the motions and only looking forward to taking the long road to Plymouth.

Unfortunately, I hadn't replaced the motor that had been crushed but a regular customer came to the rescue and let me have his rather nice Ford Capri for a few days. I decided that I would go down straight after the New Year's Eve session if I hadn't partied too much.

Trouble was, I did party too much....so much so that I came within an ace of blowing up the sound system itself. I thought it would be appropriate after Auld Lang Syne to mount the DJ rostrum and spray our beloved patrons with champagne. The crowd were all in full voice bellowing out, *'Mull of Kintyre'*, yet again. It used to seem that that song was going to be Number 1 in the charts for eternity. Nine weeks it managed in the end – who were these people who were buying it?

I'd seen the Formula 1 drivers do it enough times, I thought it would be a cinch but the cork stubbornly refused to pop out causing me to get a bit frantic with it. It eventually exploded alright, right over the decks causing Paul McCartney to give way to a gentle 'phut' as the sound disappeared and died. The crowd carried on regardless with endless verses of that nauseating tune which I did come to appreciate on that occasion, as it gave us time to wipe down the gear and coax it back into life. I'll not forget the first 20 minutes of 1978 though, thinking that I'd really cocked up big time!

The next day I finally laid eyes on our baby. She looked wonderful as did her mother who now seemed contented and at ease with herself. Sure, there would be difficult days ahead but for now she could bask in the pleasure of the company of our yet unnamed daughter. Seeing the two of them there, I felt so proud. Nothing else mattered now, not trouble and strife in nightclubs, not company politics such as I'd also been experiencing, nor wondering what our families would think of the baby's arrival. She was here, she was lovely and she was loved and adored.

My visit was all too fleeting though and soon I was driving back again. Nothing would ever be seen the same again, I knew that much. Everything from that day onwards was viewed in a slightly different perspective and I suppose that must be the same for every new parent. I was troubled though, because already I felt matters were out of my hands. I knew her family would take control and would do so in the best interests of mother and child. It mattered not what I felt about it all, there was no point in challenging the situation as I was just not around. It was a sinking feeling but one I knew I had to get used to.

For the next few days back in Redhill, I couldn't get the pair of them out of my mind and I became detached from everything going on around me. On one occasion, I found myself in the spirits cupboard doling out stock to one of the bar supervisors. I was just not taking in her orders and it was driving her to distraction.

'What's up?', Ros finally asked of me and when I turned to face her I found myself collapsing in tears.

The stress had finally got to me and I could see no way out. I had achieved quite a lot at Busby's but now it was as if it was all to no avail. What was the point of it all when the things that really matter in life should be getting one's full attention? Here I was in this crazy, artificial, hedonistic world trying to make a living out of people having a good time when I realised I was just not enjoying it anymore and worse still; I just didn't care anymore. The situation was exacerbated by the worrying fact that my stance with the Thai doormen had not gone unnoticed and some sort of backlash was bound to occur.

Their arrival was an undoubted success in so many ways. Those boys did their job so well with good grace and excellent discipline and their respectful manner to patrons and management alike was a revelation. It was an object lesson compared to the previous regime and I knew if I could hold it all together for a few more weeks then we could set a course for growth and prosperity in the business. I wanted to be able to move on from the security issues and to promote the club's offering in terms of music, food, atmosphere…..and coolness. It may have sounded idealistic but on the surface, things really were that good. It could be a great place to be and to work in, but all the time there were sinister undercurrents which I dreaded coming to the surface.

The Ops Director and his team were taking a very close look at the operation now. One might have hoped for support and encouragement, perhaps some sort of acknowledgement for the excellent revenue now being produced. Instead, it was the total opposite; they seemed to see me as some sort of maverick who bent the rules. There may have been some credence in their assertion but instead of celebrating a remarkable turnaround, I found myself subjected to endless nit picking. If it wasn't an error on one of the endless paper returns I had to file, it was a deficiency in the standards of maintenance or cleaning. All transgressions were sent via the dreaded 'House Notes', Rank's internal system of communication which was copied to a myriad of people in the chain of command. On one occasion, I was asked why an Incident Report had not been filed for a fight which had apparently taken place outside the premises. As there had been no fights to my knowledge I sought clarification on this one. It turned out that one of the Ops Director's spies had reported specks of blood near to the entrance.

Thinking that my team had failed to report the incident to me, I reared up on them only to be told that a drayman had merely cut his finger when delivering the day before! My explanation was not acknowledged, nor do I expect, even believed. Such a discourtesy would hardly have been tolerated by the great J Arthur Rank himself!

It was a climate that gradually led to me contemplating an exit and if it meant leaving the industry altogether; so be it. A few nights later I was approached by a customer who had previously had a chat about the club and the nature of the business we were enjoying. I thought no more about it but he was to reappear and set me on a different course.

The following Saturday night we were enjoying another capacity session at Busby's. The place was buzzing and I realised that all the ingredients were now in place. We now had an excellent resident DJ, Dino, the guy I had hired a few weeks before. At last I now had someone in this key role capable of setting the tempo and steering the crowd without simply regurgitating whatever was in the charts. I sometimes used to take myself up to the old cinema balcony from where I could take in all the action below. The whole arena was framed in scaffolding which extended the length of the room above the dancers' heads. Even though there was a huge void above them, the placement of the speakers and lighting rigs gave the impression that they were dancing in a very compact bubble cocooned from the rest of the world. Though I was very proud of what had been achieved here, I knew I could never be content here. I had to move on.

Walking back down to the club area, I wandered up to the front door to check out the numbers. The guys were just doing the 'changing of the guard' when the boys inside the main club area would be summonsed to take up a position on the front door for an hour or so. The changeover meant that for a minute or so we would be under strength but on every other night the process was almost seamless. Not tonight though. The situation was exacerbated when I invited Peter Langley to go to the office and watch his beloved Arsenal on *Match of The Day*. He said he wasn't that bothered as it had been a goalless draw but I insisted knowing that he'd been on the door all night and was due a break.

I stood alone on the front door with Pat, one of the Thai guys, whilst we waited for our reinforcements. Pat was a very quiet, softly spoken student who always went about his duties conscientiously and that perhaps explained why he was especially well liked by the rest of his colleagues. He had a pencil slim figure which betrayed his strength and the fighting capability which his countrymen assured me he possessed. Working at the club was a necessary means to an end for Pat. He wasn't interested in the women or anything else which attracted others to work in such an environment. He just needed to earn enough to get by whilst he completed his studies. With a degree under his belt he knew he could get on in life back home….and make his parents and family proud of him.

I used to like to chat away to Pat about how he found life in England and the comparison with home. He had been here long enough for the novelty to have worn off, but it was clear that he questioned the values of people he was meeting in this job. Many of them certainly used a different moral compass from his to steer, or lurch, their way through life.

We looked out from the door and noticed three guys negotiating the dozen steps up to our front door. As they drew nearer, I recognised them as three of the local villains our previous doormen had been too frightened to make sure they paid for entry.

'Be careful, Pat', I whispered, 'these fellas could be trouble'.

'Awright mate?' chirped one of them I knew as Val. I'd never witnessed him as one responsible for causing trouble, but he had an uncanny knack of always being in the vicinity of it. 'Brought a couple of mates wimme, it's ok to go in innit?' I didn't have a reason to bar them, especially not knowing the other two at all, but their silence unnerved me.

'Sure', I said, 'you're very welcome - 3 quid apiece' and gestured towards the cash desk.

'You're making US pay?' said the large, dishevelled figure beside Val, 'we NEVER pay no one'.

I wasn't about to debate his use of a double negative as he stood staring, first at me and then at the pencil man alongside me. He looked at Val and then at the fit looking character on his other side who stood smiling as he looked down at his shoes.

'Are you going to let us in mate?'

'No mate', I heard myself saying back to him quite emphatically trying hard to conceal the heavy rumblings of fear I felt in my stomach, 'things have changed here, if you want in, you have to pay'.

I braced myself for his reaction and was expecting to catch a flying fist. Where the hell were all the doormen?

He shuffled slightly on the spot, looked at his mates and then behind him to check if anyone else was witnessing our little dispute. There was no one.

He unzipped the Harrington jacket he was wearing, put both his hands across his chest...and then pulled out two enormous machetes.

I took a step backwards and then felt a punch to my left cheek from Val and immediately another to my right cheek from the fit guy. I felt the crunch but no pain, the machetes had effectively anaesthetised me and I continued to walk backwards focusing on the blades.

When the first blow landed, I was aware of Pat disappearing from my peripheral vision and assumed he had run to save his skin. I was very much alone now and as The Fat Man raised both machetes, I thought my very life was about to be extinguished.

Still the punches were raining in on either side, my head veering one way and then another which was probably making it awkward for The Fat Man to take aim.

I could hear screams but despite there being nearly 800 in there that night, no one was on hand to help my resistance which was all but shot now.

I had retreated backwards along the entrance passage which was adorned with framed portraits of Spencer Tracey, Humphrey Bogart and all the Hollywood greats, and then I felt myself falling. My last recollection was of looking up from the ground and seeing those machetes coming down towards me from a great height. I must have passed out at that point for the next I knew was a flurry of people coming to my aid asking if I was alright. I was, but I couldn't quite fathom it out. I had seen the machete drop, so why wasn't I dead? Perhaps I was dead!

I was taken into the manager's office and was amused to find Peter Langley still sitting there watching the Arsenal, completely oblivious to the chaos which had reigned just a few feet away from him on the other side of the wall. He recoiled in horror when he saw me and as I caught sight of my battered face in the mirror, I could see why. I was battered beyond recognition but I had all my teeth still and as far as I could make out my head was still stuck to my shoulders.

Three CID officers who had been drinking in the club that night came in to try and interview me and slowly I was able to piece together exactly what had happened. Pat, who I thought had run off in fear, had in fact saved me from further damage and quite possibly had saved my life. Instead of fleeing he had run to find something to defend us with. All he could find was a free-standing ashtray which sat atop a two foot pole. You never see them nowadays but they always seemed to be a prop in the older James Bond films. As I fell to the floor, The Fat Man had apparently sat astride me as he picked the spot to bring down his machete. Pat brought the ashtray down on the back of his head which led to him getting a pummelling from the two accomplices. The Fat Man then brought one of the machetes down square on the top of Pat's head. He was now lying covered in blood in an ante-room whilst we awaited an ambulance. It was a quite horrific sight and I feared the extent of his injuries. The screaming and commotion were by now at fever pitch but Pat and I sat in silence at the centre of it all. Whatever had happened we were still alive and I think his mind, like mine, was concentrated in prayer.

The Fat Man and Val had both already been arrested but the third had made his escape and the weapons too, had disappeared. The uniformed police now arrived in numbers but there didn't seem to be any co-ordination. It was a scene of utter chaos and confusion but my only thought was to get a clean shirt on.

Soon, the ambulance arrived and I finally experienced what I often wondered. What would it be like to speed through the streets and have the blue lights flashing just for you? Pat was doing his best to act stoically and he constantly asked about my wellbeing. I was more worried for him though. His injuries looked very serious and I was concerned when his speech slurred and his eyeballs rolled back into his head. The ambulance crew and myself did our best to keep him talking in an effort to stop him drifting into a state of unconsciousness. There were moments we felt we were losing him and as he lay there I thought of those hopes and dreams of his we had discussed earlier in the evening and I dreaded the thought of his parents receiving tragic news from across the world.

As soon as we arrived at the hospital, Pat was whisked off to the intensive care unit and I was prepared for an X-ray examination.

It's all a very surreal experience in these situations but the upshot is that Life suddenly comes into much sharper focus. I thanked God that I appeared none the worse for the hammering I had endured even if I was going to look pretty gruesome for a little while. It occurred to me that Pat and I had literally put our lives on the line in the course of our job and for what? To ensure that some low life would pay £3 if they wanted to come into our establishment.

I knew we wouldn't be thanked for it. I could hear the commentary that would follow, that we were unlucky but then it's all just a part of the job. 'Not any more' I resolved to myself. Other things in life were far, far more important and as I lay in the hospital cubicle I knew I had to start to control my own destiny from hereon in.

Eventually Pat emerged after what seemed like several hours of treatment. With his head swathed in layers of bandages his appearance was akin to that of the walking wounded in that grainy old film footage that survives from World War One.

Fortunately, his skull had held firm but the machete wounds were deep and gaping and required extensive delicate stitching. The cops had turned up at the hospital and I heard them discussing the charges that would be levelled at our attackers. At the outset, they feared the possibility of a murder charge but once Pat's condition had stabilised this was reduced to attempted murder. They decided this might still be too hard to prove so reduced it further to GBH (Grievous Bodily Harm) against the pair of us.

I prayed very hard that night in the hospital. I prayed for Pat's life and welfare. I prayed that I might be steered on a path away from this silly life and I prayed most of all for Carrie and our infant that I could somehow do right by them. It was then that I shot up with a jolt as I realised that I had to be in Plymouth on Monday to register the birth. Get me out of here – quick!

Chapter 9

'Uptown Top Ranking'

There wasn't too much sleep that night as the medication I was prescribed failed to make much impression on the aches and pains that ravaged my entire body. My feelings though were those of intense relief. I had been expecting trouble because of the stance that I'd taken but I'd come through it in just about one piece and given that Pat's injuries appeared to be a lot less than feared, then I calculated this was one severe boil that had now been lanced.

Of course, the company was bound to conduct a post-mortem but with my attackers subject to quite severe charges – conspiracy to causing an affray had been added to their list – I knew at least that they'd be out of the way and I didn't envisage too many more taking potshots at us.

The bambino was due to be registered at 3pm that day and with the journey to Plymouth taking up to five hours in those days, I couldn't afford to hang about too long. I called Peter Langley telling him to deal with the Ops Director, I didn't expect tea and sympathy from that quarter but I hoped that he might at last begin to appreciate the risks we had undertaken on behalf of the company on a nightly basis. Any press inquiries I told Peter would have to be met with a firm 'no comment'. To do otherwise would only invite them to put their own spin on a story which would invariably portray the club in a negative hue. We couldn't do very much if the police chose to give them a story but Detective Sergeant Robbie Crawford promised me that they would try to keep the lid on it all as best they could. As horrific and frightening as the incident had been, it would all be old news in just a few days.

It seemed to take an eternity to reach Carrie's house that day. Her family lived just outside Plymouth in a picturesque little village sited atop cliffs looking out towards Plymouth Sound. I'd walked the five miles or so to it back and forth from Plymouth a few times and thought nothing of it...even when I'd get home at 2 in the morning; but what's a few miles for Love's young dreamer? Events, unfortunately, had seemingly overtaken us now but I was still mighty relieved to turn into her drive once more. Carrie's mother answered the door but my smiling greeting was not reciprocated. Saturday night's beating was clearly written all over my features and she stepped back in horror when she saw the ghoul stood in front of her. I should have rung ahead to warn them maybe but I didn't think my looks would be so bad as to frighten the horses....and Carrie's mum!

There were a few words of what sounded like sympathy but I couldn't help feeling that it reinforced any concerns her parents might have had about my pursuit of the unsuitable occupation I was engaged in. I couldn't really disagree with them at all about that.

It was great to see Carrie and the baby once more. Emmeline, she was to be called; I had no say, but no matter as I thought it was a just dandy name. She was smiling and gurgling away and in that magic moment along with Carrie and her mother, all the angst that had afflicted us all in the past few months just dissipated. The power of the innocent child has no equal.

A couple of hours later the registrar also gave me a double take as he entered the details of Emmeline's birth. Carrie had decided to add a middle name which again came as a surprise to me. Never mind, perhaps I'd have more input should we have more issue some day!

We didn't get too long to play happy families before it was time to hit the road again to resume my place on life's treadmill. Carrie did though agree to come up to Redhill for a day or two when we might be able to discuss what course we should embark on. Away from the rest of the family I hoped that might mean the two of us could talk somehow of the future, maybe even of being a proper family.

Somehow or other an air of calm appeared to be descending on activities back at the club. Peter Langley was settling in well and had started to take a good bit of the weight off my shoulders. With Mark taking care of the bars and the Thai Army being so resolute with security, I could relax a bit and even start to enjoy some outside pursuits.

With a mainline station just outside the door, I took the opportunity of catching some regular Saturday afternoon football and checking out some grounds. Queens Park Rangers' Loftus Road ground was one I was especially keen to get to. QPR were an interesting team in the 1970s, Terry Venables had proclaimed them to be the team of the '80s no less and with the likes of Stan Bowles, Gerry Francis and all; they played some great football. Not too much was known of their opponents on the day I went up; the newly promoted Nottingham Forest. That was soon to change though. Brian Clough was assembling a team that would shake the football world not only in England but across Europe too. They won 2-0 that afternoon and finished that season as champions. It was not the football I remembered most that day but the sight of seeing a priest I knew from Kettering in the crowd….with a woman!

That season too, some of the lesser London clubs were enjoying very good FA Cup runs and on March 11th, 1978 I set off for Cold Blow Lane in south east London, to The Den, the home of Millwall FC. It was something of an historical occasion as Millwall were enjoying their best Cup run since before the war and their opponents were the excellent Ipswich Town team assembled by Bobby Robson. There were many great players on view that day who I had been looking forward to seeing, the likes of Paul Mariner, Alan Brazil, John Wark, Terry Butcher, Mick Mills etc., internationals all but unfortunately it wasn't Ipswich's football that was to be seared in my mind thereafter.

A few weeks before, BBC's *Panorama* programme had run an edition focusing on the problems of football hooliganism and how it was a serious issue with Millwall in particular. Some of their fans had taken to wearing the surgical garb of characters from Stanley Kubrick's *'Clockwork Orange'* film and enjoyed celebrating the sickening violence depicted in the film. The programme also highlighted the presence of The National Front who had been seen propagating their fascist message by distributing their material outside The Den. The club had of course disassociated themselves with any links to that organisation and hoped that this match would see the club represented in a far more positive light.

George Burley's opening goal for Ipswich dashed any hopes they might have had of that. Ipswich oozed class that day and it was only a matter of time before they registered their second goal. Any notion of the Millwall Clockwork Orange brigade celebrating a famous day in their team's history was soon dispelled but they were well aware that the larger football world was looking at proceedings that day…and it was simply too good an opportunity for them to miss.

I was at the very far end of the ground from where the trouble first started behind the Millwall goal; too far to get an informed view of proceedings. I'd seen crowds give way and open up before when a fight or disturbance breaks out in their midst but when that happened at The Den that day, it was a contagion that seemed to spark a chain reaction amongst literally hundreds of Millwall fans seeking 'aggro'. It wasn't clear who their victims were as the two sets of fans were strictly segregated but I soon learned that identity and loyalties were incidental when a certain faction were intent on sparking a riot.

Play was still in progress as some spectators spilled onto the pitch to take refuge. A trickle at first, then a surge before panic and pandemonium completely took over. The referee, Mr Gow, took no chances and immediately whistled to abandon proceedings, temporarily at least.

All around the pitch perimeter, police had been stationed to face the crowd, but now they looked quizzical not knowing whether to stay in their posts or to run to the assistance of their colleagues locked in the trouble zone. I noticed one young policewoman moving cautiously along the cinder track by the side of the pitch when she was called over by one of the crowd in the paddock. As she stooped to hear what the problem was, a young thug jumped up and punched her viciously rendering her unconscious with a single blow. No one came to her aid and indeed that section of the crowd started singing lustily before a number of them clambered over the perimeter fence and headed for the real aggro.

Moments later I was to witness the sight of an elderly black lady staggering down the touchline drenched in blood from a head wound with a St. John's Ambulance first aider valiantly trying to help her. A nearby photographer captured the image and it was the one used to illustrate the riot on the TV news bulletins and in the Sunday papers the following day. Thankfully the section of the crowd I was in didn't share the enthusiasm of what seemed at least a couple of thousand agitators. Like me they were stunned at what they were witnessing. Hooliganism was an ugly stain on British football in that era but what happened that day plunged new depths of mindless depravity. I wondered what would happen next and then the cavalry arrived...quite literally. Police reinforcements were at last on the scene and only the actions of the mounted police arriving from the Ipswich end forced the mob to take stock and quickly retreat.

For a few moments, a certain stillness fell on the stadium. Had we really borne witness to such chaos? Had the police regained control? Would we be able to get away from here safely? Whilst I and many more wondered such imponderables, the stadium PA system suddenly crackled into life and the match referee announced himself. Striding onto the pitch was the noble Mr Gow along with the two managers. The match by now was running at least half an hour late, maybe more. Perhaps the referee was going to announce its abandonment and we could all go home and forget this nightmare. That was probably the outcome the hooligan element hoped for too, maybe thinking their team could live to fight another day with the Ipswich score expunged. Mr Gow was to disappoint them though when he boldly announced that the match would be played to a conclusion that day….'even if it finished at midnight!'

'Good man', I thought and the cheers that resounded reassured us all that there was indeed a silent majority of peaceful, law abiding spectators present that day. There was also a rather irked Ipswich team present too who proceeded to stuff Millwall by going on to hammer them 6-1. If ever actions spoke louder than words, it could not have been better illustrated than by the events of that afternoon.

Throughout my tenure at Busby's I continued to keep up my subscription with Blues & Soul magazine and I looked forward to every fortnightly edition. It allowed me to keep tabs on everything in Soulville and in particular what was happening on the Northern Soul scene which had been so much a part of my awakening. The Torch had sadly closed in March 1973 when I had witnessed the closing of proceedings with appearances from The Detroit Emeralds and Sam and Dave and now I was reading of the new Mecca for the scene, Wigan Casino.

It was hard to imagine anywhere being better than The Torch or even of The North Park in Kettering as far as I was concerned but I resolved to get there one day. Why, oh why, was that music not celebrated 'down south'? It finally did make it, but it was to take a long, long time.

In the meantime, the so cool Soul aficionados of London and the South were just getting into the jazz-funk scene and I decided to take a close look at it to see if it was something that could even be introduced to Busby's. The music at the club had improved immeasurably since I arrived but it was still very much a 'handbag scene' appealing to most of the people most of the time…and really, that's as much as anyone can hope for.

Scamps in Sutton and Scamps in Croydon offered the jazz-funk fayre in the middle of the week and there were some great tunes being dropped there including the likes of Roy Ayers's *'Running Away'*, Eddie Henderson's *'Say You Will'* and Dennis Coffey's wonderful *'Wings of Fire'*. Occasionally there was the opportunity to hop on a train to Brighton to catch an appearance of a touring soul band. The Ohio Players and Brothers Johnson were two I caught in this period. On another occasion, I found myself at The Lacey Lady in Ilford where Chris Hill was carving out a reputation for himself as a pioneer and leading influencer on the jazz-funk scene.

I loved the music but it was interesting to compare and contrast the attitudes of Soul fans north and south. For the Northerners, the music was everything and the comradeship of sharing a passion was a massive bonus. Things just evolved like the fashion, the talcum powder, the accessories like discotrons, sports bags etc. It was a living, breathing organism of its own. A strange and quite crazy world in many ways, but once you were in it, you were hooked and as time has since proved, you were hooked for life!

The music was almost an accessory on the Southern scene. It provided a sound track for a time and a place perhaps and whilst it could be hugely enjoyable it was for the most part very transient. The people liked to pose and 'to pull' in a way that was never a feature of the Northern scene.

A few, very few, embraced both scenes and a handful of DJs, most notably Colin Curtis, carved out a reputation on both scenes. There was I found, naked hostility on the part of the Southerners towards the followers of the other scene which was regularly vented on the pages of Blues and Soul but occasionally it could be seen at venues where the two scenes overlapped.

Reading was one of the 'frontier towns' where the two scenes met at the local Top Rank Suite and I was there on the notorious occasion when the Sounds of Understanding and Love were anything but.

The event was a Sunday Bank Holiday Alldayer when Northern Soul was being staged in the larger downstairs ballroom whilst the jazz-funk session took place in a much smaller upstairs area. There may have been a lot of counter attractions going on for the Northern Soul fans that weekend for they were very much in the minority on this occasion whilst the jazz-funkers were jam packed into their zone.

Just prior to starting his slot; Chris Hill became aware that the DJ in the lower ballroom was about to announce a dancing competition which was a regular feature at Northern sessions. Whether it was a sense of mischief that got the better of him, I'm not sure, but he certainly displayed a distinct lack of judgment.

A couple of tunes into his set he suddenly started berating the crowd who were enjoying themselves downstairs. It was all the usual stereotypical rubbish that the Southerners tended to brand the Northern Soul crowd with. That they were living in the past, had no fashion tastes, worked in mills or mines etc. All very amusing to some perhaps but he crossed the line when he suggested that the jazz-funkers make their way downstairs to sabotage the dancing competition.

For the most part, the Northern Soul crowd would profess to love all good quality soul music even if they particularly celebrated certain strands represented by particular artistes or labels. They liked what they liked and have always been passionate and quite protective in relation to it. So, they didn't take kindly to the toerags who sauntered onto the dancefloor during the competition to start taking the p**s out of their passion.

It was an ill-judged intervention and highly provocative. Pushing and shoving soon started before the sound of smashed glasses signalled that a tipping point had been reached. Millwall fans rioting wasn't that surprising but what depths had we reached when similar mayhem was on show at a soul music event?

I would have liked to introduce a proper Soul event at Busby's and thought with the right connections it was eminently feasible but the events at Reading helped to support a strand of reasoning that was starting to gain credence amongst The Rank Organisation's hierarchy.

Soul music attracted black people they reasoned and black people meant trouble! The policy, for certainly it became a policy, was never documented as such in formal communications but it certainly became acknowledged and sadly, was adhered to for the most part in some of the company's venues.

At Reading, the DJs were actually told to play no Soul and no Reggae. It worked; the black people stopped coming…as well as 80% of their regular patrons. I told my DJs to ignore such an instruction which was easier than I imagined owing to the policymakers not really knowing what soul music actually was!

Sad to say there were other times when we were actually told not to let in Paddys, chinks, pikeys or ragheads (Arabic looking patrons!). I used to wonder what J Arthur Rank himself would have made of that policy given that the company he originally founded with a religious ethos had a mission to promote wholesome family friendly entertainment without any discrimination or favour.

Despite all the problems, life in Redhill could be fairly enjoyable if one could put aside the politics, the violence and the continuous hassles. I found some very good people there who helped and supported me immensely. The kindness of certain individuals who welcomed me into their homes and spent time with me away from the madness really helped to alleviate the pressure I was feeling which just seemed to be relentless.

The violence was never quite as bad again….even when a policeman's son from Guildford took umbrage for being turned away and returned armed with a shotgun! Every week produced some kind of drama which would have seemed too incredible for the average TV soap opera.

One morning I arrived at work to find the police waiting for me, but this time it was in connection with the death of a patron who died in an incident after leaving the club the night before. The chap concerned was one of the Irish gang working on the M25. He and his friends had become regulars at the club and were well liked by all the staff who had come to know them. Unfortunately, a wrong word or a misunderstanding over a bag of chips had cost the lad his life in a Chinese takeaway. One of the staff there had called out to a colleague when he felt he had been insulted. The colleague lunged at the Irishman who collapsed in a heap after being stabbed in the heart. At times like that one cannot comprehend the futility and senselessness of actions no doubt fuelled by alcohol and of course the terrible impact and loss felt by family and friends left behind.

On another occasion, Betty asked that I return a call she had taken that morning but with the Motown rep turning up I said I'd do it after lunch. The Motown man was always very good company and that day he was in a particularly ebullient mood as he had been assigned to look after Stevie Wonder on his forthcoming British tour. It was to go so well for him that he was promptly appointed Stevie's personal assistant and he subsequently went off to spend the next few years in the States. I noticed later that he even managed to get a credit on all Stevie's albums during this period!

When I returned from a very convivial lunch, Betty immediately reminded me to make the call, saying that it was from someone in Kettering. Her insistence suggested this was more than a routine courtesy call. I was right; it was a call with devastating news from home which left me in a state of deep depression for a long, long time.

It was hard to take in the detail of the call which came from my best friend's fiancée. Apparently, another of our friends had become embroiled in an argument with his girlfriend's mother who disapproved of the relationship with her daughter. No one will ever know the sequence of events but the mother's body was found wrapped in a carpet in her own home whilst her assailant set off in his car and crashed it into a tree in what appeared to have been a suicide attempt.

He was arrested at the scene and taken to Bedford police station for questioning. After being detained in the cells there, he was put on suicide watch. The police officer in attendance found his lifeless body hanging from his bunk bed when making his second check of the cell. He was just 22 years old. He was a guy loved and admired by all who knew him. Years later people in Kettering never fail to smile at the mention of his name, Stefan.

In between times I was still travelling down to the West Country to see Carrie and Emmeline but I felt things were slowly changing and understandably so. Life had to move on without me around and much as I longed to see them, I started to feel that my visits were something of a disruption to their family life and I knew I had to accept this. Perhaps it was this realisation that caused me to acknowledge some of the girls in and around Busby's. I went out with a few of them on my nights off but whether or not it was the company I was seeking I'm not sure but I certainly wasn't inclined to forge any meaningful relationships.

One Thursday evening, the club had an unexpected fluky success when one of the PA acts that the record companies used to foist upon us suddenly struck gold. A week before they arrived, no one had heard of the two Birmingham teenagers, Althea (Forrest) and Donna (Reid). We hadn't bothered to publicise their appearance as their presence, we figured, would offer only a small diversion during proceedings that evening. The two girls had only recorded *'Uptown Top Ranking'* as a joke. The joke continued when Radio 1 DJ played the track by accident and when the station received numerous requests for repeat plays, the girls were added to an edition of *'Top Of The Pops'*. I couldn't quite believe our luck when this act, who didn't cost us a penny, were Number 1 in the charts by the time of their booking resulting in another full house. Happy days. The girls themselves, were just as stunned, and I'll never forget their bewilderment as they looked out from the stage that night. Sadly, they were unable to follow up their success but at least they were one of the great One Hit Wonders!

That same night, a suited character who looked like he had come straight from his office struck up conversation with me and asked if I enjoyed my job. I was a little taken aback but then realised he was the same guy who had remarked on how well the club was doing just a few weeks earlier. I answered something to the effect that it had its good and bad points and thought no more about it as he chatted a little more before wandering off.

The following Saturday evening he was there again and I remarked to him that he must be enjoying it here.

'Very much' he said, 'I think you've cracked it here'. Again, I thought no more of it other than that was a nice compliment to pay.

Later though he came over again and after a few more probing questions he revealed that he was a Regional Director for a major leisure company and he had a post that he needed filling. In the circumstances, I had to consider any way out if the role was substantial enough and was suitably rewarding.

'Tell me more', I found myself asking him and listened intently while he outlined the opportunity he had to offer.

The position was for a General Manager to run Reeves, a venue in Bristol consisting of a nightclub, cabaret bar and a restaurant. It was a pretty big deal alright and it had just been awarded Club Mirror's 'Club of The Year' title. I had to take a look and I agreed I would go down to Bristol the following week.

However, the very next day another opportunity presented itself when Rank's internal mail brought news of a similar role in Bournemouth at The Village, a nightclub and bowling alley complex. This was more up my street, I liked Rank as a company and would have preferred to stay with them. A posting to sunny Bournemouth certainly appealed and I knew I would be working for a different Operations Director, a guy I knew I could get along with. I hurriedly signalled my interest and almost immediately I received a call inviting me down for interview.

I had every reason to be feeling pretty optimistic about life now. Still the youngest manager in the company, I was now in the running for two of the most prestigious roles in the industry at that level. Onwards and upwards surely?

The interview in Bournemouth went very well. I felt very comfortable with the Director, even moreso when he concluded the meeting by offering me the position. He qualified the offer by saying it had to be ratified by my Ops Director but my thinking was that he would probably be glad to part company with me, given all the friction there had been between us. I walked around the streets of Bournemouth before heading home thinking how much I would enjoy coming to that town.

The only serious competition in Bournemouth was Le Cardinal which I knew to be owned by the Radio 1 DJ, a certain Jimmy Savile! His stewardship of the venue was legendary with certain rules imposed such as always playing two slow records at the top of the hour. That was designed to stimulate bar sales; there would either be a rush beforehand to fuel Dutch courage for guys or people would flood from the dancefloor straight to the bar. He it was who also advertised 'Free Admission to Skirt People'. Thus, sidestepping the sexual equalities legislation and ensuring plenty of paying Non-Skirt People! Corny perhaps, but at the time that sort of advertising drew comment – if only to condemn the practice – and it worked!! I'd been in the business long enough now to appreciate that this business relied heavily on such lateral thinking....and Savile was a master at it.

I was hoping that my appointment would be quickly ratified and there would be no need to flee to Bristol but once again Fate decreed otherwise.

I had wanted to cancel the Bristol trips but deferred the appointment instead with the intention of withdrawing altogether once the Bournemouth job was confirmed.

The following morning Ulrika, the boss's secretary, called to ask me to come and see him immediately. 'Here we go', I thought for what I anticipated would be a bitter-sweet encounter. I was dying to get away and leave the hassle and the politics behind but I hoped that we could part cordially at least.

Terry Samuels had a large intimidating presence which he liked to deploy to great effect. With his thick black beard, one felt they were dealing with Goliath. I had found his style pernickety and incredibly ignorant but I knew having seen him at play with his young family there was something of a tender heart in there as well. I doubted that that would ever be revealed to me though and the way he started the meeting confirmed as much.

He looked at me angrily before asking what on earth I was doing applying for other roles. Why did I not have the sheer courtesy or respect not to have informed him beforehand? I thought to myself that respect was a two way street and it had never been forthcoming from him. He berated me for my immaturity, my lack of judgement and a host of other heinous sins but then he suddenly stopped, turned and completely took my breath away.

'No!'

'No?', I queried.

'No, I'm not agreeing to your transfer...and I've told JC that he can't have you'.

'But, why?' I asked, 'you're always moaning at me, surely it's better for everyone?'

'I said NO!', he bellowed again. 'You drive me up the f*****g wall sometimes, but I know you're the best man for the job'.

I couldn't quite believe what I was hearing from this man who had been my absolute nemesis all the time I had been in the role.

'I know you work hard, I know you've dealt with a lot of trouble and I know you've been in real danger. You've been a bit green but I can see you've turned the place around. People like you, the staff like you, customers like you and damn it, I quite like you really. I want you to stay....so you're staying!'

Still I was speechless.

'OK then? he said, 'get out my office and get back to work!'

I was totally unprepared for what I had just heard and as I walked back to my office, my mind was in complete turmoil. He had actually complimented me but I was so disappointed to learn that he had been in touch with his opposite number to deny me the Bournemouth role; I was in a state of absolute despair. All I could envisage was further wrangling; I doubted very much that a new day was dawning on our relationship. In retrospect, perhaps I should have persevered but things were moving quickly now and I was in no mood to hold back. I picked up the phone and told the people in Bristol that I was coming down.

Chapter 10

'Mind Blowing Decisions'

For the first time, I took Peter Langley into my confidence. I was literally at a crossroads now...should I stay or should I go?

Despite all the run-ins I had had with the boss man, he had just given me a massive vote of confidence. Perhaps now, I could use the endorsement and run the club the way I wanted whilst looking forward to better remuneration and a plum appointment within the company in due course. That would have been the ideal scenario for me but I just didn't expect this leopard to drastically change his spots. Peter agreed that was unlikely but I thought it was pointless to speculate until I had at least had the chance to evaluate what Bristol had to offer.

On the following Friday night, I was deep in thought in my office when there was a sharp knock on the door and a large burly figure strode in. It was The Fat Man!

'What are you doing here?' I asked as I reeled back, totally startled at seeing my assailant from a few weeks ago, 'who's with you?'

'Whoah, whoah', he said, holding his hand up in a gesture that said he was coming in peace, 'I just want a quick word with you and I'll be straight out'.

The door burst open again with two of my door staff asking if I was ok. I was annoyed that The Fat Man hadn't been stopped at the front door but I'd look into that later. 'It's ok lads', I found myself saying, 'this won't last long'.

They left the room and I gestured to The Fat Man to sit down but he chose to stay on his feet.

'Thanks', he said, 'I know I can get done for coming here but I had to try and have a quick word with you'.

I knew it was a condition of his bail that he was to keep away from me and the others involved that night, so I had to ask what he had in mind.

'Look, I've just come out of the nick and I don't want to be going back again'.

'I can't help you with that', I said.

'Yes, you can', he insisted and then started to explain.

'I'm not afraid of doing time, but it has to be worth it. If I'm knocking over a supermarket or a post office for £40k, that's the risk you take….but not for belting a nightclub manager with nothing to gain'.

I could see his logic alright, but failed to see where I came into the equation.

'I need to make out the fight was a lot fairer'

'What?', I still couldn't see how that would change things.

'All you have to say is that there were two or three bouncers on the door with you, my brief says that if you do that, he could persuade a jury that it was just an argument that got out of hand'.

'If I get off or get a result, then there's a monkey in it for you…that'll come afterwards in an envelope'.

I wasn't 100% sure but reckoned he was talking of £500 being my payment.

I was about to ask him to leave but he pre-empted me; 'I'll be off; just you have a good think about it. No one will ever know. I'm sorry for what happened but I just can't face doing another long stretch'. He stretched out his arm and I found myself shaking his hand before he turned on his heel and walked out.

Perhaps a part of me felt a little bit sorry for him. Perhaps he had been swept up in the moment when his pals suggested the confrontation but now he faced a long period of regret it would appear. The feeling didn't last long though because I knew too, that he could well have been facing a murder charge.

That night I realised this was all a nightmare that threatened to go on and on. I thought of the implications if I did nothing and just forgot about the meeting and I thought of the implications if I did do something; namely to report him.

The next day I had arranged to meet Peter Langley, his father and some friends at Stamford Bridge for the FA Cup semi-final between Arsenal and Leyton Orient. Ordinarily, I would have expected a match like that to have been forever ingrained in the memory yet the only recollection I have of that day, 8th April 1978, is of meeting the guys in a pub in Pimlico and relaying the details of the dilemma I was faced with. There was little doubt on their part of what I had to do; I had to tell the police.

The match ended in a 3-0 win for Arsenal by the way, taking them to a final which ended in an inglorious defeat against that Ipswich side

I had so admired a few weeks earlier. At Victoria Station, I called Reigate Police and advised that I probably needed to make a further statement.

At 10pm that evening three detectives arrived at the club to hear my account. Their response was one of sheer delirium. My attackers were due to enter pleas at a preliminary court hearing at Reigate Magistrates Court on Monday morning, now the police would be able to add an additional charge against one of the defendants – perverting the course of justice.

They later told me that uproar broke out at the court when the defendants learned of the new charge. They had agreed to take a common approach and all expected to go in and enter a not guilty plea hoping that bartering between prosecution and defence counsels would lead to diluted charges. If one of them tried to gain an advantage for himself; the others saw it as weakening their defences. After much hurling of abuse one of them decided to cut his losses and, to the chagrin of the other two, he suddenly entered a guilty plea. The Fat Man had not necessarily been the worst offender on the night of the attack but he now found he was facing the most serious charges and the outlook for him was ominous.

The trip to Bristol which I had rearranged now took on greater significance and I knew I had to give it my best shot.

Bristol was a city I had little knowledge of although I had been there nearly a decade earlier to see Bristol Rovers knock my beloved Poppies out of the FA Cup.

I was surprised to find Reeves was situated in Brislington on the outskirts of the city. It was part of the Arnos Court Hotel complex and there was no doubt that the business there was pretty robust.

I was wanted to run Reeves disco and cabaret club as well as The White Swan bar and restaurant. The neighbouring building was the Harlech TV studios and my brief also included all their catering requirements. It was a seven nights and seven days operation and on Saturdays we were expected to cater for up to five wedding parties simultaneously.

They were certainly out to get their pound of flesh from the appointee but at the time I saw it as a prestigious appointment offering very good money….a whole £100 per week!

I was duly offered the role and drove back to Redhill pondering the huge upheaval that lay ahead for me. I felt I was at the end of my tether with Rank and the court case had just about put the tin hat on it.

When I told Peter Langley that I had decided to take the offer, he said I had to do it reasoning that the wages alone made it all worthwhile, yet the differential was probably only £15 per week from what I was now on after Rank had revised my package. Even so, I thought it would make it easier for me to provide for Emmeline and she was still foremost on my mind.

I put in a call to Ulrika asking her to arrange an appointment with Mr Samuels and then I prepared to break the news to The Boss.

He was not totally surprised but he was generous in his comments and seemed to genuinely wish me well. He must have known my departure was largely due to our difficult relationship but he made a point in saying that the door was always open should I ever consider a return. I couldn't imagine that happening at the time but his offer was taken on board as was his warning that the grass isn't always greener on the other side.

When I drove home from the club that day, I was somehow consumed with trepidation with what lay ahead but kidded myself that it was a brand new challenge in a big city and all that that had to offer. Glancing in my rear view mirror, I noticed the car behind me had his lights on and I momentarily wondered if it was a Volvo, one of the few cars back then whose lights were always on permanently whilst the vehicle was in motion.

At the traffic lights, I stole a glance in the mirror again to see if the car had that distinctive grille, so characteristic of the Volvos. I wasn't sure so I kept looking but thought I wouldn't find out if I had to take the road across Reigate Common. I was surprised when the car followed me along the Common road but even more so when it followed me into the railway station in Reigate where I planned to pick up some milk and groceries at the neighbouring corner shop.

Now, I was getting very uncomfortable. I was just a short distance from the flat I was renting on Reigate Hill. I decided that if it followed me into the communal car park there, then I would set off for the police station. It did!

I pulled in and contemplated if I should just drive on to the police station. Before I could do anything two guys jumped out of the following car and ran up to my door before I could get out. 'Here goes' I thought, but they didn't look like thugs.

'Hello boss', smiled the taller of the two, an immensely fit guy who I figured could probably take me out with little more than a stare.

I didn't answer and waited for him to explain himself. 'We're keeping an eye on you my son; we can't be too careful, so don't be alarmed'.

'Uh, ok, thanks', I bumbled which didn't conceal the sheer terror I felt at the thought that the police were so concerned that they felt it appropriate to monitor and guard me.

'That's alright', he went on before completely gobsmacking me when he added, 'oh and rest assured the Bristol police have already been briefed and will be taking care of you down there'.

I had only told two people of my intention to quit and move to Bristol and yet welcoming parties were already on standby. I felt like I was the central character in the sort of thrillers I couldn't bear to watch!

It wasn't hard to bid farewell to Redhill. I'd had some great times there and I knew the experiences I had endured would stand me in good stead. Right now though, I needed to recharge the batteries and set off for the comforts of hometown Kettering before embarking on the next adventure in Bristol.

The people I grew up with often talked of Kettering as being the original 'one horse town' and if I spent too long there I might have subscribed to that view too. But in the two weeks I spent there after Redhill, I really did appreciate the notion that home is where the heart is. The nightlife was never glamorous but it was always fun and you knew that you'd always find some Soul there! It's a town with a real heart and soul of its own and nothing could better going back to bask in the company of friends there once more. It was wonderful too, to recall how pleased my mother and father were to have me back home again. I used to feel so guilty knowing I couldn't talk freely of the troubles I'd experienced but nothing could be so bad as denying them the news of their new grandchild.

The sojourn in Kettering was all too brief and so it was that on a wet Monday afternoon I landed in Bristol Temple Meads station and took a taxi to the Arnos Court Hotel complex to start my new assignment.

The welcome was understated to say the least. There was no one present to meet or greet me. Instead a note left at Reception instructed me to go to lodgings that had been arranged for me in Wick Road, Brislington, about half a mile away.

It was the home of a very nice elderly couple, Alice and Leslie Edwards; who had converted the top floor of their home into a self-contained flat. The furnishing was a little sparse but it was clean and tidy and contained all that I was ever going to need...but it suddenly felt very lonesome. Maybe I was feeling a little melancholy but it was during this period that I realised I was really pursuing quite an itinerant lifestyle. I was now embarking on my third posting in little more than three years and once again would need to be establishing new contacts and new routines. Many of my contemporaries back home reckoned I was leading a fabulously hedonistic lifestyle and whilst there were occasions like that, most of the time it could be pretty mundane.

One couldn't plan a proper social life because work consumed all your time. The regular hours were anti-social to say the least and one was usually too tired to make much of any spare time you did have. In Bristol I was to find, that spare time was very much at a premium.

The first morning was spent being introduced to all the full-time staff at my disposal...and there seemed to be hordes of them. There was a Promotions Manageress and her assistant whose job it was to toddle around the city doling out flyers and complimentary tickets to all the key businesses and employers in the city. They also co-ordinated the placement of adverts and various public relations activity the club would get up to.

There were two full time DJs, one for the discotheque and the other for the cabaret room. The latter also booked in the acts and produced a monthly newsletter which reviewed activities and broadcast future activities. The newsletter was distributed internally on club nights and externally via the promotions girls.

One had to be impressed, all the angles were covered and by any standards it was a well-oiled commercial operation. The Arnos Court Hotel itself was very busy with a very high occupancy level and it soon became apparent that the two businesses certainly complimented each other.

In the office, there was a secretary who apart from carrying out normal secretarial duties proved herself adept in all aspects of financial control. This included reconciling the daily takings, preparing wages etc., and for good measure she also managed the club's membership system which was the backbone of the customer base. Through that we were able to issue such as birthday invitations and make provision for party bookings, private hire etc.

The schedule was exhaustive with revenue pouring in every day. On top of the regular nightclub operation we were also utilising the premises during the day by providing all the catering needs for Harlech TV next door and of course there were also all those weddings every Saturday. Once again, going to football matches would be a rare treat.

It was however, Britain's Nightclub of The Year that I was now in charge of……and I was actually quite proud that I was entrusted with it. I knew well there would be downsides but for now I was happy to congratulate myself, I was heading in the right direction….wasn't I?

Chapter 11

'Ring My Bell'

My first night on duty at Reeves was also the official last night of the outgoing manager. Fair play to him he had obviously done a great job in getting such widespread recognition for the venue and he was evidently held in great esteem by just about everyone I spoke too.

I didn't want to steal his thunder so we agreed that I would make a brief appearance wherein I was to be introduced to all the staff before being shown the routine adopted for setting up prior to the night's activity. I was glad to leave it to him that evening but I lingered long enough to appreciate that this was to be a challenge radically different to anything I had yet encountered.

I was back in my flat by 10.30pm; a rare treat for me on a work night but of course I could never sleep properly, so rigidly set had my body clock now become. Decades later, nothing much has changed in that respect; much to my wife's chagrin. I so admire those who effortlessly set themselves in motion in the early hours of the day and at the other end of the day are fast asleep hours before I can even contemplate the prospect.

The following night I prepared for my first session 'in charge'. Looking back now, one appreciates what a different country Britain was just a relatively short time ago. From Redhill to Bristol, it was barely 130 miles and yet in terms of fashion, music and attitudes the distance was enormous. I had had the chance to compare the same in Stoke, Plymouth and Surrey but here in Bristol I found the gap to be a chasm.

It probably sounds very patronising but it really did seem like one was taking a step back in time by at least a decade. The pace of life was a lot slower which I found quite endearing as people had more time for you than in slick Surrey but everyone seemed to dress the same and sport the same hairstyles. Individuality was at a premium and the audience we attracted seemed to take their lead from whatever Top Shop or even C & A deemed appropriate garb! It was the same with their musical tastes; they just wanted the current Radio One playlist and we probably could have played a tape of the weekly chart rundown on 'Pick Of The Pops' and kept them all quite happy. Gloria Gaynor's *'I Will Survive'* was the hen party anthem down there and Anita Ward's, *'Ring My Bell',* used to seem to be on a loop, so often was it heard.

For me it amounted to tedium in the extreme but it was an interesting exercise in social observation.

The place was vast though and with several parts of the premises offering simultaneous variations of music and entertainment, it was at least very diverse in that respect and represented very good value for the punters, who I was to find, were exceedingly loyal.

There were about six bars on the premises to make sure everyone had the opportunity to imbibe themselves easily and indeed, compared to Redhill, the patrons consumed copious amounts of alcohol. Unlike in Redhill though, there was rarely any trouble. Even with 800 or more punters on the premises, there were never more than 3 or 4 doormen or 'bouncers' but they seemed to know their customers very well indeed and their agreeable attitude seemed to resonate well with people.

The rest of the staff too were extremely diligent and rarely if ever did I have to cajole them. Many of them had been there a fair time and it was evident that newcomers were soon indoctrinated to conform to the practices which were proven and found agreeable by the majority.

I was standing in the reception area that first night reflecting on the differences I'd observed when a couple of doormen uttered a low cheer as another coach disgorged a party of young ladies to join our revellers.

'Do you know them?' I innocently inquired.

'It's the Wrens boss, they're always up for some fun….they won't all be going home on the bus either!'

I watched in awe as the ladies of The Women's' Royal Naval Service, based in Yeovilton, Somerset, whooped and shrieked as they made their way in and prepared to enjoy themselves. There were some very elegant ladies amongst them and I did wonder if they'd appear the same by the end of the night. Suddenly one of the group lunged at me and proceeded to plant her scarlet lips on my cheeks smudging the collar of my pristine, new white shirt in the process.

'What are you doing here?', my assailant wailed. My jaw dropped when I saw it was Katy Coyle from Kettering, the fantasy girl for just about every young man of my generation in that town. I had known her since she was about twelve and had watched her blossom into one of the finest examples of womanhood a man could ever imagine. She was considered out of everyone's reach but I remembered the snog we had shared at the North Park Christmas Party. It had promised to get a whole lot better when she let me walk her home that night....but her dad had called proceedings to an end when he found us at the back door when he came out to use their outside lavatory. Dreams can be dashed for the oddest of reasons, but his call of nature was pretty unfortunate!

Never mind, she was here now and positively blooming if a little er....loud!

The staff were amused to see their new boss so quickly embarrassed and it was with them in mind that I stammered and stuttered quite uncontrollably before responding to the fragrant Katy. No need for that, she just took up the baton and yanked me into the lounge so we could 'catch up'.

She was well impressed that she now had a friend who was the General Manager at the place she and her friends used so often; but I wondered if in time she might find that a little inconvenient.

We quickly exchanged news about our lives and the gossip from K town but I had to do my rounds and I said I'd catch up again later in the evening.

The night passed without incident and at around 1am I looked for Katy again before commencing the shutdown routine. However, she was nowhere to be seen and I felt a twinge of disappointment when I learned the Wrens' coach had departed a few minutes earlier.

The last hour soon passed and I was delighted to find that by ten past two the crowd had all but dispersed and the tills were already counted and reconciled. It might be nice, I thought, to arrange a drink for all the staff whilst they awaited their taxis just to thank them for their efforts and to say how I looked forward to working with them. So far so good until Richie the Raver, one of the young glass collectors advised me that he had found someone in the toilets and thought I'd better attend to this person.

You've guessed it; it was Katy who had deliberately gone AWOL from her party.

'Why?', I asked.

'Cause I figured you would come to my rescue!' she simply smiled.

Richie found this highly amusing of course. Given the regard I had for the lady; I should have been thrilled instead I was mortified that I was descending into a situation which would see me lose all credibility with my new staff on my very first night with them.

Richie though, to his eternal credit, could see my discomfort and suggested I see to all the staff whilst he sat with Katy. I duly returned to the gathering and told them all was in order after which they quickly dispersed.

Katy was on a mission though and simply asked;

'You can put me up tonight, can't you?' 'What more can a boy do?' I thought, 'they'll never believe me back home anyhow?'

My little tryst with Katy turned out to be one of the more memorable features of my time in Bristol. For whatever reason, it was just not my kind of town and my time at Reeves seemed to lurch from one crisis to another.

Initially, it seemed quite satisfying. A pretty good venue, very busy and very successful but the physical demands were relentless and I soon feared for my health and perhaps even my sanity.

I was working seven days a week and no breaks meant it was hard to keep tabs on Emmeline and Carrie and any other social or recreational activity was out of the question.

I demanded a meeting with the company directors to beg for an assistant manager and they eventually relented. A guy from North London was recruited and he promised to relieve my load considerably. He claimed to be an experienced bars and catering manager and he certainly talked a good game. He started off being very willing and helpful and after a couple of weeks I decided to take a Sunday night off and left him in charge of the session.

The following morning, I arrived at work just after 9 o'clock to be met by the secretary giving me a very troubled look. She took me through to one of the bar lounge areas and pointed to what looked like a bundle of clothes in the corner. It was my assistant manager....fast asleep, surrounded by empty beer bottles and detritus from the night before.

Money was still in the tills and nothing had been cleared from the night before. The well-oiled operation I had inherited seemed to be visibly crumbling and I knew the buck would only be stopping with me.

Once my devoted assistant sobered up he pleaded for a second chance pledging his undying devotion from hereon in. Well, he did try, but perhaps more to hide his addiction than anything else. It was a losing battle though, the guy was a hopeless alcoholic and as much as I wanted to help him, I feared he would bring me down with him. He knew as much and within a couple of days he tendered his resignation with immediate effect.

It was probably my first real experience of seeing the ravages of alcohol destroying a person's life. We've all walked past the hopeless cases for whom it is hard to spare any sympathy but seeing this guy at close quarters brought it home to me how quickly the descent can be. My understanding was that the guy was already estranged from his family and there in Bristol he had no friends or any kind of support network. I knew losing his job would have knock on effects for him and I feared he was only one step from the streets.

A few weeks later, I received a reference inquiry for him from a hotel in Somerset. I did write him a very decent one in the hope that he would be given another chance and an opportunity to turn his life around. However, I remembered the glowing reference I had received about him just a couple of months earlier from a previous employer. No doubt they too had hoped he would redeem himself in my employ.

As it happened, Richie the Raver stepped into the breach and became an unlikely, but totally dependent right-hand man. Unlikely, because he was a young lad with some learning difficulties who was an easy target for the few, less kind folk who thought it amusing to mock the afflicted. He was also from a broken home and to say he had low self-esteem would be an understatement. He valued his job as a mere glass collector but I noticed that he was always willing to do the odd task at my request. Just being a tiny part of the set up at Reeves meant a lot to Richie and I thought that the pride he had in the job and his place of work should be acknowledged.

Richie started to show up during the days as well to offer help in distributing flyers or to do such as preparing the venue for functions. He gave his time freely and never sought remuneration.

I started to show him the ropes of cellar management and stock control. He was quick on the uptake and proved to be a willing and attentive student. It wasn't long before he became a full-time fixture, so I decided to put him onto the payroll and reward him properly. When I told him this news, he was quite overcome. His efforts were being appreciated and up to that point in his life, he had had little experience of that.

'Go home and tell your mum that you'll be paying her more from now on' I told him. He did just that and I think she was as thrilled as he was.

Some of the cynics amongst the full-time staff at Reeves thought I'd taken leave of my senses with this appointment but I'd found someone who I could totally trust and was happy to do things my way. I had long come to realise that in that world, it was rare to find one you could totally depend upon.

Around the same time, I had reason to call Dino, my old DJ in Redhill who lamented the fact that things just weren't the same since I'd moved on. I invited him down for a couple of days to give him a break and allow me to converse with someone more on my wavelength than most others around me at that time.

Dino found the place fascinating and the city too. Maybe he was tiring of the London scene and saw this as a nice departure; but I think too, he rather liked the idea of putting his very own stamp upon a place. He knew I'd support him with this and when he made his feelings known we were both delighted at the prospect of renewing our working relationship.

Slowly, I was beginning to mould an effective team around me which was a good amalgam of the best that I'd inherited allied to a few I brought in to take on key roles. Being an already successful operation, it didn't need a radical overall just a bit of tweaking here and there to see if we could build upon what we had.

One weekend I managed to get home to Kettering and catch the Poppies in action. They were on the rise at the time having come second in the league and made it to Wembley for the FA Trophy final a few weeks earlier. They were always the bridesmaids though as they never actually won anything. Yet our hopes were high that for the first time since their formation in 1872, maybe, just maybe, they could reach the Promised Land which was The Football League for us!

Ironically when they played at Wembley, there was only one Kettering man on the pitch - and he was captaining the opposition! That was Bob Ritchie with whom I'd enjoyed many playground matches at Kettering Grammar School all those years ago.

Whilst at home that weekend I read a fascinating article in the local Evening Telegraph about a local man, Peter Dowdeswell, from Earls Barton, who possessed a rare gift. Peter was generating tremendous media coverage and huge public fascination for his ability to disgorge huge amounts of food and drink at a record rate of knots. In fact, he was setting eating and drinking world records on an almost weekly basis and The Guinness Book of World Records was having a job keeping up with him. I'd had dealings with Peter before when I brought him to Redhill when first he started to demonstrate his prowess. On that occasion, he had brought the house down when, after downing yards of ale and piles of doughnuts, he decided to snack on electric light bulbs and razor blades. It was a lightbulb moment in itself and I knew if I could get him to Bristol he would be a sensation.

Peter was up for it straightaway and guaranteed he would set another world record in the process! Absolute gold dust as far as I was concerned. I knew I would be able to get the local press and radio on board and with the Harlech TV association, perhaps even the telly as well! Not bad for an outlay of just £200 plus a bed in the lodging house across the road.

Not surprisingly, the very nature of Peter's act gave rise to a huge chorus of disgust. How could this be regarded as 'entertainment'? I expected no less and of course it was exactly what I wanted. Only a couple of years previously I had witnessed how The Sex Pistols had demonstrated that outrageous behaviour and negative publicity could be translated into morbid fascination and great business.

Sure enough, the local media lapped it all up and the citizens of Bristol seemed to be fascinated at the prospect of the freak show we were about to stage. Strange as it may seem, gluttony and speed was proving to be a heady mix!

Harlech TV proved to be especially accommodating and their commissioning editor was happy to provide me with five minutes of his scheduling on their daily regional magazine programme. I was surprised when the BBC too gave me a call. They were an altogether tougher nut to crack and over the years I had only ever utilised BBC radio. This time though they couldn't avoid the buzz being generated by The Guzzler who was Peter Dowdeswell. I was happy to accommodate them too; it was just a matter of deciding what Peter would choose to gorge on. I think we decided on soft boiled eggs for the BBC, 13 of them, and prunes and pickled onions for HTV.

'It really doesn't matter', Peter used to say, 'I'll bring it all straight back up!' What a man!

As stunts go, it was one of my better ones. The place was packed with many visiting the venue for the very first time and Peter revelled in it all. He was a very humble guy in many ways but he proved a natural showman. Food, drink, lightbulbs etc., it was all in a night's work for him but he also put his body through unbelievable stresses. He'd been joking with the bouncers beforehand when on a whim he suddenly decided to involve them.

He wrapped a rope around his neck before handing one end of the rope to three of them on his left and the other end to the three on the right before ordering them to….'just pull it as hard as you like'.

He just tensed his muscles and comfortably held them all at bay before clapping his hands to signal release. Then, spreading a mat on the floor, he asked for three glasses of water. He drank the water then smashed the glasses spreading the shards of glass on the mat. He took off his shirt, lay on the mat and said; 'Ok guys, come and walk over me'. After they duly obliged, he then turned to me asking if I'd be so kind as to pick off the glass that was still embedded in his bare flesh. Now, that's entertainment!

Such little time as I had outside of work had to be planned meticulously in advance but being the 'Billy No Mates' that I was at the time, it meant I could indulge in whatever took my fantasy.

I was quite fascinated by the St. Paul's district of the city which was a complete no-go area for most that I spoke to at Reeves. It was the most ethnic area of the city but I could see it had a wonderful vibe and was the only place I was likely to find a bit of soul….as well as a lot of roots reggae and ska. It was a big regret that I was unable to get down for a session at The Star and Garter where the late lamented, DJ Derek, was establishing himself as something of a cult figure.

A tiny newsagent's store in St. Paul's was the only place I could be sure to find a copy of *Blues and Soul* every fortnight. I had devotedly purchased it every fortnight since 1969 and it was my only means of keeping in touch with what was going on in the soul scene in the rest of the country and particularly 'up north'. I knew that there was an oasis for Northern Soul not too far from Bristol in the sleepy backwater of Yate. There, some pioneers of the scene had established an all-nighter at The Stars and Stripes Club - and I was determined to get there.

I eventually did at 4am one Saturday morning after another session of 'disco' at Reeves. It took me an age to find it but hearing the strains of Richard Temple's, *'That Beatin' Rhythm'* wafting through the night air as I made my way through deserted streets in that lonely Somerset town sure gave me a high that no chemical concoction could match. A few years before I had befriended a clutch of West Country soulies from Cheltenham and Gloucester at The Torch in Stoke-on-Trent so it was great to soak up the sounds on their patch.

I had also made it a mission to make sure I took in some football games at Bristol City and Bristol Rovers whilst I was in the city and at Ashton Gate I expected to see some quality football as City were then in the old First Division and entertaining the very top teams of the day.

Those were heady days for City in their very neat stadium which was packed that season for games at a level they haven't played at since. However, it was a game at 'The Gas', Bristol Rovers old ground at Eastville Stadium, which remains permanently lodged in my memory.

I was one of 8,120 who gathered there on November 18th 1978. A strange ground; it lay in the shadow of the M32 flyover with a speedway track encircling the pitch. As I recall there was precious little at stake in that match but it fairly rattled the old teleprinter on BBC's Grandstand that afternoon.

It was a truly ding-dong affair which, at 5-5, ended in the highest scoring draw seen in The Football League for 12 seasons and it has only been surpassed a few times since then.

Over the years I often wondered if I'd imagined it, but there were cameras there that day and the goals from the game can now be viewed on You Tube – including the dodgy penalty which gave Rovers their 5th and equalizing goal.

By now, Reeves was settling down under my management regime. It was still a pretty joyless place as far as I was concerned but business was extraordinarily good and as I wandered from the disco, to the cabaret bar and back to The White Swan bar and restaurant I could reasonably claim that I did indeed have a very good number going here and even if I wasn't enjoying it greatly, better things surely lay ahead. If not here in Bristol, then certainly elsewhere. I just needed to be diligent, keep my head down and act beyond reproach. That was the instruction I gave to myself to stay on course and to be prepared for the right opportunity once it presented itself.

Of course, it was possible to have enjoyable nights at Reeves, particularly in the cabaret bar where you just didn't know what to expect. Some were awful beyond belief - but then that was amusing in itself – whilst some were actually very good and went on to better things. I remember the likes of Marti Caine who went on to have her own TV show and Carol Lee Scott who found fame as Grotbags the witch. There was one pretty good comedian by the name of Pete Conway who later became famous for being Robbie Williams's dad!

Jethro, the West Country comedian, was an act I used to continually rebook as he always went down a storm. He has gone on to have a more than respectable career but I'll never forget the night he appeared whilst the Jeremy Thorpe scandal was dominating the newspapers. His entire act revolved around the affair as he never let up with a stream of what would now be regarded as completely unacceptable homophobic material but on that occasion at least, he completely nailed it!

I used to like it when I could become totally immersed in the job. It was my vocation really and when it was all going well, then you'd kid yourself that there was no need to worry about anything. But then came the letter I was dreading, I was being summonsed for my day in court!

Chapter 12

'I Will Survive'

Ever since leaving Redhill, I had felt physically safer but I knew the day of reckoning was looming for my assailants and now I just wanted it all over and done with. My injuries had healed but my mind was still very scarred by the events of that night and to some degree they have remained ever since.

I had warned the directors of Reeves that this would be happening and as I was obliged to set aside two weeks for proceedings, another manager was drafted in from their club in Camberley. The trial was set for The Old Bailey and I knew then that it was likely to receive a lot of attention and may even be of interest to the national papers. This presented me with something of a dilemma. I hadn't told my folks what had happened and hoped I wouldn't need to. I knew my mother would panic and worry but it would be so much worse if she heard of it all through the media. It was still a few weeks away yet though, so I resolved to tell them just before the trial got underway.

A couple of days later, I was visited by two Bristol detectives who had been asked by their counterparts in Surrey to visit me. I was told that I had to travel by taxi to the trial and that I would have to stay in a private house. If I couldn't find somewhere suitable then the police would arrange my accommodation. This raised my concerns considerably but the police insisted they were just being cautious.

Further visits from them ensued and a couple of days before the start of the trial, I was informed that proceedings were being transferred to Kingston Crown Court instead. The trial of the Liberal Party leader, Jeremy Thorpe, was also taking place at The Old Bailey and such was the interest of the worldwide media, that all the other scheduled trials there were being moved.

I found accommodation with one of my old customers, John Jeffries, a zany, extrovert character who had spent the past 30 years as a waiter in the sky for the airliner, BOAC. I imagined I would find John's company therapeutic after the grilling I expected to be subjected to. It was a good decision, John proved to be just the right man at the right time.

The police took no chances ensuring I was dispatched by taxi and sent directly to Kingston Crown Court where I was met by more police and told to wait in a secluded area. The investigating officers on the case, Sgt. Robbie Crawford and his cohorts dropped by to make sure I had been suitably delivered. I knew they were especially keen to see my assailants off the streets for a very long time and they had the air of men confident their wishes would soon be granted.

Things never quite go to plan though and I was astonished when Crawford suddenly turned the air blue with a torrent of cursing and swearing. Seemingly the two teams of lawyers had been called to a briefing and the prosecution counsel returned to tell the police that one of the trio had absconded. Unless he was found quickly, this could have thrown the whole trial into jeopardy but surprisingly it was decided in minutes to proceed without him.

The two remaining defendants, The Fat Man and Val, were charged with actual bodily harm on me, grievous bodily harm to another (Pat) and conspiring to cause an affray. The Fat Man was further accused of conspiring to attempt to pervert the course of justice.

It didn't help The Fat Man that Val had entered a guilty plea and his defence was to struggle in garnering any sympathy from the jury.

I waited for hours on my own in the ante-room with only a tattered old copy of the Daily Express to help me pass the time with. It's a paper I have always detested. The TV listings are usually the only pages in it that I ever agree with. One of the court assistants made sure I had plenty of tea then, just as I rose to seek out the toilets, I was summonsed to appear.

'Can I just use the….'

'No, hurry along please'.

I was feeling distinctly uncomfortable as I undertook the oath and even wondered if I should ask the judge for a natural break.

One doesn't get too much time to think and take in proceedings when standing in the witness box. I've been in that position several times now and it never feels less than intimidating at best.

I soon found that a full-blooded attack on the prosecution witnesses was to be the strategy of the defence barristers. My statements were dissected in minute detail, personal accusations were levelled at me and conspiracy theories were also raised. They just fell short of calling me a bare faced liar, but for the jury, the message was clear enough. I had been expecting it all, but was still pretty shocked at the sheer aggressiveness of the questioning and the scenarios they were suggesting.

On and on it went. I couldn't believe that an incident lasting barely five minutes or so could have required so many hours of interrogation.

The halt to proceedings for lunch came as a mighty relief for my brain and bladder alike. Even though the questioning was relentless, after a while one does get conditioned to it. After all, it's not you who is on trial, so you just have to tell it how it is to the best of your ability.

I found it interesting to watch the reaction of the two defendants. They had both glowered at me when I took my place in the dock but after that Val, having pleaded guilty, sat impassively with a look of resignation. It must have all seemed a good laugh when the trio met that night at The Bell in Reigate. The court was told that Miller (the absconder) was the instigator. He had taken umbrage a few weeks earlier when he was refused entry into Busby's by one of the new Thai doormen. As he drunk with his two old friends he grew increasingly agitated about being denied entry into a club in 'his manor'. When he said he wanted to go down to 'sort them out', the other two didn't dissuade him but they probably didn't reckon on Miller packing the two machetes he was to reveal later.

It must all have been a nightmare for The Fat Man. He hadn't been at liberty very long since serving a lengthy sentence for a supermarket raid. It was bad enough going along with Miller's thirst for revenge but in his desperation to avoid the inevitable, he had aggravated his position still further. The court would surely take a dim view of his attempt to pervert the course of justice even though it was more an act of stupidity which didn't actually harm anyone.

After lunch, I was tackled with a new line of questioning which I hadn't been expecting. A statement had been made by one of the young, female staff members who claimed that I was as much to blame and that it was me who started the fighting.

I found it very sad that someone had managed to coerce this young lady into helping their case. She was a nice girl, a young mother who needed and valued the job. She had never caused me any bother and I knew her role in the kitchen that night meant she was far from the scene of the trouble.

On that charge and every other, I just had to stay resolute and play a straight bat as best as I could.

The questioning went on into a second day. I rather hoped that The Fat Man would bow to the inevitable and re-enter his plea. It would surely have saved a lot of time and expense and the likelihood too, I'm sure, of a considerably shorter sentence for him.

Eventually, there was a pause and the defence barrister signalled that he had no further questions. I was mighty relieved of course but the most memorable aspect of my days in court had yet to be played out.

I was ushered out of the court room and back to the ante-room where a court official offered me a welcome cup of tea and asked if I would fill in a form she had put in front of me.

It was a schedule of the expenses I had incurred to attend the trial and I duly sat down to complete it. Just as I did so, Robbie Crawford bounded into the room looking very pleased with the course of proceedings.

'How are you feeling, you were brilliant….never wavered. Job well done', he enthused and speculated at the sentences that the defendants were in for.

He didn't doubt that there would be a unanimous verdict and said he was hoping The Fat Man would get five years in view of his record. 18 months was his prediction for Val.

'That would be a decent result' he concluded and even though he had raged when Miller didn't show, he now figured his eventual appearance was a formality and the outcome for him could only be improved if he pleaded guilty.

'How much are you claiming then?' he asked.

'About £40, I said, just the taxis there and back'.

'What about your meals? Your accommodation? Your loss of wages?'

'I didn't lose any wages and John hasn't charged me'.

'Oh, you, dickhead', he said, 'you're entitled to it – give it me here!'

He grabbed the form and put his own figures in. 'Is that better for you? he asked.

'Yeah, sure…£280…thanks'.

'OK, sign it then and we'll get that out the way'.

We went along the corridor to the court office and Crawford waited whilst the clerk processed my claim and paid me in cash.

We were just by the entry to the building and I was about to bade Crawford farewell when he said there was another bit of business to attend to first.

I followed him back along the corridor whilst he chatted away amiably to me. Standing by the ante-room once again, he looked around but the place was deserted.

'Get in here', he said and pushed me into the room.

'What's up?' I gasped, I thought he was going to start thumping me.

'You asked for 40, I doubled it for you, the rest is mine!'

It would have been nice if a *'News of The World'* reporter had appeared at that moment to see me bunging £200 to a copper but it doesn't quite work like that. He pocketed his bunce for the day and left the room saying;

'See ya'.

A few hours later I was back in Bristol so glad to have the experience behind me but I wondered if Sgt. Crawford would be dining out that night with his little bonus.

The next day the jury was sent out and they didn't spend too long deliberating. Half of Crawford's double came up – Val got 18 months but the judge settled on 3 years for The Fat Man. He probably felt he was guilty of stupidity more than evil intent.

Thanks to Jeremy Thorpe, the story never made the nationals. The local paper, *The Surrey Mirror* did splash the story prominently with the headline; 'Saturday Fight Fever'.

Not bad I thought, very topical and besides, wasn't I John Travolta's doppelganger in those days?

Where it all began. The Top Rank Suite, Plymouth on the right.

*Pictured with my parents and sister, Maureen,
at Plymouth Top Rank Suite.*

**TOP RANK SUITE
UNION ST., PLYMOUTH**

Invites you to an evening of

NORTHERN SOUL

on Monday 18th April 1977

· *in the*

Disco One 50

This Ticket admits one or two persons
free before 9.30 p.m.

The night Northern Soul came to Plymouth.

'The Godfather of Soul', James Brown, pictured in 1981 at Brighton Top Rank Suite.

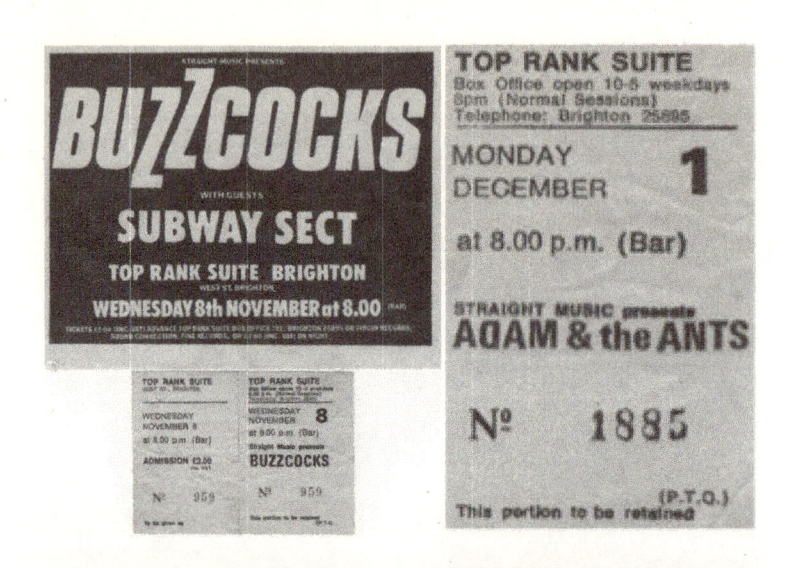

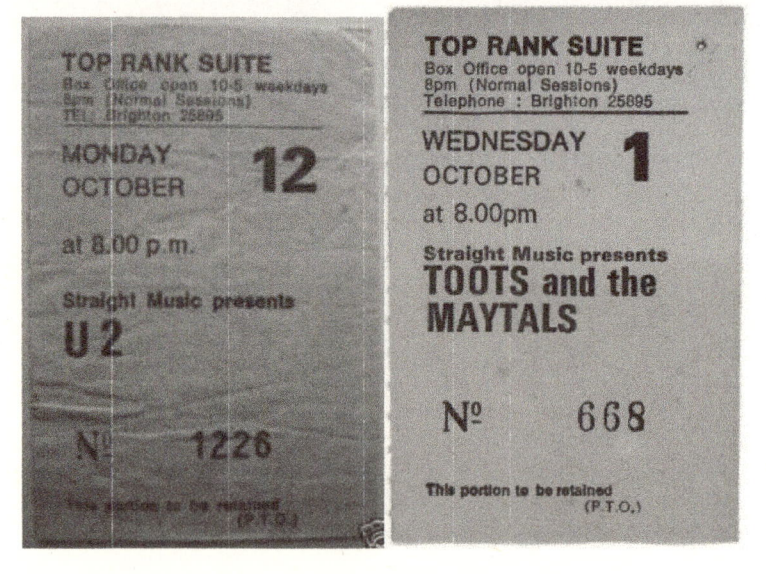

Every week would see top line bands appearing at the Top Rank Suite.

Yet another street stunt in Lincoln!

Christmas at Cinderellas' Rockerfellas' in Lincoln

It wasn't very PC by today's standards, but there were any number of competitions to get girls into various states of undress.

The Lincoln crowd take to the floor for 'Oops Upside Your Head' - The Boat Song.

Brighton's Kingswest where both the Top Rank Suite and Busby's were housed.

Peter slips his way to record

Peter Dowdeswell, the world eating and drinking champion – a marvellous character, who I brought to several venues.

Popeye power formula is put to the test

I YAM what I yam — and I'm only pretending I'm Popeye the Sailor Man! Pat Shevlin, deputy manager of

The suite is holding a Popeye evening, and world eating and drinking champ Peter Dowdeswell will be trying to set a new personal best in spinach chomping.

So far the champ has two challengers, in the burly shapes of a couple of Worthing firemen. Olive Oyls are welcome to compete — provided they can put away a few pounds of power-giving spinach.

Another costume, another promotional stunt.

With my trusty partner in crime - Clive Rayson, here supporting a local pirate radio station.

Another often repeated promotion for St Valentine's when the area's longest married couple were sought. Along with Lesley Brett, I met this couple in Brighton who had been married for 72 years. Their nephew was the entertainer, Frankie Vaughan.

*The staff at Busby's, Brighton not looking too bad
at 3 in the morning!*

Erika Roe was the talk of the nation after taking to the field at Twickenham - 4 days later she was appearing at Busby's.

The young Andrew Ridgeley and George Michael of Wham! who appeared at Busby's for the princely fee of £10.

Miss Brighton, Julie Dawn Elliott,
who went on to much better things.

'80s man pictured with Karen Greer at The Restoration in Brighton which I ran for a period with Clive Rayson.

Chapter 13

'Stuff Like That'

It was strange going back to Bristol. I had just reached the end of one of the most tortuous episodes in my life and it would have been nice to reflect upon it with someone, but here I couldn't have been more detached from proceedings if I had lived in the Outer Hebrides.

I started to take the view that really, I was a loner in life, a drifter even. Outwardly, I was a very social animal but my job and my routine meant I was destined to plough a lonely furrow. When I started in the entertainment industry, I thought it would be a sociable way of earning a living. Sure, there were the highs, many nights of fun, the girls of course and some would say there was kudos in being in control of such a diverse and challenging venue as Reeves.

But where was it all leading to? What was the point of this life of hedonism? I liked to take myself off to Mass every Sunday and I would often call in at the beautiful church of St. Mary-on-the-Quay in the centre of Bristol. Hypocrite though I undoubtedly am, my faith has always been important to me and looking back I know now it was the crutch that sustained me. I so admired the priests who were inspirational and made a difference in their community. 'Could it be me?' I often wondered; but I knew the answer was 'No'. When I was 12 or 13, my parents had taken me to a seminary in Co. Roscommon one summer when holidaying in Ireland. Such was the way back then, they would have been proud to offer their son to the priesthood. I was intrigued, but I experienced no calling and nothing more was ever said.

Being the grammar school boy, I had been encouraged to take up a profession or go into banking or the civil service. Safe, secure, respectable position – 'with good pensions don't forget'- but those roles didn't appeal one iota and I let the opportunities pass. Now, I was here in a city not of my choosing, doing a job that not only often bored me, but it was one I was asked to put my physical wellbeing on the line for on a pretty regular basis.

I began to envy the shop assistants, the postmen, the taxi drivers – people in so called dead end jobs. They had lives, they ate their meals with their families, they socialised, they had regular hours and they were safe. Yet, they were supposed to envy me.

It wasn't much better for Dino, although he did have his girlfriend with him. He was telling me one night about this mad woman, Ma White, who was his landlady. She was heavily into the occult and the spirits guided her in all that she did. I was intrigued enough to want to meet her and so it was that I ventured up the Whiteladies Road one afternoon for the rendezvous that Dino had arranged. Her appearance suggested that she truly was as mad as a sack of ferrets; but she immediately locked her eyeballs on me saying we needed to talk.

She told Dino to go and take a walk whilst she started to interrogate me closely. Interrogate is probably the wrong word as she soon delivered her assessment of me and my life. It was damning in the extreme but her analysis and reading of my state of mind was undeniably accurate. Whilst talking in full flow she reached for a pack of tarot cards and then delivered my Fate.

Her interpretation of them was that I had to leave Bristol as soon as possible. My health was in jeopardy and my wellbeing even moreso. There were people out there who hated me and would do their best to bring me down. It was futile to fight them as I had no chance of changing the situation. I had to leave as soon as possible. She told me Life would be difficult for a long, long time and tragedy would visit my family. I would get through it, but I had to keep my Faith and be true to myself. I heard Dino coming back in through the door and Ma stopped abruptly at that point.

Dino wandered cheerily in and checked himself just as he prepared to launch one of the pointed barbs that he was so adept at producing. One look at me, told him that Ma had obviously hit home to me in some way. I didn't know what to make of Ma's reading but I did know I'd reached another crossroads in Life and staying put was not going to be an option.

One can ponder all they like weighing up the pros and cons of a situation or the implications of a decision to be made but when Fate intervenes, your destiny is out of your hands completely. Leaving Ma's that afternoon, I figured I would be weighing up all my options – even if at that juncture, there didn't seem to be any that appealed.

Back in my lonely room that night, I asked myself what could I do if I were to get out? Journalism maybe? That was the boyhood goal but surely I'd blown any chance of getting into that now. Retail store management was another option, I had the qualifications and knew I'd have a chance of getting in but then I remembered the tedium of life at International Stores…..nah. Banking? The Civil Service? Suddenly I was hearing the advice of my Grammar School teachers and career advisers. Maybe they were right? At least I would be safe, the money would be ok and I'd surely find a nice girl eventually – if it wasn't going to be Carrie – and I'd settle down to a respectable middle class life in a middle class area, have nice hobbies and go to the football whenever I pleased.

I began to think what areas of the Civil Service I could get into. Inland Revenue? Social Security? Jobcentres? Customs maybe? Or perhaps banking would be a good idea after all. I'd get a cheap mortgage and I could just see myself calling the shots in an anonymous small town branch somewhere.

How about teaching? Yes, I'd be good at that…..and I'd love the holidays of course.

I went to sleep that night resolving to give it all some serious thought. I'd write a few letters, set up some interviews and see what might materialise. I was still young, quite well educated and you know what, I didn't have to be dictated to by anyone anymore.

The next morning the alarm clock rang at 7.30am as usual and I reached out to reset it for half an hour later…..except I couldn't. The clock continued to ring, louder and louder but I couldn't stop it. I couldn't lift my arms, I couldn't lift my legs. I panicked, what was happening? I started to sweat and I could feel my skin tingling. I thought I was having a stroke. I took some deep breaths, cried out to God and offered up a Hail Mary. I lay there motionless trying to assess what had become of me. The clock stopped ringing and in the silence that followed I could feel my heart thumping and my neck throbbing. I tried to be calm, but I was scared. Now my head was throbbing and still my skin was tingling but my limbs just weren't responding. I clenched my fingers and wiggled my toes…at least I'm not paralysed I thought.

I didn't know what to do but figured I needed help. The old couple lived downstairs and I prayed they were up and about.

'Help!', I kept shouting…and wondered how they'd react. Did they think I was having a fight with someone? There was no answer so I tried again. 'Help! Please help'.

'Are you alright me dear' said old Leslie Evans in his rustic Bristol accent as he climbed the stairs and tapped on my door.

'No', I shouted, 'please come in, I can't move'.

Dear old Leslie, he was well in his 80s and just getting up the stairs must have been a mighty effort for him. His wife Alice, came up behind them. The two of them crept through the door silently, no doubt scared stiff of what they might find.

'I don't know what's wrong, I just can't move', I tried to explain. They were both visibly shocked at the state they found me in but tried to act as calmly as possible. Alice went to phone for a doctor whilst Leslie sat beside me to see if we could make sense of the situation.

The tingling and throbbing continued, but slowly I was able to move my limbs. That had to be an improvement and I started to relax a little, even taking a sip of the water that Leslie proffered.

Within half an hour the doctor duly arrived. He took my blood pressure, asked a few questions and then delivered his verdict.

'You've had a breakdown'.

'What?' I said.

'A breakdown; certainly physical but hopefully not mentally'.

He asked what I did for a living and when I told him, he said I wouldn't be doing that for several weeks. 'You need complete rest; you cannot be subjected to any stress'.

I knew the governors at Reeves would take a pretty dim view of this situation. I had regularly been working 70-80 hour weeks. They had no one to cover and I couldn't see them being content to pay me sick pay whilst I recover. But that was a concern for another day, right now I was under doctor's orders and to my bed I was confined.

Whether or not it was the medication the doctor prescribed, I've no idea but I certainly slept the sleep of the deep over the next two days. I guess the body has its own way of signalling when enough is enough and it certainly decided it wanted to take time out from the schedule I was following at the time. Slowly, I felt normal service was resuming and bit by bit I regained my strength and was starting to pad around again.

Alice had notified the club that I would have to have an enforced absence but my feeling was that they must have received the news with some indifference. Significantly, no one from there called to check on my wellbeing or otherwise. Only the loyal Richie took the trouble to do that. He brought me up to speed with all that was going on and happened to mention that the Camberley man was moving to Bristol.

After a few more days, I felt ready to pick up the reins again but I knew changes had probably been made whilst I was away.

Just the routine greetings I received from the office team were enough to tell me that my foresight had been vindicated. An awkward, embarrassed air seemed to prevail over all of them and no wonder for I went through to my office to find that Camberley Man had been making himself very comfortable in it.

A custard stained dress suit hanging from the stationery cupboard was the first slob sign I noticed. Then a dirty shirt chucked in the corner. It was one of the cheap, crimplene, frilly efforts that C & A used to knock out at £5.99. No class obviously and the stale reek of Old Spice aftershave on it just about summed up the impression it gave me. My desk was strewn with tea stained paperwork, cufflinks and a crumpled copy of The Daily Express. That alone was enough to show me that this was a guy I could never be matey with and the overflowing ashtrays and empty bottles of Holsten Pils merely confirmed as much. Have people no respect when they're on someone else's territory? Not when they've appropriated it and it was becoming clear that this was nearer the truth of the situation I found.

I called in Sandy, the secretary, and asked her to bring me up to date with all that had happened in my absence. She looked at me and hesitated before saying…'I'll just make a pot of tea.'

Sandy was one of those indispensable characters that every good business needs. A person you can totally depend upon, who knows what you need even before you thought you needed anything. I'd been fortunate to have similar people like that in both Plymouth and Redhill. They knew every nuance of the business, they second guessed the priorities and when necessary, they'd be blunt and tell you where you were going wrong. Without them, you couldn't take your eye off the business for a moment. You needed them to be your eyes and ears and you had to know you could trust them absolutely. In return, you had to be sure you demonstrated your sincere appreciation. I had long since learned that when you had someone like that on your side you could always get by. DJs were supposed to be the poster boys of your business, but they were all dispensable and replaceable compared to the Sandys.

The politics at Reeves were unlike anything I'd previously encountered but if nothing else the experience I had gained in this industry gave me a certain 'sang froid' attitude. People were either with me or against me. It's nice to be a friend of everyone but it was impossible to spend a lot of time persuading people to conform to your way of working and your way of thinking. For the most part, one just had to be single minded in the course one pursued and hope that you had enough of the right people on board.

I knew Sandy would give me the truth, however awkward and inconvenient it might prove to be.

It turned out that Camberley Man - or Mr Sheridan as he had apparently insisted upon being addressed – was very much 'the insider', having been an associate of two of the company's directors for several years. Two directors, who I learned had opposed my appointment because they had wanted their man, Sheridan, to take the role.

With my illness and the court appearance, they had an opportunity to put the cuckoo in my nest. Sandy told me that it was looking like Mr. Sheridan was staying with me being asked to work alongside him. I knew that would be impossible and if he held sway with these people then the writing was probably now on the wall for me.

Sandy told me what an unbearable, ignorant creature he was. In his mid-fifties, it seemed he had led something of a nomadic existence drifting from pubs and hotels to clubs and holiday camps. There had been a failed marriage or two along the way but he obviously had friends in the right places. Sandy spoke disparagingly about his brylcreemed barnet, his scruffiness and a perceived lax attitude to personal hygiene. It seemed he opened and closed the premises but did little more than spend each night in the office chain-smoking and drinking Pils. Yet, he was dangerous according to Sandy. He had made a point of going through the books checking every item of expenditure with items charged to me being meticulously catalogued.

I could see he had probably been asked to prepare a charge sheet against me but I knew I wasn't guilty of anything untoward. Her description of Mr Sheridan chimed with the kind of man I had feared on becoming myself – the kind of middle aged drifter sadly drifting from club to club getting more out of touch at every port...and eventually losing all respect if not actually becoming something of a figure of ridicule.

I feared for my immediate position of course but I actually wasn't too unhappy with how I thought things might be panning out. Others might have thought my situation was potentially disastrous but I had never settled in the city, I really didn't like Reeves that much and hang on, hadn't Ma White only just told me that people were gunning for me?

My health was uncertain too and if I was serious about restoring my physical and mental wellbeing then I should face up to the fact that I was in the wrong game.

The time I spent in Bristol coincided with a period of depression and discontentment in the country generally. When I arrived in Bristol, the Prime Minister was 'sunny Jim' Callaghan but there was little to laugh about. He had taken over in 1976 following Harold Wilson's sudden resignation and by 1978 his Labour government was limping along sustained in power by virtue of a pact with the Liberal Party and even that had collapsed by August. The Tories in opposition were not an attractive option as memories of the miners and power worker strikes were fresh in the memory. In 1975, they had jettisoned their leader, Ted Heath, and replaced him with one Margaret Thatcher who had yet to make her mark. Despite their problems, Callaghan's government was still ahead in the polls and so it came as something of a surprise when Callaghan decided not to call a snap election which many thought would have secured him an overall majority.

In the winter of 1978 the unions decided to flex their muscle power demanding double digit wage increases for their members to offset the effects of a 10% inflation rate. When they failed to broker a deal with the government, the infamous Winter of Discontent was the result. In Bristol, as elsewhere, rubbish went uncollected and stories emerged of the dead going unburied. Such a state of affairs was seized upon by the right wing press whose cause was greatly helped when Callaghan was asked for a comment about the situation on returning from a summit meeting in Guadeloupe. Looking tanned, he tried to offer calming words to the press but *The Sun's* sub-editor put his own spin on his words and in bold headlines proclaimed Callaghan as saying 'Crisis, what crisis?'. Though he never did utter that phrase, the die was cast and the government was flailing on the ropes from hereon in.

They had been relying on the support of minority parties to prop them up but when a crucial devolution vote was lost in farcical circumstances, a vote of 'No Confidence' was called. Their subsequent defeat in that vote triggered the General Election of 1979 which swept Mrs Thatcher into Number 10 and the Tories into power for the next 18 years.

There was a certain irony for me, for only a few years earlier when studying for my A Levels; I witnessed a vigorous debate amongst fellow students over the education policies of the then Conservative government. Most of us present that day were at least left of centre in the political spectrum and thus unanimously opposed to measures planned by the then Education Secretary – Margaret Thatcher. To say the consensus was one of acrimony towards her would be an understatement, until one guy who had hitherto remained silent suddenly rendered us into silence when he roared 'Stop!'.

All eyes turned to Dennis Bagehot from Barton Seagrave who paused, gathered himself together and ever so softly said;

'I couldn't agree with you more chaps, but this woman you're talking about happens to be my auntie!'

Little did we realise then, that Dennis's Auntie Margaret was to become one of the most famous figures in the world; indeed, she seemed to many at that time to be not much more than a novelty turn. Many, even in her own party, thought as much when she challenged Ted Heath for the party leadership. Her victory then was more of a surprise than when she eventually won the 1979 election.

The mood of the country in the spring of 1979 was one of quite high emotions as I recall. One knew there was change afoot but where was it taking us? The same uncertainty was besetting my own life and the choices I made but that election was a mighty diversion. In those days, local hustings were still a feature of election campaigning and I thought I'd make a point of going along to see how our local MP, Tony Benn, would handle such proceedings.

Tony Benn, or the former Sir Anthony Wedgwood-Benn, was a man of immense standing and intellect but he was also a very divisive and yes, quite destructive character. In the years to come I was to lament his behaviour as the Labour Party shifted so far to the left it prompted a few stalwart figures to go off on and form another party, the short-lived SDP (Social Democratic Party).

At the local level, it was another story though and it was fascinating for me to witness this certainly charismatic character getting down to the real nitty gritty. I had often heard that Benn was a master of the minutiae but I could never have imagined to what extent.

He breezed into a packed assembly room at a local primary school on this particular evening to face a largely supportive crowd but one peppered with opponents intent on tripping him up.

His opening words addressed national and international issues on which he was well versed to comment having been a Cabinet Minister since appointed by Harold Wilson in 1964. This was the man who had helped to establish the Girobank, given the green light to the development of the Concorde project and who, one thought at the time, still had an eye on taking control of The Labour Party and maybe even moving into No 10 itself.

He was a natural and supremely competent orator with a compelling turn of phrase which demanded the rapt attention of his audience. I remember the audience being particularly in awe as he relayed the story of his arrival in Bristol taking over from Sir Stafford Cripps in 1950. He recited a string of names of local party activists and supporters, many surely long deceased, citing their jobs and addresses – even giving the house numbers. He trotted out the names of local policemen, doctors, small businessmen etc. It was a marvellous feat of memory in itself, but he succeeded in conveying the impression that these were 'his people' and he would always do his best for them.

The hecklers sought to attack him on a wider front though and one lady seemed to have landed a blow when she posed the question;

'Why is the Labour Party so keen to abolish Grammar Schools and remove our choices in education?'.

When Benn paused, many thought she had succeeded, but he looked at her and said;

'Madam', before taking a long suck on his pipe. Looking back at her he waited whilst the room stilled itself, 'Madam', he repeated, 'what choices in Life does an 11 year old boy or girl from Brislington have if they fail the 11 plus examination?'

He paused whilst Madam and the audience waited for him to answer his own question.

'I will tell you that the boy may hope for a job at the St. Anne's board mills, he might become a garage mechanic, be a labourer or try to get himself a trade. The girl? Perhaps she'll find herself in a nice office job or will land up in Woolworth's behind the counter. There is nothing wrong in these positions but why can't our 11 year old children dream of going to university and strive to become doctors, lawyers or whatever they want to be? Because madam, they failed a test when they were 11 years of age that took away their hopes and aspirations and denied them ever dreaming that they could achieve anything better than going beyond the lower rungs of society'.

It was a precise, succinct answer that all could relate to and the effect was spellbinding. I thought of how my own sister had managed to reach university, in spite of the system not because of it. How could it be right that she and her friend were the first to ever go to university from her secondary school? I thought of bright kids I had gone to primary school who were now holding down dead end jobs…..and how had I escaped? Well, I and a few more like me accepted the bribe of a bicycle from our parents for passing that wretched examination.

I was to disagree with a lot of Benn's philosophy in the years to come but I have never forgotten his condemnation of selective education. It can never be justified.

A few days later Mrs Thatcher arrived in Downing Street and the best I could hope for was that The Labour Party would get its act together. I was to have a very long wait.

Back at Reeves I decided it was time to bite the bullet. I had no idea what lay in store but I feared for my health and maybe even for my sanity. I met with the directors and tendered my resignation with immediate effect. I had little money, no car and certainly no immediate prospects, but the relief was enormous.

Chapter 14

'Is It Love You're After'

Bristol was a city that I never took to. It was not that it was unappealing; indeed, it's a place with a whole lot going for it. It was just a place that I seemed to flounder in and unlike any other town and city that I have stayed in for any period of time; it was one where I failed to make any real connections and a place I just didn't empathise with.

On leaving Reeves, I should have retreated home for a little while at least but when you're feeling low you don't necessarily want people to know just how bad it is for you. I was in a real mess one way or another and how the hell was I going to make any meaningful provision for Carrie and our child?

Carrie's family were wonderful though. They supported her completely and Carrie for her part did not admonish me. Both she and her family were nothing less than civil and respectful when I got down to Devon which, because of my circumstances, was all too infrequently.

Not knowing what to do, I answered an ad in the local paper to join a Life Insurance company. It was a commission only role which paid well on results but there was no regular income. A kindly Scotsman there, Bill Meikle, persuaded me to give it a go whilst I decided which way to turn next. He and the branch manager, an avuncular South African called John Suter, introduced me to the rest of the team who did indeed seem to be deriving a very good living from the business.

I found it very difficult indeed but I worked exceedingly hard at it to prove that I didn't have to get back on that nightclub treadmill again. I hated the fact that we had to do a lot of door knocking but gradually I refined my approach and soon I began to write some business. The rewards were certainly there but I was uncomfortable with some of the ethics of that type of business. Whilst I could talk convincingly of the need for the products; life insurance, pension plans, investment bonds etc., I was uncomfortable to see that for many of my colleagues, the potential personal reward for them far outweighed the benefits for their prospective customers. I came across stories of agents who would pay the first month's premium for a customer after signing them up so that they could get their commission the following month. If they could be introduced to a neighbour or a friend, then they would pay more instalments. That to me was akin to a glorified Ponzi scheme and I wanted no part of it. Though I did meet some very good people in that line, it certainly wasn't the way I wanted to spend my working life. But the experience did me no harm at all.

At the end of the summer I had two weddings to attend to in Kettering, one being my sister's. Once again, I just loved being back home and when I returned for the second wedding I admitted to my folks that I found myself in something of a hole.

My parents were always nothing less than 100% supportive but I used to think I'd let them down badly. Only a few years before I was seen as the college kid with all to play for but here I was back home again and jobless. I'd been on a tour of nightclubs around the country and what had I to show for it? I was potless with no immediate prospects and the secret of their grandchild was now becoming such a huge burden that I knew I was damn close to completely cracking up. In the meantime, the peers I grew up with were establishing themselves in their careers, getting married, starting families and buying houses. I thought I'd been doing so well but now here I was back home with the parents with no clue as to where to turn.

Home though, really is where the heart is and slowly I began to get my act together. My health improved and I found solace in returning to Kettering's still buoyant social scene where of course the sweet soul music sounded better than ever.

I needed to earn some money though...and quickly. Dad had mentioned a mate of his who drove for Headland Taxis and who needed someone he could trust to drive his opposite shifts. That appealed to me instantly. I liked driving and I liked the idea of being able to do the job when it suited me, allowing me to get away for interviews for 'the proper job' which would surely come. I picked up the phone to make the inquiry and was simply asked when I could start. Yesss!!! It was only as a taxi driver but the pleasure of that moment was as good as anything I could have imagined at that time of my life.

That evening a very nice old boy, Roger, turned up at our house in his winged Vauxhall Cresta. This was to be my chariot and I loved it.

Beautiful leather bench seats and the fascinating column gear change was what I remember most about the vehicle.

The deal was simple enough. I would take one third of the takings and Roger would pay for all the petrol and overheads out of his share. Any tips were all mine. Roger would drive during the day and the car would be dropped off to me every evening at 6pm.

In those days there was no formal taxi training to undertake, nor was there a need for any background checks. I had a driving license so I was in business. Our company had sole access to the taxi rank at Kettering Railway station and that proved to be the bread and butter business. Other jobs would be phoned through from the controller and at the weekends there was ample work to be generated from the town's pubs and clubs.

The other drivers made me very welcome and I soon enjoyed the banter and their way of working. Some liked the longer, out of town journeys and others preferred the short hops. I realised that it was possible to do three or four short hops around the town in the time it took another driver to do the 7 or 8 miles to Corby and back. Although the fares would be a lot less, they usually meant considerably more tips and they started to mount up very quickly. If someone asked to go 15 miles to Northampton, I would often pass that job to one of the guys who liked the longer trips. They then would reciprocate and it made for a very good working relationship with all the boys.

Soon I was getting my regulars and I enjoyed the repartee that resulted as people liked to chat away and often sought my opinion on their particular problems or situations.

One fare asked me to take him to a village near Oundle which was a good 45 minutes away. He seemingly had it all; a highly paid job in the city, a beautiful home which I took him too and a young family who meant everything to him. But he was evidently paying a price for it all and during the journey he lamented the stress he was feeling and the sheer exhaustion of it all every day. I was merely a receptacle as he unburdened himself on the journey but he undoubtedly felt a lot better for having done so and proffered me a £10 tip when we finally reached his home.

I was quite taken aback but he thanked me for listening and being so helpful. We shook hands and he bounded from the taxi ripping out the backside of his trousers as he caught it on the door! Oh dear.

A young lady who commuted daily to London became another regular. She was immaculately groomed and the scent of her perfume would leave a pleasant aroma in the taxi for the rest of the shift. The first few times conversation was limited with her, barely going beyond exchanges about her journey or the weather but gradually it widened and she began to reveal more of herself every day during what was never more than a 10 minute trip.

She had moved to the town to take advantage of the cheaper property available but she knew no one and felt rather lonely. Her life was solely concentrated on work and it was beginning to depress her.

After a few days, she said how much she looked forward to our daily encounters and I said as much to her but maybe in a rather nonchalant way. She was a beautiful woman in all respects and I was beginning to become rather smitten with her. The way she talked, maybe she liked me too but where once I would have been bold enough to ask her out; now my self-esteem was somewhat lower. I told myself that I was but a taxi driver and that I shouldn't even entertain the notion of asking such a classy lady out.

It got to the stage that the other drivers noticed it too as she would let others in the rank go ahead of her until she found me available. They too thought she was absolutely gorgeous and asked what had I got to lose; but I guess my fear of rejection was all consuming and I let the opportunity pass. If indeed there had been an opportunity. It was that lady I thought of when I later learned of the words used by Franklin D Roosevelt in his inauguration speech;

'the only thing we have to fear is...fear itself —
nameless, unreasoning, unjustified terror'.

The other guys were so right and their advice – and the FDR quote – is one I have doled out to so many others over the years. Yet then, and too many times after that, I have failed to act. What is it with human nature that stops us from even to dare?

The taxi driving worked for me on so many levels though. It only lasted for a few months but it got me functioning once again so much so that I was in absolutely the right frame of mind when one evening the phone rang....

'I'm looking for Patrick', the caller began. Heck, I thought, what trouble am I in now?

'Would that be senior or junior?' I asked.

'The one who might be interested in a very attractive position I have to offer in a fabulous establishment about to open!'

It was a gentleman called Gordon Hubbard, the Operations Manager for Mecca Leisure and he needed an experienced hand for the new joint they were opening in Northampton, 'Cinderella's Rockerfella's'. I still have no idea how he knew of my availability, nor how he acquired our ex-directory telephone number, but no matter he got through to me and yes, of course I was interested.

Now I had tried to tell myself to stay away from this environment but the nightclub industry had become something of a vocation for me and it really was my natural environment. Like punch-drunk boxers, I had seen others return to clubland when surely, they should have moved on. Like the boxers, we're all suckers for punishment. I feared the same happening to me but against that, I was still young, I could still make strides in it and besides what else could I really do? More than anything it still gave me a buzz and when Gordon outlined his plans I knew I wasn't going to be able to resist. It also appealed to me that I would be near to my home comforts too – mum would be happy to do my washing every week...and indeed she was.

Mecca was in something of a state of flux at the time. For years they had been dictated to by 'Chairman Eric'. Eric Morley had established a nationwide network of Mecca Ballrooms. They were not unlike the Top Rank Suites and their flagship brands were the Tiffany's and Locarno Ballrooms. They were vast dancing emporiums capable of housing 2000-3000 patrons. Most of them tended to have their own resident band who were capable of both knocking out covers of the pop hits of the day as well as strict tempo ballroom dancing numbers.

Like Rank's venues they tended to be multi-purpose operations with nights for different age groups, dinner dances, sports events and occasional pop concerts.

It was a formula that had worked well for decades, but by the late '70s, times were changing rapidly. They were seen as too mainstream and too vast. The smaller, intimate discotheques and nightclubs were now the order of the day. There the DJs could respond more easily to customer demand and be much more 'cutting edge' with music policy and the sounds of imported soul and funk resonated far better with the discerning youth than did mainstream pop music which the larger ballrooms used to feed their patrons on. As for the resident bands, they were now a total anachronism. It just wasn't on for middle aged sax and keyboard players to even attempt the raw funk riffs so characteristic of James Brown & Co at the time. It was even more ridiculous to see some of the old crooners pleading to the next generation to;

'Get on up, stay on the scene like a Sex Machine;
Get it together, right on, right on!'

Mecca Ballrooms in short, were synonymous with an age long gone characterised by Chairman Eric and such as his Miss World beauty pageants. They were both once a staple of mass market entertainment in Britain but now they were beginning to look like elderly relatives who had lingered too long at the party.

Unfortunately, Mecca was lumbered with vast sites they couldn't adapt for modern usage and many of the bands were locked into long term contracts.

Rank Leisure had stolen a march on them with the development of smaller scale nightclubs where overheads were a fraction of those of the ballrooms and the revenue yield was considerably greater. Indeed, hadn't I managed one of the very best of them in Busby's? The management headcount was of course much less and they could dispense with such as engineers and maintenance personnel who were always a heavy cost for the larger operations to bear.

Now though Mecca was set to make its play and money, in relative terms, was no object. The 'Cinderella's Rockerfella's' format had already been pioneered in the north and again in Lincoln, Purley and Guildford.

Some of them were still fairly large venues but the aim was to offer a twin scene nightclub operation to patrons. The intention was to provide a plush, upmarket facility unlike anything else in the locality. The door policy was crucial; it had to be rigidly enforced and patrons wanting to use the club were expected to dress and behave accordingly. And they did!

A few days after his call, I met Mr Hubbard at the club in Northampton. I had known the premises as the old Salon Ballroom in Northampton but had only been there a couple of times. My recollection was that it had had a pretty raucous atmosphere where the sound of breaking glass chimed pretty well with the music that pounded out there.

One of my visits had proved unforgettable; it was the night I bumped into an ex-army boy from Kettering who I found in a pretty alarming state. Looking wild eyed and gap toothed, I wondered if he'd dropped some speed or had maybe taken a slap from someone.

'No, no', he spluttered, 'worse than that!' What could be worse than that I wondered but Squaddie Boy's story did make me wonder…once I'd stopped laughing.

It seems he'd asked a girl for a dance earlier in the evening, leaving his pint on a table. When he returned, the pint had gone so he was obliged to buy another one for himself. A little while later he went for another dance and once again he returned to find his pint had been pinched. This wasn't funny, it was spoiling his night and he made up his mind that it wouldn't happen again. By now he had pulled a young lady, with whom he was getting on famously with. She then heard a tune she liked and tried to drag him back out onto the dancefloor.

'Hang on darling', he cried to her, 'there's something I need to do'. He didn't want to lose yet another pint so she looked on in astonishment as he took out his dentures and put them in his pint! 'OK baby', says Squaddie Boy, 'let's boogie'.

They had a couple of dances before returning to the table. Squaddie Boy was relieved to see his pint still there…. but then hit the roof when he found his false teeth weren't!

We hoped this sort of behaviour wouldn't occur in the new and very refined 'Cinderella's Rockerfella's', but you really can't legislate for a good prankster.

A management team of 6 had been assembled for the new operation and I was to be joint deputy to a guy called Ross, an experienced Mecca manager who had come through the ranks with them. The other deputy, Tony, was another Mecca man who had worked with Ross previously. Two young assistant managers, Robin and Sue, were recruited locally and were new to the industry. Their primary concern would be the bars and catering operation. They seemed very capable but both were newly married and I wondered if it was wise for them to be taking up their positions.

The launch of Cindy Rock's, as the place came to be referred to by the locals, was well trailed in the local press and we could tell when dropping promotional literature around the town that there was a real buzz of anticipation. Many firms were making block bookings for the restaurant and the private hire calendar was filling up rapidly.

To enhance the cachet of 'exclusivity' we decided to introduce a membership scheme. Members would get priority admission and be able to queue jump - and they provided us with an invaluable database of addresses, birthdays etc., to allow us to target promotional activity much more precisely. All this is quite commonplace now of course but back then it was quite radical.

Prospective members were invited to come down to the club to have their photographs taken for their membership cards and were given a sneak preview of the facilities. There was an awful lot of chrome, green planters, pink neons and Tivoli lighting in the design schemes of nightclubs in that era but Cindy Rocks took it to another level. The burgundy velvet wallpaper seemed to many of the patrons to be the last word in luxury and fine taste!

When an advert was run seeking part time bar and waiting staff and door attendants we were totally overrun by applicants but we wanted to see them all and decided to run open evenings to meet prospective candidates.

We had different nights for the door staff, restaurant staff, and the bars and waiting staff were recruited over two evening sessions. Tony had told me how he planned to save time in selecting the waiting staff but I thought he was only joking.

On arriving all were told to fill in the application forms, then Tony, Ross and I visually graded the candidates according to gender, appearance etc. The finer detail was to be determined in the one to one interviews.

When it came to the waiting staff, there was only one criteria as far as Tony was concerned they had to be female, young, fit and look extremely attractive in the uniform provided which was a high cut leotard with high heels. Very PC I don't think!

Tony handpicked a couple of dozen girls out for the role and they were invited into the office half a dozen at a time.

Ross and I sat either side of Tony whilst he conducted what turned out to be a communal interview.

'Would you all like to work here?' he asked.

'Yes' they all chorused.

'Would you all like to earn massive tips?'

'Yes' they all naturally replied.

'Well to do that, you've got to have the right attitude and be able to smile a lot and relate to the customer. Do you think you could do that?'

'Yes' they answered as one.

'Good, I'm sure you all will. Now all we need to do is to see you all in the uniform!' and then Tony proceeded to throw a tiny nylon garment to each of them. 'Hurry up please; we've got a lot to see!'

It was a tiny office and it was plain there was no obvious changing facility so the girls looked at each other blankly before one took the initiative.

'Right here sir?', she asked and was naked in a flash on Tony's nod. The rest followed suit in an instant. It was a job they wanted and modesty would have to be temporarily abandoned. I had to applaud Tony's chutzpah and most of the girls had a good giggle too at the cheek of the man who managed to process 24 naked young girls in barely half an hour!

After a week of intense screening we'd finally assembled a small army of staff and were ready to roll. We brought them all in on the night before opening and gave them a full training session during which we also trialled the sound and lighting systems. Perfect.

We thought we'd covered every likely scenario and were ready to meet the public with a well prepared, well drilled team ready to serve them. In such situations, one does learn to expect the unexpected but we never expected that to be delivered by the Managing Director of the company.

There was a lot riding on the success of Cinderella's Rockerfella's and the powers that be were pulling out all the stops to ensure the success of the new operation. It would determine the direction of the company and we learned that a number of the company's major shareholders would be present on the opening night.

That was no big deal as far as we were concerned. We were as prepared as we could be but we reckoned without the intervention of Mecca's big chief at the time, Michael Guthrie.

Guthrie had succeeded Chairman Eric and was the man who had approved the format of Cindy Rock's. For him it HAD to work. On the night before opening we learned that Mr Guthrie would be inspecting the premises at 9.30 am the next morning.

This was a bit of a pain as a lot of preparation can only be done on the final day. All the food and drink was being delivered and a flotilla of catering staff were due in to prepare the VIP buffet as well as prepare the restaurant for its first night of operation. Decorators, electricians and joiners all had a full schedule of last minute 'snagging' tasks to attend to and of course there was the media to attend to as well as ensuring all the staff, DJs, engineers etc., were all fully versed and prepared.

Mr Guthrie's last-minute visit would be an unwelcome diversion; but hopefully it would all go swiftly and smoothly.

The great man duly arrived at the appointed hour and was greeted by Ross with little more than a grunt in return. He had three or four aides with him armed with clipboards and ready to act on his every utterance.

He swept through the premises nodding as he went along and giving little more than a cursory glance at all the features pointed out to him. As he was leaving Rockerfella's, he stretched out a hand to feel the texture of the velvet wallpaper which had become so much of a talking point, especially as we had now learned it cost more than £50 a roll.

Ten yards further on, he did the same again, then stopped.

'Hang on' he said in an irritating fashion, 'that's not right'.

Oh Gawd, our hearts sank, what was happening? Back ten yards he went, then he crossed the room squinting back at the area he had just left.

'Take it down, take it all down'.

No one knew what the problem was and no one dared to ask. The decorators were sent for and told to take it all down. Soon Rockerfella's walls were bare; stripped down to ugly grey plasterboard complete with graffiti and obscene artwork now revealed.....as the artist never intended.

'Shocking', said Guthrie as he walked out of the building. Where to? We had no idea.

'What's the matter with it boss?' one of the decorators asked Ross, but Ross was temporarily spellbound. He hadn't got a clue. 'What are we going to do now?'

Ross gradually got some self-control back, looked at the mess caused by Guthrie's order and softly said to the decorator; 'Would you mind putting it all back up please?'

A few hours later it was all back in place and we were at last ready to roll. I was posted to the VIP entrance waiting to meet and greet a host of local dignitaries and our special guests of honour that night. What on earth these celebrities were doing there, I still have no idea, but I warmly greeted the Second World War forces sweetheart, Shelley Winters who was accompanied by the comedian, Dickie Henderson.

A few minutes later Michael Guthrie arrived with those same aides. He grunted his way in on arrival and walked straight to the section of the wall that had so aggrieved him earlier in the day. He looked it up and down, then turned around and beckoned me over. 'Here we go' I thought, 'what now?'

He looked approvingly at the very same wallpaper he had ordered to be stripped down earlier, then after the most pregnant of pauses smiled and said;

'Much better, so much, better'.

'Thank you', I found myself saying and walked back to the door wondering if in some strange way, behaviour such as he had displayed was the secret of his success.

Back on the front door, I could see that we were going to reach capacity very early. The locals really did make a magnificent effort in dressing up for the occasion, especially the guys. You know that people are always going to be better behaved wearing their best threads and it occurred to me that the local men's' outfitters must have been enjoying a huge boost to their business on account of Cinderella's Rockerfella's arrival in town.

It was a surreal night all around made all the moreso with the arrival of the guest of honour that night, one Anthea Redfern, who, at the time was very much an A List celebrity.

The Generation Game' was then the biggest show on British television and Miss Redfern, as a hostess on the show had become an instant star. She had embarked on a relationship and then married the show's star, the evergreen Bruce Forsyth. At the time of her appearance, she was never out of the tabloid press.

There couldn't have been a more high-profile celebrity in the country. Who wasn't aware of her? Well we found someone. It was the staff member who had been entrusted to check in the VIPs that night. We only realised that when Miss Redfern, who had arrived alone and unnoticed, was met with an uncompromising barrier who told her bluntly; 'No invitation, no entry!'

'No, no, no, no', I found myself gasping as my heart sank. Although Anthea had arrived at the door unnoticed, now there was a plethora of photographers who had arrived as if like flies to the proverbial jam jar. I had visions of this all blowing up on the front page of The Sun the following morning, though I suppose any publicity can be good publicity.

Fortunately, Anthea saw the funny side of it all and was a model of good grace. I apologised, resisted the temptation to say, 'Nice to see you, to see you, nice' and whisked her through to the restaurant where she joined the other assembled guests.

Our guest checker was totally perplexed and couldn't understand the fuss. She had no idea of who Anthea Redfern was, had never seen The Generation Game and hadn't seen any coverage in the press.

Thankfully the rest of the premiere evening went off perfectly smoothly. We shared a drink with all the staff at the end of the night and congratulated ourselves on a job well done.

We knew the real test would come in the next days and weeks when the novelty effect would gradually fade. Instead though, we found that we had achieved real momentum and our attendances were sustained, indeed swelled, by patrons coming from way beyond our immediate catchment area.

Groups from Leicester, Coventry, Bedford, Milton Keynes and Luton became commonplace and it was interesting to see how many other club operators dropped in to take a look. It was certainly a rare phenomenon to find a provincial nightclub attracting vast numbers of patrons all quite immaculately presented.

The buzz was back for me, it was a great environment to be working in and, as there was a sizeable management team, it was easier for us all to have sufficient time off to recharge the batteries.

I was able once again to catch plenty of Poppies matches with them being just 15 miles up the road and soon my old social network were making the short journey to catch up with me.

Initially I was travelling to and fro from Kettering every day but of course it meant getting home very late after the sessions. There was a guest house across the road from the club which was mainly used by construction workers but I enquired to see if they could cut a decent rate for me. It wasn't too posh but it was clean and it was handy and meant I didn't have to worry too much about drinking. And I suppose I did realise it might be handy for entertaining too.

By now I was resigned to the fact that Carrie was getting on with her own life and inevitably I started seeing one or two girls again. In that environment, it was easy to meet people and if you just wanted to have fun, it was very easy. I did succumb on occasions but I didn't feel good about myself for my actions and I'd berate myself for my shallowness. Thankfully, there were no hearts broken though. I guess my behaviour then was par for the course and I'm just glad that none of the girls involved took exception to anything that happened. One though used her knowledge of my guest house to great and quite amusing effect. Though on the night in question; I didn't quite see it that way at first.

I had maintained some contact with people back in Redhill and word came back to me that one of my attackers had just been released from prison. It momentarily occurred to me that maybe he might seek an opportunity for retribution but I figured I was too far away and anyhow, he probably needed to get on with his life.

At the end of one Friday night session, I went out to see the staff who were sitting around relaxing after their shifts and waiting for their taxis. I used to make a point of making sure they had all booked their taxis, if not, it always caused a delay in locking up for the night.

I noticed one girl, Anne, hadn't got her name on the list and asked if she was alright for getting home to Brixworth.

'She's fine', piped up Gloria Beesley, who was probably the gobbiest of all the staff; 'she's got someone taking her home tonight!'

'Ooooooohh, lucky girl', said a few of the other girls and Anne herself shyly smiled and nodded to me indicating that was the case.

I thought no more of it and within ten minutes all the staff had disappeared, I locked up the premises and sauntered across the road.

A very low wattage bulb in the porch generated just enough light to make sure one could negotiate the steps into the house which was always unlocked. My room was up the stairs and the first on the left. Although my door was always shut, I tended to leave it off the latch.

That night I crept up the stairs as usual and felt my way along the corridor to the first door. I opened the door, but before stepping in I found myself suddenly gripped with fear. Something wasn't right and I stood stock still at the entrance to my room as I tried to take in what was causing me to be so alarmed. I opened the door a little further and with the aid of a shaft of moonlight; my eyes gradually took stock of the surroundings. I could make out my clothes hung on the wardrobe, I could see the bags I had left out earlier but what was the noise I was hearing?

I felt a presence and tried to take in the rest of the room. Then I clearly heard breathing. I thought it must be from another room, one of the pipelayers who had checked in that day perhaps? This didn't make sense. But no, the noise was nearer than that. I looked towards the bed, had I left it unmade? I knew I hadn't. There was someone here! I immediately thought of the guy who'd got out of prison. Panic set in and I reached for the light switch.

'Hello', said a voice.

'Jesus, Mary and Joseph, who's that?' I shouted.

Then a head emerged from under the bedclothes. It was Anne.

'What are you doing here?' I asked. I was shocked but mighty relieved at the same time.

'Gloria said you liked me and that you'd want me to come'.

'Oh heck', I thought, 'what do I do now?'

She was stark naked and obviously expecting a night of passion. I knew I couldn't do that. She was a nice enough girl but very, very impressionable and Gloria and some of the others would have been having a hell of a laugh at what they'd set up. On the other hand, I had had quite a few drinks and wasn't fit to drive. Now, what would any guy do?

Well, maybe I should have but I didn't. 'Come on girl', I said, 'get dressed and I'll take you home'

'Don't you want to…..', she started to say and she was nearly in tears.

I cuddled her and gave her a little kiss and she realised she had been set up. She then felt very humiliated and I realised that a joke is only a joke when no one is hurt and she was very hurt.

Anne got dressed but was still very distraught. I tried to tell her that it wasn't that I didn't like her but this wasn't the way to be doing things when other people are having fun at our expense.

'What shall I say?' she asked.

'The same as me. Nothing!'

I figured Gloria would tell all the staff including the bouncers and if we weren't careful it would be damaging for both of us.

'Say nothing, smile and touch your nose. If you do that, they will wonder but let that be our secret'.

'Oh ok', she said cheering up, 'but in that case, we might as well go back to bed!'

'Come on', I said, 'let's get you back to Brixworth!'

Sure enough there was plenty of giggling going on the next night but Anne and I kept our pact and everyone was left to wonder.

It was a pretty good stunt though and I had to admire the sheer brass of Gloria who apparently had a chance conversation with a girl who had been over to my place previously. 'Brassy' is the most appropriate term I can think of to sum up Gloria. Her cackle rings in my head as I write this as does her reaction to the news stories of the Abingdon rapist who was prowling Northampton at the time.

Two or three rapes had been carried out on the old Abingdon Racecourse site in very quick succession and there was a heightened state of alert amongst many young women in that area but they didn't include Gloria.

'I've been down there four nights this week – and he still hasn't come for me. What's wrong with me?', she wanted to know. She was a real force of nature with a compelling wit and presence.

Gloria's stunt was almost a carbon copy of the one I had experienced in Plymouth some years before but this time it was not the work of a sadistic woman but a fun character out to give everyone a laugh.

A few years later, I read in the papers that Gloria had died following a domestic incident. It was hard to think that the voice of this bold, brazen, outrageous young lady had been forever silenced.

The weekly routine was quickly established at Cindy Rock's and unlike some of the venues I operated, we didn't have to work too hard to keep pulling the punters in.

We knew it wouldn't always be so easy and to that end we worked vigorously in signing people up for memberships so that we could later mine the data and information they supplied us with. In the meantime, we could concentrate on the invaluable private function business which would generate incremental revenue on nights when the premises would otherwise have been closed.

For my own part, I was finding my own role less stressful than any I had held down in this sector. No overbearing bosses, no physical threats, no exhaustion and no real business pressures. In some ways, I was finding it just too easy and in truth many days were becoming a predictable routine, maybe too much so.

I spent a lot of time promoting the venue in Northampton and further afield. It was important to build relationships with the bigger businesses and the likes of Barclaycard, Debenhams, Beatties and the County Council offices became crucial to our sustained success. A few concessionary tickets dropped into somewhere like Debenhams could trigger as many as 40-50 people attending from just one outlet and I made it my business to keep as close to these key outlets as was humanly possible.

It was on one of my regular visits to Debenhams that I spotted one of our bar staff working there in the Clinique concession. Carol was a particularly vivacious girl, full of life with a killer smile that would melt your heart. I'd noticed she was a girl people would gravitate towards though she was quite modest and unaffected by the attention she seemed to attract. She absolutely loved working at the club and she did a great job in promoting the place to her friends and colleagues.

I knew that every time I went into Debenham's I would get a great reception from both Carol and Lucy her friend, who had also come on board with us at the club. Carol then asked me to let her know when I was likely to drop by and she started arranging her breaks so that we could share a coffee together. I think we both knew that feelings were starting to grow towards each other but at that time, commitment was something I was studiously avoiding. Or so I thought! She had such a magnetic personality and to me she seemed the Real Deal. Very beautiful in an understated way, immaculately groomed and very demure but at the same time with a perkiness and quirkiness you just couldn't help smiling at.

One Tuesday night we had arranged to take a coachload of the staff down to the Cinderella's Rockerfella's at Guildford as a thank you to them all and to let them compare what we were doing with another operation which was meant to be similar. As usual on these occasions some staff behaved better than others and some didn't behave at all! You do factor that in of course but compared to other 'jollies' I've been on, no one disgraced themselves.

I'm not sure if it was by accident or design, but Carol plonked herself down beside me on the coach and remained by my side for the rest of the night. We were now an 'item' it seemed. After the roller coaster ride of recent years, Life suddenly seemed very nice and settled again and I was as comfortable as I could be with it.

I made sure that Carol knew all about Carrie and Emmeline who by now was three years old. She was surprised of course but seemed to take it all in her stride. I would see Carol three nights a week at work and I'd look forward to going out with her on a couple of our nights off. Her family made me very welcome and I began to wonder if we were on course for something rather more.

We didn't talk about that as I recall, but I hoped she was feeling the same way as me and certainly her demeanour suggested she was quite content with the way things were going. It was all very easy and I can't ever recall any stresses in our relationship but once again I found I had no plans for the unexpected turn of events which eventually presented themselves.

An SOS had gone into Mecca Head Office from the Cinderella's Rockerfella's in Lincoln where the General Manager found himself at breaking point after the resignation of his previous deputy and assistant managers. Northampton was top heavy with management and it was no surprise when they looked at our pool. Because I was the most experienced it was felt that I was the only one who could step into the breach. I made it clear to Gordon Hubbard that I was not happy to go but given that he had given me the break a few months earlier I did feel obliged to help him out. He was a very decent man, a little pompous and affected in a certain way but one who I had found to be as honourable as anyone I'd found in this game. Gordon, for his part, recognised that it was a big ask but promised that it was his aim to give me my own venue as soon as a suitable position became available. I knew too that if I didn't accept, I was very likely to be overlooked in the future.

I was going to miss Carol and wondered if she would feel the same. Whatever happened this was going to be the test for us both. If we proved that we were right for each other then I would eventually have to consider a proper job outside of the mad world of nightclub management. I said as much to her and we agreed that we'd take each day as it came and still try to see each other as often as possible.

It was therefore with a very heavy heart that I started to make plans for my departure to Lincoln. I had been to the city a couple of times and I actually had relations there but it always seemed to me to be a little remote and slightly off the beaten track even though it was only a short hop from the city of Nottingham.

Carol and I spent as much time together as we could in our last few days together but I was getting that gnawing, agonising feeling that this move wasn't going to be good for our us, as a couple. I thought she was special but sometimes, somehow you just know that something good is about to slip away.

Lincoln wasn't that far away I kidded myself. Only 90 miles or two hours away in theory but it may as well have been 900 miles. I was only going to be having Sundays and Tuesdays off so that wasn't conducive to be planning time together.

Once again, I was on the horns of a dilemma but I knew I had to obey my orders.

Chapter 15

'And The Beat Goes On'

Lincoln for sure is a beautiful city and after a quick spin around it, I looked forward to exploring it fully as soon as I had an opportunity. For now though I needed to bed down in my new role and I needed to do that as quickly as possible.

Fortunately, the club was not in a state of crisis. On the contrary, business was quite buoyant and as far as I could see it was a well-oiled operation that functioned pretty smoothly behind the scenes.

The General Manager, Chris, was a young guy in a hurry. Originally from the Potteries area, he had come through the Mecca ranks very quickly and it seemed to me he was destined for a very senior role within the company if that was his desire. I wasn't surprised when I later heard that his real aim was to run his own enterprise which he did eventually manage to do.

In his office he employed a secretary, Rosie, and a membership secretary, Jools; two ladies who worked very well together despite being polar opposites in both character and attitude. Rosie was the settled family lady who carried out her duties diligently and without any fuss whatsoever. She had been doing the job for a long time and Chris obviously trusted her unconditionally. She was another fine example of that key member of staff who knew the operation inside out and could be relied upon to flag up any issues and concerns.

Jools, in her late twenties struck me as quite a light-hearted, zany character who took nothing too seriously. That much was certainly true but her outlook belied the true feelings of a woman who had experienced a very real catastrophe of quite tragic proportions just a few months previously. Jools hadn't long been married and believed herself to be in a strong relationship which promised so much for the future. Unfortunately, her husband had his personal demons. What exactly they were, no one will ever know, but they caused him to take his own life when he went out for a late night drive before driving to a local beauty spot and carefully connecting a pipe to the car's exhaust emission. Carbon monoxide poisoning resulted and his body was found the next morning by a man out walking his dog.

No note or explanation was left and Jools must have agonised over what led him to that state of mind. She rarely spoke of him but instead threw herself into her work where at least she was in the company of some good, caring people. As I had found in Northampton, her role proved to be a vital function and the hours she spent combing the data to identify such as people's birth dates, addresses and occupations was justified with the sheer weight of numbers attending as a result of the invitations that she had been sending out. Indeed, her efforts allowed us to achieve huge attendances on otherwise quiet nights which many operators would have considered were not worth opening for.

Because the operation was meant to be similar to the one I left behind in Northampton, it was no surprise to find that the two clubs shared some of the same DJs who could be relied upon to deliver the musical content that the format demanded.

DJs at Rank were often employed on a whim and their quality was variable, but they were usually all local to the venue. Mecca took a different and probably more enlightened approach. They believed in looking after the good ones and rewarding them very well if they were prepared to travel and conform to the company's edicts. Initially, I was a little sceptical but I noticed that these guys were invariably very polished performers and surprisingly innovative in their ways of presenting to and controlling a crowd. The fact that two or three would be used per night also meant they sparked off each other and adopted each other's better routines and stunts. Their presence also had the effect that good young local DJs could be schooled in best practise too.

A Mecca DJ in those days was expected to be an accomplished all-rounder. He needed to know his music thoroughly and be capable of keeping up with current trends; but beyond that he needed to be capable of acting as an MC for such as the endless beauty pageants that used to be staged or one of the impromptu competitions that they were urged to do occasionally. The John Wayne lookalike contest used to go down especially well in Lincoln! He needed to be the man in charge capable of entertaining a works party private function when all ages had to be catered for and he needed to have the ability to launch into a suitable party set for whoever was in attendance. His appearance and presentation was equally important. 'Smart casual' was de rigeur but his wardrobe needed to house a dress suit and the necessary accoutrements too.

Certain technical ability was also essential in those days of vinyl turntables when a tiny ball of fluff could wreak havoc, never mind a spilt drink!

The DJs across the country would have their own controllers who would advise them of their assignments, timings and the nature of events. It was a system that worked very well and it certainly took care of what had been a regular headache in other venues I had worked in.

Big Al Mayfield and Pete Charles ruled as two of the DJ Godfathers and together they laid down the framework of the Cinderella's Rockerfella's policy. The two of them regularly worked Purley, Guildford, Northampton and Lincoln and helped to develop a second tier of DJs who usually lived closer to some of these venues. One guy I particularly appreciated was Paul Bentley from Mansfield who was covering Lincoln and Northampton.

He had a voice like velvet and was the consummate professional in his execution of the role but what I liked about him was that he was a real maverick who liked to take a risk. He also looked like a bag of spanners sometimes - for a mannequin he was not! It was no good relying on Paul to be anything of a fashionista, he would probably have turned up in his overalls over custard stained bri-nylon shirts. Instead Paul was always instructed to wear a dress suit and bow tie. Although his velvet jackets and bow ties invariably clashed with whatever colour of fake frill dress shirt he wore; it did use to look like he'd made an effort and if you closed your eyes….well, everything else was perfect.

Paul never claimed to be a music aficionado either. He might take a glance at the charts but other than that he ploughed his own furrow. However, it always seemed to work quite seamlessly. He might give some spiel as a James Brown track was coming to an end, but somehow, he'd keep a full floor for a totally contrasting choice such as Cliff Richard! Absolutely no other DJ used to even carry a Cliff record with them but Paul would raise the roof when he dropped 'The Young Ones' or 'Bachelor Boy'.

We used to chew the cud between his sets and I found a fascinating and intelligent guy who was to become a firm friend. He was married and had at least five children but he was one of the least stable men I have ever encountered. He hadn't a clue where he was coming from and where he was going too. All his actions were the result of a whim or a notion, yet he was immensely well liked, tremendous fun to be with and was very, very good at his job..

After the days of the 3 day week and relative austerity in the 70s, these were boom years for the disco industry and in Lincoln we were really enjoying the ride. It was hard and tiring work but one didn't mind when things were going relatively smoothly and the work for the most part was a lot of fun.

I was happy to socialise with the staff there too in a way that I hadn't allowed myself previously. As a result, I got to know the rest of the social scene in Lincoln very well too.

I also made a point of catching up with relations I had in Lincoln and they in turn introduced me to the City's Irish life which was very buoyant at that time too. Just after I started mixing with that set a very tragic accident befell that community which sent a shock wave searing through them all. A 22 year old lad who was the only son of a major Irish contractor was killed when he embarked from the wrong door of a train pulling into a station.

Although I hadn't known the boy, I had met his family a few times. They happened to hail from near my own people in County Mayo. The family were devastated as you can imagine but I wasn't prepared for the huge outpouring of grief I found when I attended the funeral and the wake afterwards at The Hop Poles pub. I saw then all that was best in people when disaster strikes and I was truly proud to be amongst them all on that terrible occasion.

Chris was very proud of the ship he was steering in Lincoln and it was a great credit to the man that he had a team behind him who were never less than supportive no matter what crazy ideas he would come up with....and he came up with quite few.

The John Wayne lookalike competition that I referred to was just one ingredient in the Western themed night that Chris proposed on one occasion. Chris wouldn't stop at merely dressing up the staff; he wanted the whole town to be aware of it. The papers, radio and TV would all be alerted when we had something going on. They may not be the slightest bit interested he would often say, but they have time to fill on their schedules and space to fill in their papers so let's help them out. If they wanted some colour, some quirkiness etc., then we would provide it. I would have preferred not to have ridden bareback around Lincoln Market on a very moody chestnut mare but that's the job we're in I thought and yes there were worse ways to make a living.

From Lincoln, it was now an awful long way to go and see Carrie and the little one but I resolved to get down there as soon as I could put two or three days together. I would phone occasionally but I found it awkward as no doubt Carrie did too and instead I'd attempt to dash off a letter in which I would try to sound as if I wasn't having the life of Riley. I wasn't of course but I used to think that was probably the assumption.

I was still harbouring hope that my candle hadn't been extinguished by Carol in Northampton but I wasn't too upbeat about that. My mood changed though the next time I called Carol when she said; 'Don't come to Northampton, because I'm coming up there!'

A few of the bouncers in Northampton thought it might be a nice little jolly to come up to Lincoln for the night and asked Carol if she'd come along for the ride. I was delighted even moreso when I realised that she would be stopping over for the night for that had never happened before.

She duly rolled up with the band of brothers from Northampton the following Thursday. I was apprehensive for sure but it couldn't have gone any better. She was on top form and I felt very happy and very lucky to be with her. She had no shortage of admirers and I was resigned to the fact that, given my circumstances, absence wouldn't make the heart grow fonder.

We bade our leave the next morning and I looked forward to meeting her a fortnight later when it would be her 21st birthday.

Two new recruits had joined the management team at Lincoln and I knew I was going to get along with them both very well. They were both newcomers to the nightclub life but as they were both unencumbered, I figured that they would settle very well.

Gerard had been brought in to manage the restaurant operation and his background had been on cruise liners. His pedigree was real quality before that, having been trained in his native France and going onto work in some seemingly prestigious restaurant operations. I wondered if he had undersold himself coming here but this was where those winds of change had blown him and he seemed to want to make the best of it.

Karen was a very nice lady indeed. She had been hired as the Bars and Catering Manager so theoretically was also Gerard's boss. She had the full accreditation but after leaving catering college she opted instead to join the police force.

She spent 8 years or so as a policewoman but the way she used to refer to it, I think there may have been a sour note at the end of it. There had been some kind of relationship too but it was evident that she was intent on drawing a line under her past and I was just keen to see her succeed in her new role.

Both Karen and Gerard were extremely diligent and utterly professional in their roles and it was noticeable that those in their charge markedly raised their game as a result. Given the nature of our operation, I knew Gerard would find our menu somewhat limited so I encouraged him to experiment and be innovative within the parameters that controlled us.

He responded superbly. We already had a number of regulars that used the restaurant, but now we started receiving referrals and recommendations. The change seemed instantaneous and that part of our offering was now a source of great pride. Change doesn't have to be dramatic but when it's done well with care and consideration; that's when people notice.

Lincoln's Theatre Royal was situated not too far from the club but hitherto there had been precious little interaction with them. Now we noticed that they were calling to ask if we could accommodate some of their visiting stars. Great, we thought and asked them to give us a call whenever they wanted to send someone. A few nights later they duly obliged and in walked as strange a combination as I could ever have imagined.

First through the door was Hattie Jacques along with John Le Mesurier. Both were household names at the time having long been film and television favourites of the great British public. Hattie was particularly known for her roles in the *Carry On* films and as Eric Sykes's 'wife' in a long running sitcom whilst Le Mesurier was best known as 'Sgt. Wilson' in *'Dad's Army'*, a series which seemed to run for years and years.

However, it was their companion that night who turned heads and really raised eyebrows. It was none other than the hell raising snooker player, Alex 'Hurricane' Higgins……and he was sober!

Alex was rarely out of the papers in those days and usually for all the wrong reasons. He was liked and loathed in equal measure. Liked for his undeniable brilliance on the green baize where his maverick approach and speed of action had completely transformed the public's perception of a game which had always been played in a quite staid and gentlemanly manner. However, he could rarely keep his emotions in check and fuelled with copious quantities of alcohol his behaviour often spun out of control. Accounts of his boorish behaviour in public and in private and his attitude towards certain other players, meant he was excluded from the snooker 'establishment' and sponsors kept well clear of him. Yet, he was box office magic and such was his impact that he probably deserved his self-styled moniker as 'The People's Champion'.

I'd met him three years before in Redhill on a night when he was almost totally out of control. On that occasion he was loud, he was brash and he was totally paralytic but the crowd had swarmed to him like flies to a jam jar. He was a flawed genius, not unlike the other Belfast man of that era, George Best.

In Lincoln though, his behaviour was quite exemplary. He was courteous and polite as he made his way through the crowd to the restaurant area with the other pair. They enjoyed a good meal, listened to the music and left quietly; after tipping very well it should be said.

I worked very well with Karen and Gerard. It was nice to work alongside two people who knew what they were doing and did it very well.

Whilst Lincoln was exceedingly pleasant in many ways, the three of us found ourselves relatively unchallenged. Perhaps we should have been content with that and maybe should have prepared ourselves for the next role with the company which promised considerably greater rewards.

In the space of just a few weeks, disenchantment suddenly seemed to set in very quickly for both of them. Gerard had been used to well-heeled customers enjoying fine wining and dining experiences. He just couldn't contemplate a long spell catering for hen parties demanding 'Sex On The Beach' cocktails to accompany their meals rather than a nice Pouilly-Fume or even a Chateau Latour! I could see his frustration building up every night but being the consummate professional, he was, he always contained himself in the course of his work.

With Karen, there was something deeper. The job was evidently an escape from something, but still she would never open up about her personal life and we would never probe. There was always a certain sadness about her demeanour. Outwardly able and efficient, she made sure the job was always done so well. There was a certain gravitas about her which meant she always commanded respect and no one would ever take liberties by making a cheap joke at her expense.

Physically, she was a very imposing lady. You would describe her as handsome rather than pretty, as she displayed well sculpted features enhanced only by the lightest of makeup which was always tastefully applied. She had a prominent port wine birthmark on the left side of her forehead which I'm sure she was always very conscious of, but I didn't think it distracted from her features at all.

She had a very sturdy physique which suggested she had probably been an excellent athlete at some time and one assumed she would have been well capable of handling herself in her previous role with the police.

Because she rarely spoke of her time in that job, I began to suspect that there had been some hurt left behind there. There was no man in her life but on one occasion when we got into deep conversation she did momentarily reflect on a boyfriend she had had 'in the job'. The way she talked of that so wistfully made me think that that episode in her life was never far from her thoughts.

Around one o'clock time every session, Karen would allow herself to relax. By that time in the evening most of the work was all but done and there would only be the cashing up and replenishing of the stock required before close of play. She'd order a half of lager, sometimes a glass of red wine, before lighting up a Camel cigarette and inhaling deeply. That was the time when she was more reflective and might open up a little. She had many admirers and plenty did try to chat her up. They were always rebutted politely but firmly as she would say she was awful busy or was required elsewhere.

I'm not sure how she spent her days off but we never saw her socialising with the staff or the management. She was her own woman alright, but she was not happy.

Working at Lincoln for me, and I suspect Karen and Gerard, started to seem like a metronome. The routine was entirely predictable and week after week we executed our duties in much the same way, at the same time and with the same results. Lots of people have repetitive working practices I know and ours wasn't onerous or unpleasant but I guess we were young(ish) people who had known better and were frightened that we were gently lapsing into predictable mediocrity. We didn't know if change for any of us would be for the better or the worse but we also knew that not changing was not an option.

Gerard was the first to make that leap. The Royal Viking Line came calling for him and though he knew that he'd been there and done all that before; it was still more appealing than the status quo. Whether to stay in Lincolnshire or travel the world, that was the question for him and it took him a nanosecond to decide. I hoped the experience he'd had with us would somehow stand him in good stead but somehow it was hard to imagine. He was a great guy and I was very sorry to see him move on.

I had negotiated to create a little bit of time off for myself and at last managed to arrange a trip down to the West Country but before that I was due to see Carol again and in truth I was aching to do so.

On the two hour drive down to Kettering, I wondered how I could somehow make her 21st birthday celebration a little more special. I was driving around now in a banana coloured Mitsubishi Colt Sigma that I'd bought a few weeks previously at a car auction. I'm not sure what possessed me to purchase it, no one had heard of Mitsubishi cars in those days, but It looked the business and I loved it.

It had all sorts of bells and whistles on it. I sure hoped she'd be impressed and I thought it would be nice to take a spin down to Luton which wasn't too far down the M1 from Northampton.

The Three Degrees were playing a cabaret club there and so I duly phoned and booked a table for two. The full works I thought and why not, she was a great girl and I quite adored her.

After seeing the folks again that night, I gave Carol a call and arranged the rendezvous for the following night but didn't say what I had planned. She seemed as buzzy as ever but made a point of asking me to meet her at the end of her road instead of calling around the house that evening. I did momentarily wonder why the change in arrangements because I had become quite fond of her parents who had always treated me very well.

The next day I caught up with a few friends and made a point of buying some flowers to take along that evening. I thought they'd be a nice gesture at the end of the night.

I arrived at the pick-up point in good time but Carol had beaten me to it. She looked exquisite as usual, she was never less than stunning as far as I was concerned but when she turned to smile it was not with her usual eager beam that used to just melt me.

She jumped into the car and gave me a quick peck and asked where we were going. When I told her, she seemed delighted but then went a bit quiet.

'Is everything OK?', I found myself asking thinking maybe she was tired and a bit pre-occupied with the events of her day.

She looked at me and tried to say something but couldn't and I noticed a tear rolled down her cheek.

I pulled over and went to hold her but by now she couldn't contain herself.

'I'm sorry, I'm sorry', was all she said. She didn't have to say anymore, I knew my time with her was at an end.

She started to say we could still go to Luton if I wanted to but that we would have to finish. She said it was because of Carrie and Emmeline; that they would always be first in my life and that she couldn't ever see herself getting used to that.

I tried to say what she meant to me and we could work it out. I said I'd never abandon Carrie and Emmeline but they had a life without me. If I'd thought otherwise I wouldn't have been with any other girl.

But her mind was made up. We sat sobbing in the car and I said I'd take her home. It was so hard to say goodbye without even putting up a fight but I knew there was no going back for her though of course I would have welcomed that. I never, ever heard from her again and hope that she went on to find the man she deserved. My gut feeling was that she had in fact already found a worthy candidate but I wasn't going to press her on that.

I never did get to see The Three Degrees that night but I drove back to K town and consoled myself with a few jars in the North Park that night. I remember thinking how ugly and charmless all the girls looked there that night. At least, I consoled myself, that I had developed some quality control along the way.

The flowers ended up with my mother and such was her gratitude I wondered why I hadn't done that more often for her.

I was feeling completely empty on that long journey the next day down to Devon. The little one was not so little any more but a fully developed 'little lady' in her own right. On the way I stopped, as I often did, in the little town of Bridport in Dorset. I've always thought it to be a neat little town and I was partial to a pint of the Palmer's which was brewed locally.

Bridport had one or two quirky little shops and it was in one of those that I came across 'a puppet on a string' or a marionette puppet to give them their proper term. I was fascinated by it. It was a little donkey puppet and it was exactly the kind of present I would have liked to receive myself as a kid.

Now that was a good enough reason *not* to buy it. My little girl was only three, how did I know if she'd like the same things as me? She couldn't possibly work it either but heck, it didn't cost that much so on a whim I bought it.

Decades later we still talk about that toy. I'm not sure that she did particularly like it and Carrie thought it wasn't suitable at all. Sure, she had Ken and Barbie, My Little Pony and all the rest but the donkey it is, who triggers the smiles all these years later.

I was thrilled to see Emmeline again. I really was rather proud to be a father, her father. How I regretted that things hadn't worked out better and that I, as a father, couldn't have given her that proper start in life. But I knew that Carrie and her family had more than made up for my shortcomings.

It was now getting very difficult making these visits to see them. Carrie was now getting on with her own life and I used to find nothing but a very happy and contented household on my visits. Emmeline in her innocence had lit up the lives of all of them and her grandparents – and great grandparents – were absolutely enthralled by her.

I was always treated with great courtesy but it was awkward and in truth my visits were probably a tad disruptive to their routine. The little one would be puzzled on my arrival but once she got used to me, we'd have great fun playing together. When I disappeared again though she often got very upset afterwards. I knew that and I knew it wasn't easy for Carrie to pick up the pieces afterwards. I knew it wasn't fair for her. She was there 24/7 and was proving to be a wonderful mother but there must have been little respite for her and I feared she must have harboured some resentment towards me from time to time.

Coming back to Lincoln after those few days off I was feeling very sorry for myself again. Affairs of the heart sure weren't going too well and it wasn't too long before I took solace from a couple of the girls on the staff who I got along well with.

One of them, Fiona, worked for the County Council there and had a wide circle of friends who all seemed to party very hard. One night I joined a load of them and found myself in a club in Nottingham where everyone seemed totally spaced out. I'd had a few drinks myself but felt totally in control. For some reason though, the music suddenly sounded thunderously loud and the place seemed to be consumed by some kind of chemical smell which started to overwhelm me.

Everyone was laughing and whooping it up and I guess I must have been going along with it because I remember being out on the dancefloor and wanting to dance non-stop. Fiona was all over me, shrieking like crazy before sinking her teeth into my neck.

'Come here', she urged me, 'have some of this'.

'What is it?'

'It's only smelling salts', she said reassuringly but by now I was too far gone to know or care. I took a deep sniff from the little bottle she gave me....and then the room started spinning.

I was laughing, going crazy, maybe shrieking like her – like them all in fact. Tomorrow would be another day, but right now I was up there on Cloud 9 and I felt like staying there.

The noise, the smells, the colours...everything was in a different dimension to anything I'd ever experienced. It was all so beautiful, so vivid, so utterly out of my control. I was spinning, I was falling but I was still laughing. Fiona's face flashed in front of me, she was doing something to me. I don't know what, I hope she did but it felt warm and kinda nice. Others around her were shrieking as well but it was all getting even louder and louder. The music was thumping now, no rhythm, no melody just crashing metallic sounds that made my body shake and tremble.

The next thing I'm on the street. Freezing. 'Where's my jacket?' I asked myself. I couldn't figure that out no more than I could work out where I was and how I'd got there. No idea, not a clue. I was totally wasted, completely out of it. I must have looked a hopeless bum. But now it seemed my senses, though shocked, were ever so slightly being restored.

There were a couple of people around me. I didn't know them, didn't know if they'd been with me earlier. Maybe they were just passing by?

'Are you alright mister? We were worried for you'.

Ah, thank God almighty. These Samaritans, for that's what they surely were, had seen me collapse in the club. The bouncers had just wanted to lob me out unceremoniously but these guys for some reason had taken me out for air and waited until I came around.

I kept saying; 'What happened, what happened?' One chap knew, he'd been aware of the same smell in the club and asked me if I'd sniffed anything?

It was all starting to come back to me and now I was able to talk fairly lucidly.

'Yes, I did, someone gave me smelling salts'.

He laughed and said I hadn't been sniffing smelling salts. He reckoned I'd snorted some amyl nitrite which was the clubbing drug of choice in that establishment.

'You're joking!' I said. I'd never knowingly taken any drugs or substances in the pursuit of pleasure even though many, speed especially, had been such an integral part of the Northern Soul scene which was such a big part of my life.

'They all use poppers in there mate, don't worry you'll be ok'

Poppers? I must have been leading a sheltered life I thought, but at that time poppers were relatively new in clubland. I was to come across them a lot in the next few years but it sure is hard to fathom how a substance developed for the benefit of angina sufferers could become such an essential part of a night out for many people.

Fortunately, Fiona and company were loyal and remained discreet about the events of that night. She and her friend, Elaine who also worked at the club, started to take an interest in my welfare and between them they ensured I had a comfortable life away from work and introduced me to a wide circle of new friends in the area. I was very grateful to these two – the original friends with benefits!

Life in Lincoln was uneventful for the most part, but though that is often a welcome state of affairs compared to the usual stress and strife which is never far away in clubland; tedium is not a state of great contentment.

So, when a surprising phone call came through from Brighton, I had to consider if another upheaval was desirable.

I had been maintaining loose contact with old friends within Rank and it seems my name was mooted with regard to a vacancy coming up in Brighton.

Brighton? Now that would be interesting. I would be back in the mainstream once again. Would that be a good thing or would I just prefer to coast along in the provinces?

There was a lot to be said for the latter choice but I knew that nothing was forever in the career choice I had taken. You had to go where the work was and there was precious little you could do about it. At least in Brighton, I thought there would be viable alternatives should I feel the need to or indeed be told that, I had to move on again.

Chapter 16

'The Second Time Around'

I never thought I'd find a reason to be back in Redhill and walking around the town again before going in to see Mr S; it did feel quite surreal.

I walked past the arcade where Phil the Flower Man had his stall and yes, he was still there. His eyes nearly popped out of his head.

'You're back!', he exclaimed.

'Can't say too much Phil, all will be revealed', and I tapped my nose before hugging him and adding, 'I've missed you, you lovely old queen!'

Over at the taxi rank I met with a crowd of the lads who used to ferry my staff home a couple of years previously before meeting their boss man, Mike Gold.

'Good to see you my man', said Mike who was every inch the archetypal Jewish businessman, though he did like to ham it up excessively so. 'What are you doing back in town?'

'Well to tell you the truth Mike, I'm thinking of getting into this taxi business'.

He sucked on his little cheroot cigar which seemed to be a permanent fixture between his lips. It allowed him to blow a circle of smoke whilst he tried to come up with a suitably witty response which surprisingly was not forthcoming on this occasion.

Although Mike had the taxi business sewn up in this part of Surrey – and woe betide anyone who might think of setting up against him – he liked to give the impression that he was into much, much more. We used to talk for hours in my office; or rather I used to listen to him for hours. He was successful, undoubtedly but he hated being known as 'The Taxi Man'. He wanted that little sprinkling of stardust to be associated with him. He wanted to be looked up to in his own community and in the wider Surrey business community. He always seemed irked that his living depended on drunks getting home and children getting to school in the mornings. I didn't think there was anything wrong in that but Mike always yearned for considerably more.

As I walked down towards Busby's, I waved to the ladies in Fortes Café where I had first started the downward spiral of gaining weight. I just loved their steak and kidney pies with apple crumble and custard to follow. I figured I'd be out of the meeting by 1 o'clock so tapped my watch and said, 'See you later!' That was an indulgence I could look forward to.

I strode up to Samuels' office and smiled at the once familiar faces there. They were all generous in their welcome and no doubt they reflected that when I had previously come into this lair, it was to have a dust up with their boss. Now I was back again and at his bidding.

I think we were both slightly embarrassed as we shook hands again.

'You look well', we both said in unison before he said earnestly. 'How is life for you? It can't be perfect if you're back here?'

I thought that was a clever opening as it was he who had made the approach, but he was right, what was I doing back there?

'I'm back, because I thought maybe you've come to appreciate me a bit more'.

'Touche!', he laughed. 'That's true, I do'.

Blimey, I thought. He would never have admitted as much before so I thought I'd better indulge him.

'I'm not doing too bad', I said, 'but you were right, the grass isn't always greener on the other side. I've had some good experiences, but I have to confess, I have missed this company'.

'Ok then, well maybe we can help each other'

'Go on then', I wanted to know what had prompted his call, what exactly did he have in mind.

'I'll give you a GM job in due course, but first I'd like you to do a job in Brighton for me'.

Well, it was nice to know there was a General Manager's role in the offing. That would be a significant boost to earnings and help me to get on a firm footing in financial terms. I didn't like the sound of the 'but' though. What was his problem in Brighton?

It turned out to be a personal one and one which Samuels had not been able to handle in his usual bullying, blustering style which I had once become so familiar with.

'Tell me all about Brighton, what needs doing?'

To his credit, he laid it on me without any ambiguity. It was almost sad as he described the frustration he was experiencing with the existing GM in his key Brighton operation, the Top Rank Suite.

The man in situ had been there 20 years – I already knew him, though not too well. Because of his experience, he had connections right throughout the company. The two of them clashed regularly on policy and direction and it seems that the GM was somewhat wilful in being obstructive and constantly undermining him. Samuels wanted him out and he wanted me to facilitate it. If that happened his job would then be mine. It was probably the most prestigious role in the company and Samuels wanted his own man there who would dance to his tune.

I could understand that. I'd have probably felt the same if I'd been in his position.

'What exactly do you want me to do though?' I asked.

Samuels then recited a whole litany of failures with the operation as he saw it and as far as he was concerned things would never change whilst this guy was in charge. Without saying as much, he also suggested there was a question mark regarding honesty and integrity.

So that's what it was all about. He didn't just need an experienced hand; he needed someone to usurp the incumbent. I didn't need that grief and I didn't want him to be under any illusions about that. Yes, I'd welcome the chance in Brighton but I wasn't desperate. However tedious things could be in Lincoln, it was still a pretty good number and no doubt in time other opportunities would arise.

'I'll do the job, but I'll do it straight. I don't want to be your eyes and ears to catch someone out. I'll have no part in any skimming or anything else and if that's what the guy really does then I won't be a party to it. There's other ways to skin the cat. Get your auditors to come in unannounced. Keep him on his toes; you managed that before with me'.

'I suppose' he said rather meekly and I realised that this was one guy who had got under his skin and had really pushed him to the edge.

'Ok, ok….but will you still take it?'

'I will if you promise me you're a different man….and if you make it worth my while'.

'I will, I'll be glad to have you back. I'll work out your deal and put it in writing'. If you're happy with that let us know when you can start.

He duly kept his word and it was time for me to get packing again.

I arrived in Brighton on July 1st, 1980 – a date I'm never likely to forget. Apart from bidding a very fond farewell to a couple of the girls

I'd grown close to, it wasn't an upset to be leaving Lincoln. On the contrary, I knew I'd be moving to a far more vibrant and lively town – that much was certain.

I was brimming with anticipation on arriving in the town. I dumped my bags in The Salisbury Hotel where I had been billeted and went for a stroll onto the beach near the West Pier. The sun was out, the sky was blue, and even the sea looked inviting for this non-swimmer. I bought myself an ice cream and thought to myself that if this role worked out then the wandering had to stop. I ambled along the seafront until I came to the imposing Kingswest building, which was actually a blot on the landscape in the eyes of many. I thought I'd pop my head into the Suite although I wasn't due to start until the next day. The GM, Tim Bland, was in his office and greeted me warmly, if possibly a little warily. That was probably understandable if he harboured suspicions about anyone Mr S was foisting upon him. However, Tim and I were acquainted from my days at Busby's and I hoped he'd at least take me at face value for I had no agenda concerning him.

Tim told me they had one of their International Student Nights that evening and said I was welcome to poke my head in and get a feeling for the place. I said I might as well work and at least get acquainted with some of the staff straightaway. We chatted briefly before we both cleared off to grab a few hours rest before the mayhem that the student nights guaranteed.

At 7.30pm that night, Tim strode onto the dancefloor and clapped his hands to signal one of the great Rank rituals – the staff parade.

Within seconds the entire staff delegation for that evening lined up in a straggly row and at a stroke I got an indication of the scale of the operation I was now a part of. The Suite boasted six bars, four of them enormous 50' long affairs which alone would require seven or eight staff on each bar on the busy nights. Tonight, there would only be a dozen or so in total as the downstairs bars were alcohol free zones, on account of the minimum age for this session being just 14. There were about 10 doormen or GAs (General Assistants) as Rank liked to term them. It wasn't that they would be expecting any trouble but the staircases had to be policed to prevent under-age drinking. Between bar staff, glass collectors, doormen, cloakroom attendants, buffet staff and at least four members of management; there must have been about 35 staff members standing to rapt attention to hear Tim's words of wisdom and my introduction to them all.

The staff parades were much maligned by some but they were a good opportunity for interaction between the management and staff. One could monitor the standards of the staff's uniform and attire, let them know of the forthcoming schedule of events and all sorts of various issues could be flagged up. With the young foreign students, the problems would be hard to predict, but there would always be some problems. Most of them were away from home for the very first time and for many it was the first time they'd meet people of different cultures. 99% of the foreign students though, displayed only exemplary behaviour and rarely caused trouble. They were usually from good homes and had parents who had indulged them sufficiently in paying for their summer breaks in Brighton, and for the fees to the language schools in the town where most of them were studying.

The real problems were with their British counterparts. Many of them would turn up in groups or gangs, very often from areas like Mile Oak, Portslade, Hangleton etc., where the foreign students tended to be staying with host families. The local kids drooled over the quite stunning Scandinavian girls but had a tendency to pick on the young male students who, with poor English and little understanding, were quite terrified of being abused or even possibly assaulted.

The extent of the problem was such that the police had started to take notice, whilst the language schools were worried the issue might escalate and students would stop coming to Brighton. At the staff parade that night, Tim mentioned the problem and asked particularly that the GAs be as vigilant and as observant as possible.

This sort of session was easy to set up; only a DJ was required to spin a few tunes and although the students wouldn't be big spenders, it was still very good midweek revenue when more than a thousand turned up, as they did on this occasion.

The evening seemed to pass without incident and after midnight when the final record was played the premises were soon cleared which was just as well as the GAs had to prepare the room for a dinner dance the next evening. This meant laying carpets over a section of the vast dancefloor and setting up around 30 large round tables with 10 chairs to each. Once dressed for a dinner the character of the Suite would change completely and it was actually, quite an impressive sight.

The task was nearly complete when four uniformed police officers suddenly arrived wanting to talk to all the doormen. A young German student, only 15 years old, had been followed by some English youths on leaving the Suite that night. As the student crossed The Royal Pavilion Gardens his followers attacked and one had apparently stabbed the student who was evidently now in a serious condition. The police asked if any of the doormen had witnessed an altercation.

One of our GAs, Hakim, immediately recalled that a couple of students had indeed complained of being harassed by some English kids. As Hakim hadn't witnessed any incident and the students hadn't been assaulted, Hakim reasoned that perhaps the students should start to make their way home early as the session was almost finished. They agreed, went back for their coats and thanked Hakim as they left. Hakim, then noticed a group of English kids leaving shortly after them but thought nothing of it although he recalled that one had been wearing an American college style tee-shirt with a prominent number emblazoned on it.

As one officer looked on, his radio crackled into life and he tuned in to take the message. The look on his face signalled that the situation was suddenly a whole lot more serious.

'He's died, the student is dead', he whispered to one of his colleagues who immediately realised there was a long night ahead. Suddenly, all their radios went off….a murder hunt was now under way.

All the GAs stood motionless in shock. Just half an hour ago, a young kid, not yet a man, had left a room full of happy young people from all over Europe. Now he was dead. I thought of how his parents in Germany would soon be receiving the worse news imaginable. It was heart-breaking to even contemplate. I asked the Bars Manager, Terry Robinson, if he would get all the guys a drink whilst we let the news sink in. Hakim meanwhile, was whisked away by the police who planned to trawl the city in the hope that the assailant might still be on the streets. The police van had only reached the Clock Tower, barely five minutes away, when Hakim spotted the guy he had described. The chap was arrested straightaway and confessed the following morning that he was indeed the assailant.

The police visited the Suite a couple of times in the following week taking statements from staff on duty that night. The media made a big fuss for a few days but it wasn't very long before the story became yesterday's news. For the boy's family though, I'm sure their hearts would ache eternally.

After a couple of weeks in the hotel I answered an ad in the local paper and found myself taking a room in a house on the Old Shoreham Road in Portslade. It was another rather eccentric character who owned it but I was always pretty adaptable and we got on famously until I moved to a house in the middle of the town.

My old Colt Sigma was proving far too unreliable so I traded it in for a rather boring Cortina Mark 4. Brown and cream it was, very much on trend for the travelling salesmen of that era but for the most part it was at least very reliable.

The Top Rank Suite was an integral part of the Kingswest Entertainment Centre, so called because it stood on the corner of King's Road and West Street. They must have been up all night dreaming up that name! Apart from the Suite, it consisted of Jenkinson's – a cabaret bar and restaurant, The Metro – a discotheque operation and The Odeon multi-screen cinema. There were quite a few other nightclubs in Brighton, most notably Sherry's in West Street but The Kingswest was essentially where it was at in 1980's Brighton and being a part of it all would prove to be a ball.

The weekly programme at the Suite when I arrived was ballroom dancing for the Over 25s on a Tuesday night, Over 23's on a Thursday night – the infamous 'grab a granny' session and Saturdays would be the Saturday Night Out disco session with a live band. Mondays, Wednesdays and Fridays were set aside for private function business whilst on Sundays the venue was usually closed.

The success or failure of the business largely depended on the private function business and the potential revenue that could be generated on those nights. Most of the private functions were either dinner dances or pop concerts when the venue would be hired out to promoters. On occasions, the venue was used for other purposes including such as conferences, darts exhibitions and on one memorable occasion a big, fat Greek wedding!

The dinner dances were usually the most lucrative in terms of revenue but they could be tricky to prepare for and execute. Teams of chefs and waitresses would have to be engaged, menus prepared and food and product sourced. Entertainers too, would have to be booked to supplement the house band and DJ and we tended to use some more than others. Roger de Courcey, the ventriloquist act with Nooky

Bear, was one act we repeatedly used. He always went down well and was very easy to work with. Roy Castle was another favourite for hirers with bigger budgets and Ronnie Corbett also appeared on one occasion...although the venue and audience were not to his liking. His act was thoroughly accomplished and well prepared but he took exception to the bars being in operation during his performance. He wanted the total concentration of all present and being a household name after decades in show business; I guess he had earned the right to make those demands.

It was far easier to just let the venue to a music promoter. All we had to do was book sufficient staff for the night and to ensure a sound and lighting engineer was on hand to facilitate the needs of the bands. Apart from clearing furniture, little else was required and after that night's attraction had appeared the crowd would quickly disperse and we'd all get an early night.

With a capacity of 2,000, the Suite was included on the touring schedule of some of the country's biggest acts. During my time there, we hosted the likes of Annie Lennox, Ultravox, The Stranglers, Tina Turner, James Brown, The Undertones, Joe Jackson, Adam and The Ants, The Specials, The Beat and many, many more. The punk and reggae acts did particularly well and we did very good numbers for the likes of The Buzzcocks, The Damned, Siouxie & The Banshees, The Psychedelic Furs, Misty In Roots, Toots and The Maytals and Yellowman.

Very often the promoters would rush into the office in a flap because they'd forgotten to read the riders on the contracts and some of the bands would be very precious about it all. Most of the requests were simple enough requiring only drinks, flowers, towels etc., but occasionally there would be a need for food to suit particular dietary needs. The Stranglers took no chances and brought their own catering team but were they really necessary to prepare the cucumber sandwiches (minus crusts) which were produced? I kid you not!

Toyah Wilcox was riding high in the charts with *'It's A Mystery'* when she arrived and her team insisted she wouldn't take to the stage without dry ice being sourced to stage the effects they desired. That request did cause some scratching of heads but we managed it courtesy of the blood bank at The Royal Sussex County Hospital. Toyah was an especially pleasant character who seemed slightly overwhelmed at the fuss being made of her in the light of her sudden success.

The visit of The Specials was a rather poignant occasion for me. Their bass player, Sir Horace 'Gentleman' Panter had been in my class at Kettering Grammar School and I hadn't seen him since the day we left school. He'd always been a nice guy and I'd been delighted and quite amazed to monitor the success he and the band had been enjoying. Their fans bordered on the fanatical and there had been reports of serious crowd trouble at their gigs just prior to their arrival.

After their sound check in the afternoon, I tapped on the dressing room door asking for Horace. Terry Hall answered and no doubt thinking I was an unwelcome pain said Horace wasn't there. However, Horace must have picked up on my dulcet Ketrin' tones and stuck his head out of the door as I walked off down the corridor.

'Oi Shev, come back!'.

We spent a little time talking about the intervening years and he told me how he had found it when he returned to our home town. He'd been walking around Wicksteed Park lake there when he saw a youth in front of him who had scrawled in felt tip pen on his denim jacket the legend, 'Sir Horace of Kettering'. Horace said they'd played in venues all over the world but seeing that simple scrawl on a guy's jacket in Kettering really brought it home to him how much he and the band were connecting with people.

That night with The Specials was a bit of a hairy one alright. Their reputation for attracting trouble preceded them and the Brighton police saw fit to warn them against inciting the crowd that night.

I soon saw that was out of the band's control though and looking down at the crowd that night it became clear that there were elements amongst them who were looking for some sport. Pints of beer were soon sloshing over the crowd and one large group started jeering me and the GAs looking down at them.

'Shall we go in boss?', big Gordon asked me. Fearless as he undoubtedly was, I knew we were on a hiding to nothing. Apart from being overwhelmingly outnumbered, it wouldn't have been easy ejecting anyone that night when they had to be taken off the dancefloor, bundled through a packed crowd and then taken up two flights of stairs.

'Not yet Gordon; but soon. Be patient'.

He smiled knowing that this was going to be another cat and mouse game which the boys so enjoyed.

Gordon and I stood watching the mob below us and we soon worked out who the ringleader was. No matter how gobby anyone was or however much bravado they displayed among their mates, they all had to go to the gents at some stage! We didn't reckon this guy was going to be any exception and gave instructions for a couple of the lads to take up a position near the toilets. Sure enough, The Gob did need to use the facility and we watched as he broke off from his mates to go and do the necessary.

The two of us headed down to the relief zone picking up two more of the GAs en-route. The team were positioned at the entrance to the gents and just waited whilst The Gob attended to his needs. As he walked out, Gordon tapped him on his shoulder and beckoned him to follow. The Gob realised he'd walked into a trap and meekly followed the instructions without a murmur. He followed Gordon to a rarely used exit sited well out of site from The Gob's entourage. The exit led into a pitch dark tunnel which ran directly down onto Brighton beach. He probably thought he was going to get a pummelling, but we were never that sadistic. Once through the exit, the door was slammed on him and another nuisance had been dealt with. I'm sure he would have fabricated a suitable tale to explain his disappearance to his mates who became a model of conformity without him.

The concerts in Brighton gave me something of a crash course in crowd control. Given that very often there were only 10 or 12 guys to take care of a 2,000 capacity crowd, there was often a need to deploy a certain degree of lateral thinking. Sometimes we would get it down to an art form.

The police became a great help with this and we took on board quite a few of their little tricks. Some bands attracted quite a few neo-fascists and skinheads and on arrival they didn't look too wholesome with their menacing Dr Marten's steel toe capped footwear. No problem, we'd just ask them to remove their bootlaces which they'd get back at the end of the night. Without their laces, they were completely impotent.

The punks, rockers and the goths who were just starting to appear often favoured studded jackets and belts, so once again we insisted that their belts were deposited at the cloakrooms. Perhaps it was a slight irritant for some but most tended to be amused ...it was quite ridiculous when you think about it!

The punk bands like The Damned, Killing Joke etc., were very little trouble in themselves despite their anti-establishment ranting and in truth their fans were the same despite their appearance. A lot of drink was spilt when they were pogo dancing and, since the Sex Pistols, spitting and flobbing at the band and each other had became a tasteless ritual. It was all quite harmless though but the mind boggles that it was all such an essential ingredient of what constituted a good night for many.

The worst trouble tended to arise with the most unlikely crowds when we were least expecting it. We always feared a broken bottle or smashed glass attack. They'd happen spontaneously and often wreaked horrific damage on the victims. Thankfully, they didn't happen too often but when they did, it might be during the course of a dinner dance or a 'grab a granny' session and usually involved people old enough to know an awful lot better.

Occasionally, there was a more sinister threat and with the troubles in Northern Ireland rampant, it was no real surprise that veiled threats arrived when The Undertones were booked. The band hailed from Stroke City i.e. Derry or Londonderry dependent on which side of the divide you were from. As the band were all from the infamous Creggan and Bogside, catholic and republican areas of the city, they inevitably caused distaste to some protestant and loyalist segments. We received phone calls warning of consequences should 'the Fenian bastards' take to the stage.

At Busby's in Redhill I had chosen to ignore such warnings, judging that they were hoaxes; here though, we erred on the side of caution. The police were informed as was Feargal Sharkey, the band's lead singer. It seemed this was a regular occurrence for Feargal and the boys who had no truck with the troubles at home. They carried on regardless and delivered a top show which passed off without incident.

Another Irish band that appeared at the Suite at that time were eagerly awaited as they were starting to make real waves. I'm sure though, that when U2 appeared there, even they could not have foretold the dizzy success that was to come their way.

The trigger for their success was largely due to their association with the 'Live Aid' concert in 1985 which introduced them to a global audience. That seemed unthinkable four years previously for both U2 and the main man behind Live Aid, Bob Geldof.

Geldof and his band, The Boomtown Rats, pitched up at The Suite one bleak Wednesday evening in early 1981. The band seemed to be over their hiatus when they'd scored massive hits with *'Like Clockwork', 'Rat Trap'* and *'I Don't Like Mondays'*. There was no buzz ahead of their appearance and indeed only 300 or so loyal fans turned up that night. I can't say their performance was memorable in any way, indeed they looked a pretty disillusioned outfit going through the motions. At the end of the night we noticed they had no road crew with them and our GAs offered to help them pack the gear away into the two transit vans they had arrived in.

They had all but finished the task and I was ready to lock up when there was a sudden burst of laughing with the band jeering Mr Geldof. A young fan had turned up asking Bob for his autograph which he duly obliged him with before saying; 'Hang onto that, it may be worth something one day'.

Just a few years later seeing him as the focus of global attention and tagged 'Sir Bob' for his humanitarian work, he earned my full respect. He's never been one to shirk a challenge and appears not to give a damn about those who mock or abuse him. Fully 35 years later, I was curious enough to take in another of his shows and realised just how much of a buzz he still got from performing and that he was still a far better performer than he's ever truly been given credit for.

Probably the most memorable gig during my time at the Suite was the time when The Godfather of Soul himself – James Brown – came to town. Of course, anything to do with that character never passes without incident.

The promoter who brought him had staged a succession of punk bands over the previous months. All did good business but they were nearly all goddam awful to my eyes and ears, so much so that I used to groan whenever the guy appeared.

'What rubbish are you serving on us now? I asked on this occasion.

'I think maybe, you might like this one', he confidently replied.

I did, I couldn't believe it. One of the very giants of Soul music through the ages…..and he was coming here!

The date was set, it was to be in early December 1980, and the response was electric. Remember, this was in a time before information and news was exchanged in an instant over the internet or on your smartphone but soon inquiries were raining in from literally all over the country.

I had a word with the other members of the Suite's management team to see if they would cover me for that night and I would return the compliment with interest. I wanted to be there in pole position and figured I would probably view the show from the engineer's gantry.

The tickets sold out very soon and we all prepared for what we expected to be a memorable occasion.

Unfortunately, James Brown, proved that all those adverse reports about him were substantially true. Just two days before the event, news came through that the great man would not be appearing. Instead he would be remaining in the United States and going out to support The Rolling Stones tour of the USA.

It was a bummer alright, hugely disappointing but at the time the consensus was that the Stones tour was so big – indeed it grossed a record $500 million – that one couldn't blame him. The Stones were the biggest band in the world and what they wanted, they usually got.

Everyone seemed to accept the explanation and we started to try and work out how we might prevent people making unnecessary journeys and how exactly 2,000 ticketholders were to be reimbursed.

Years later, I found out James Brown did *not* appear on that Stones tour after all. Tina Turner did, The J Geils Band did, but James Brown did not! I guess he just didn't fancy it!

The promoter of course had to bear the wrath of disappointed fans, some I recall, who had travelled from as far as Edinburgh and Exeter.

A rearranged date was announced almost immediately and James duly arrived at the end of January. However, many believed he wouldn't show again and only 1,100 turned up for the rescheduled gig.

On the day in question, his band duly arrived in good time, set up and prepared for the great man to drop in and run through a sound check. I hung around until about 4pm that day but needing to go home and change, I asked a young part-time worker if he'd stay during the interim until I returned.

When I got back at 7pm, the building was open but empty. No one was on site, certainly not young Ian who I'd entrusted to keep an eye on the shop. I was livid to think that he could have walked off leaving the place unattended.

The staff duly arrived and we set up for that night's business before opening the door to let the punters stream in. Suddenly, there was something of a commotion on the front door when a long wheelbase, black Cadillac Sedan drew up. We figured The Godfather himself would emerge from behind the darkly tinted windows and so he did with his two bodyguards, his physician, his minister and……little Ian, my gopher!

Apparently, Mr Brown had turned up shortly after my departure, grunted into a mic by way of a sound check and then asked where he could eat. When little Ian suggested they might try the steakhouses in Preston Street, The Godfather insisted he had to come with them. Ian claimed he had protested, and I believed him, but The Godfather always called the shots. He duly went along with them and was told that he had to have a steak and had to have copious quantities of bourbon to wash it down with. The boy became a man that night!

Suitably fed and fuelled, James Brown delivered a tremendous performance. Completely over the top in every way, it was fascinating to see how tight his band was and how everyone within it had their eyes locked on the main man throughout. When he signalled, the band responded instantly. Clearly the stories of him fining musicians for any bum notes had to be true.

The same demands were made of every member of his entourage and to what extent we soon found out. A part of James Brown's fee was to be paid in cash that night but the promoter had taken a nap that afternoon and failed to get around to the local record shops and ticket outlets to pick up monies due. It mattered not that the situation could be remedied the following morning. James had been performing his signature mock collapse routine when he would be shrouded with a cape before being helped from the stage. He was supposed to bound back again but someone told him in the wings that there was no cash. End of show there and then!

The band played on but when there was no sign of JB, they just walked off. It would be disrespectful to an audience at the best of times but it was even moreso when one considered how many people there had already gone to great expense and inconvenience for the same man only a month previously.

Chapter 17

'Make That Move'

These were pretty heady days in Brighton. Not only was I immersed in a stimulating, albeit totally crazy way of life but I was seemingly cocooned from 'the real world'. Maybe, that was just as well for the real world at the time, seemed to be going through unprecedented upheaval both home and abroad.

Margaret Thatcher was finding life very hard in 10 Downing Street though it's hard to comprehend now that she was actually 24% behind Labour's new leader, Michael Foot, in the opinion polls at one time. Both were to visit the Suite during my time there.

Inflation was running at over 21%, bankruptcy was rife and the unemployment rate went over 2 million for the first time since 1935 but Mrs Thatcher insisted 'the lady's not for turning'.

The SAS was called into action to break a siege at the Iranian Embassy. The Iraq/Iran war was raging with tens of thousands of deaths being reported yet the one story of continuous speculation in the press and amongst many of the great British public was just who had shot JR? JR Ewing was the villainous lead character in *'Dallas'*, the weekly American soap drama which seemed to cause the country to grind to a halt whenever it was aired. It turned out to be Bing Crosby's daughter by the way!

The Iranian situation did impact on us however, as many of our door staff were Persian guys who had come to Brighton to study. Most of them had undertaken aeronautical engineering courses. With the Shah of Iran deposed and the Ayatollah Khomeini coming to power, it left our fellows in limbo. Most of them were from relatively middle class backgrounds whose families supported the old regime. They were worried for their families back home and feared that if they returned, they faced conscription into the armed services and being pitched into their country's war with Iraq which was raging at the time.

Remaining in Britain was the preferred option for most of them but in the coming months we were to find out that this was not going to be easy. The Home Office must have also been worrying about the situation for soon they began making direct and indirect contact with the guys. One of the Iranians, Said, I had a very high regard for and he came to me with a letter he had just received from the Home Office. It was advising him that he had to attend an interview a few days later and Said asked if this was likely to be a problem.

I didn't like the way the letter was structured but advised Said he would have to attend. However, it kept preying on my mind so the next day I went around to see Said and suggested he might consider seeking asylum.

Said himself was at a loss to know what to do but we both agreed he needed to move fast. I made a couple of quick inquiries and within a couple of hours we were at the immigration offices in Gatwick to make a formal application for asylum for Said. At his subsequent meeting with the Home Office he was questioned by an official who produced a thick file on him which contained minute details of his private life including names of girlfriends and places he frequented. Just to prove how literally 'on the ball' they were, his interrogator finished by congratulating Said on the two goals he had scored when playing football a week earlier!! And we always thought we had nothing like the Stasi in this country!

Others among the Iranian boys were taking matters into their own hands although it was some time before I was to establish this. Most of them proved irresistible to English girls who fell for their good manners and swarthy looks so it was no surprise to learn that a couple of the guys went the whole hog and quickly married a couple of conveniently available English girls.

I was to witness the effect that it had on some of these girls later when they were let down gently and realised that they had been 'used'. It was perhaps beyond the pale alright but I guess desperate times called for desperate measures.

October was always Party Conference time in Brighton when one of the two main political parties would stage their conference at the Brighton Centre next door to the Kingswest. We could always expect to stage a ball for them and many fringe meetings were held on our premises too.

One of the more right wing factions of the Conservative Party was The Monday Club whose ideology tended to grate with me severely. However, I treated them as just another private function client when they asked to stage a meeting one lunchtime during the conference.

Although there were perhaps 350-400 people in attendance, very few staff were needed and I called in only Hakim, with a view to helping me shift the furniture after the event. The Conservatives were handling their own security so there seemed little for Hakim and I to concern ourselves with as we sat at either side of the stage to listen to what I imagined would be some distasteful rhetoric.

We were both at right angles to the speakers on the one hand and the audience on the other and I sat there wondering just why they were all so enchanted with views I found so abhorrent.

As I looked out at the audience, I reflected on just how they chimed with the image of the stereotypical Conservative Party member. All were suited and booted; they were all white males and very few of them were under the age of 65. So uniform in their appearance were they, that they were not unlike a gathering of the Chinese Communist Party in terms of their conformity.

It was that very conformity which made one young guy stick out like a bottle of milk in a crate of coke. Well, he was young for a start. His hair was long and bedraggled and his clothes equally so. I knew there would be some journalists there and momentarily excused him on those grounds; perhaps he was writing for someone, maybe even a student mag. Except, he didn't appear to be writing.

I then watched him rise to his feet, everyone could see him now. I think most thought he was leaving; I couldn't blame him after the dirge the panel on stage were spewing. I looked across at Hakim. He was lost in his thoughts; I knew he hadn't seen him.

I looked back towards the Hairy One...I couldn't see him, he must have gone. Suddenly there was a shout and the Hairy One was level with the front row and running. Running full tilt towards the stage!

'Hakim!', I urged, trying not to shout and thankfully he stirred.

In an instant he saw the danger and we both jumped up just as the Hairy One bound onto the stage. The stage was 3 feet high so it was a huge leap and he stumbled as he landed. That allowed Hakim and I the vital couple of seconds needed to get to him before tackling him in a pincer movement. He was barely a foot away from landing a haymaker on Teddy Taylor, a hero of the Tory right. It would have earned him considerable kudos and even hero status amongst the Militant Tendency who had infiltrated the Labour Party at that time but it would have been huge embarrassment for us.

Hakim and I held the Hairy One down until he finally stopped struggling. It was at that point that I realised that I (and Hakim) were receiving a standing ovation from the Conservative Party in attendance. Irony of ironies surely?

That conference was the first as leader for Mrs Thatcher and already she was beginning to polarise people. Being the first woman Prime Minister, she was in many ways, quite fascinating for many, so, though not a fan myself I must admit to being a little curious when I heard she was coming to the Suite.

We received a briefing earlier in the day telling us what to expect and what was required. The Prime Minister would be arriving at the Suite after attending a function at The Sackville Hotel in Hove. On arrival, she was to be taken into our Function Room where she would have a drink of her tipple of choice, bitter lemon. From there, she was to be taken down the rear staircase to the stage door. The band was to be alerted and would strike up *'On A Little Street in Singapore'* as soon as she took to the stage. It was, we were assured, her favourite song.

The band really nailed that song in rehearsals and Steve Lewis the lead singer was probably hoping that he'd feature on *'News at Ten'* that night.

All the arrangements were in place and Tim and I waited patiently at the front door with a couple of party officials and a police officer who was in radio contact with the police helicopter which was monitoring the Prime Minister's progress. We heard every word that was exchanged on the radio and when it was announced that she had left The Sackville Hotel, two of our GAs blocked off the parking space for the limousine we were expecting.

'The Prime Minister is now passing The King Alfred' was heard over the radio; 'ETA is 9.15pm'.

'8 minutes', said Tim, 'are we all ready?'

'Yes boss', replied Gordon, the GA who was to accompany the Prime Minister throughout her visit.

We looked out expectantly when a very shrill Tory lady from the shires came up from behind us.

'Excuse me...'

'Not now Madam, we are just awaiting The Prime Minister, can you come back in ten minutes please?' Tim answered her very politely but very firmly.

'But she is already here, would you like to come and meet her?'

And there she was, already in the room behind us.

Tim and I stood agog. The party officials dropped their jaws and the police radio continued to monitor the progress of what could only have been a decoy.

We never, ever worked out how she entered the building that night!

Tim was a fan, so I said; 'Get in there and meet your hero, I'll mind the shop'.

Twenty minutes later, it was time for her to make her way to the stage. I escorted The Prime Minister along with her husband Denis and the then Chancellor of The Exchequer, Geoffrey Howe and his wife, Elspeth.

Mrs Thatcher did smile in acknowledgement to me but I resisted asking her about Denis Bagehot from Kettering who had claimed years earlier to me that she was his aunt. It was quite possible as her family had lived in that area before they moved to Grantham in Lincolnshire.

On the way through, it was Geoffrey and Elspeth who were the most animated with Elspeth urging her husband not to make any comments about anything!

The band saw me coming down the stairs towards the stage and prepared to take their cue for the Prime Minister's song. By the time, the party had mounted the stage I had made my way to the front of the audience and watched as Mrs Thatcher appeared to rapturous applause. She stood stock still to soak it up with a look set in stone before she turned to stare at the band and Steve Lewis in particular. Steve had really been in good voice and now his big moment had arrived. The Prime Minister was up there beside him, the cameras were trained on them both but the look she was giving him was not one of approval, it was one of withering disgust….and Steve's voice wavered.

'Give me that', she hissed, and snatched the microphone from his hand.

She turned to her adoring disciples and proclaimed; 'I don't want to be on a street in Singapore, I only want to be here in Britain!'

That was the cue for more rapturous, near hysterical applause which continued unabated when it was announced that the night was the 21st anniversary of her being elected as an MP and it was also her birthday that week.

Steve Lewis looked down at me quizzically as if he'd been cruelly set up. What could I do but shrug my shoulders?

One abiding memory of that night was the total lack of concern the Conservative Party had for security on that occasion. It's easy to be wise after the event but I remember how the party officials positively recoiled when we suggested it might be prudent to at least conduct a rudimentary body search of all entering the building that night. They had no security detail and relied entirely on our 'bouncers' and the police beyond that.

This was surprising for me as it had only been a year since Airey Neave had been assassinated but with the Brighton bomb four years later and the murder of the minister, Ian Gow; things would never be quite the same again.

Michael Foot's appearance at the Suite during the Labour Party conference a year later was much lower key. He was evidently a very nice chap who was obviously adored by most of the party faithful but he had no time for fuss and ceremony. I remember how he ambled into the venue with his wife Jill Craigie……and his dog! He apparently brought 'Dizzy' (named after Benjamin Disraeli) everywhere. After just a few minutes greeting supporters, he just ambled back out again.

After just a few months, I was coming to the conclusion that I could do a lot worse than make this town my permanent home. I was loving the job but knew the time would come when I needed to get out of the business. I reasoned that if I was to forge a new career in a different field I would be better using Brighton as a base rather than some of the more remote or unattractive outposts Rank may have wanted to dispatch me to in time.

I was also contemplating 'settling down' at some time. It was a prospect that unnerved me most of the time but whilst there were many hugely enjoyable occasions there were as many rather lonely nights when you wondered, 'Is this it?'

I'd get fed up to going home to beans and toast or pot noodles which seemed the limit of my culinary skills when I was on my own. I'd spend far too many nights in The Market Diner enjoying their big breakfasts at half past three in the morning and climbing into bed as the rest of the world were getting up.

I was getting fatter, lazier and more lethargic but I kidded myself I was having 'fun'. I'd still go to Mass every Sunday and I prayed that I could make my parents proud of me. I knew that they were but I meant really proud. To be a proper man, doing a proper job with a proper family around me. I was on a treadmill where I was smiling at the world but crying inside.

I was ashamed that I couldn't do enough for Carrie and Emmeline and constantly hoped that they wouldn't condemn me. I hoped that Carrie would find the man she deserved and that Emmie wouldn't be damaged by the start in life she had had. Thankfully my hopes for the two of them did come to pass and I couldn't be more pleased and proud.

I was actually trying to avoid relationships in Brighton but in that environment, there would always be encounters and sometimes you just tend to go with the flow. Nicky was just 17 when she pitched up at the Suite and I loved her company but got cold feet at the prospect of getting serious. I just felt a girl like that deserved better than the likes of me. Years later I was delighted to find that she'd gone on to make a very good marriage and was blessed with a very happy family around her. I was quite proud of myself when she said I'd always behaved like a gentleman to her. That was a relief!

Dorinda was different though....and how!

To say she was a force of nature would be an understatement. She was quite breathtaking in both appearance and attitude and had an aura about her that caused I and my colleagues at the Suite to be completely bowled over by her. She was though, well aware of her effect on men.

Every Tuesday afternoon she would arrive at the Suite to empty the fruit machines for her company, Cherry Leisure. Though of course we tagged her the Cherry Pleasure!

She would breeze in, empty the machines, exchange some banter and breeze out again. Left in her wake would be the scent of Estee Lauder Youth Dew which seemed to linger for the rest of the day. I don't know whether it was by accident or design but all the management seemed to be on duty whenever she called and all of us seemed to be momentarily paralysed such was the effect she was capable of.

Most weeks I would spend a few minutes with her when buying change from her. For a few charged minutes, I'd exchange small talk with her whilst looking down at heavily jewelled fingers counting out the change. Her skin was always flawless and I'd notice her tiny darting blue eyes as she'd change her gaze up and down from the coins. I'd look at her teeth as we were talking, I daren't make eye contact. They were perfect too and contained within a perfectly formed mouth that you just wanted to be sucked into.

She really was the real deal but funny with it and oh so sassy. After she left, eyes would roll but little was said. She used to manage to stun us all into meek surrender.

Of course, I'd wonder about asking her out but would never quite manage it. Sometimes she looked at me as if to say, 'Go on then', but I never would until one day I found myself saying;

'I don't suppose….'

'Go for a drink? Yes I would….are you off on Friday? That'd suit me'

She'd answered my question before I'd asked it…then she finished the job.

'I'll see you in the car park out the back at 7.30. Ok?'

Before I could answer, she leaned forward, gave me a quick kiss and shot off.

I walked back into the office and Mike Williams, the assistant manager asked me if I was feeling alright as I looked so pale.

'Er, yes, I've got a date with Dorinda', I said.

'In your dreams!', he laughed and I didn't contradict him because he was probably right.

Friday rolled around and I duly went to the car park. I didn't expect to find her there. Maybe it had all been in my dreams.

But no there was her company car. Dorinda hopped out and just said 'In you get'.

I climbed in, probably in some sort of state of shock which was to get even worse.

'I thought you'd never ask', she said, 'let's make up for lost time'. Then the assault began but I wasn't going to report it. She was all over me, like a rash some would say.

'Where are we going?' she said as she finally came up for air.

'I dunno'.

'Well, why don't we just stay here all night?'

I thought that was as good an idea as any and just hoped we wouldn't get arrested.

There was never a dull moment with Dorinda and I wondered how it might all pan out. She was nothing like I'd ever encountered though. She knew exactly what she wanted it seemed, and nothing would stop her getting there. She said what she wanted, was volatile in the extreme and seemed to defer to no one yet underneath it all, there was a certain vulnerability.

She wanted to be loved not lusted for which she feared she would always be. She'd had an unsettled upbringing with her parents going to and fro from Australia and perhaps previous relationships had taken their toll on her. But to me she was a beautiful woman inside and out. I doubted whether or not I could handle her but we were getting high on each other and I just liked her company.

I suppose it was getting pretty serious alright, but there was a day of reckoning ahead. Dorinda told me at the beginning that she was booked to go to Australia six months later. At the beginning, it had seemed so far off and we had no idea how our liaison would pan out. Now though with the relationship getting deeper and more intense, her departure date seemed to be the elephant in the room which we both avoided talking about.

It was Dorinda who finally broached the subject. 'I love you, you love me; what are we going to do?'

I didn't know what to say, I had dreaded this moment and now here it was D-Day.

'If we were to get engaged', she said, 'I'll cancel and stay here with you'.

It was probably what I wanted to but in truth I was scared. It had all happened so fast, it had been so intense, so full on but I just couldn't answer yes or no. I had agonised over the decision that had to be made but I knew that I didn't want to lose her.

'I think we should put each other to the test. I do love you but I want to know if you'll feel the same way after you've been out there 6 months'.

I expected her to react badly but she agreed. Since we'd got together there had been no breathing space. That's the way we'd wanted it and we loved every moment. I was sincere in what I said and I truly hoped it would come to pass. I was conscious too though that there was every danger that we would be overtaken by events and if that happened then so be it.

Chapter 18

'Never Too Much'

The best laid plans tend to rarely come to fruition for me and in Brighton, there was to be no exception.

Throughout my working life, I have been on countless courses where I have heard the mantra to always plan and prepare to give yourself the best chance to succeed with your goals and ambitions. Another twist on the same theme would be that failing to prepare amounts to preparing to fail.

Each time I hear those pearls of wisdom, I'll look around and see people sagely nodding in agreement. But it isn't true! It's true in controlled classroom conditions perhaps but in the real world there are any number of factors that can, and will, conspire against the best laid plans.

Harold MacMillan knew this very well when asked what could blow his Government off course; 'Events, dear boy, events'. One of his Labour successors, that wily old fox, Harold Wilson, always geared himself up for the unexpected and he is remembered for his famous observation that, 'A week is a long time in politics'.

When I arrived in Brighton, the pathway was clearly marked out. Do a little stint at the Suite, keep my nose clean and bide my time until a suitable General Manager role came up. I was enjoying life so much that I wasn't setting any deadlines but nothing had occurred which suggested my aims would be thwarted.

Chaos theorists argue that the simple effect of a butterfly flapping its wings can cause a far more consequential effect further down the line. It seemed much the same for me when Rank Leisure's Head Office sent out a memo indicating that the company's regional structure was to be realigned. It sounded like a desktop exercise unlikely to affect the course of our business in any way, nor any of our patrons upon whom, we all depended.

It was different though when we heard that Mr Samuels would no longer be our Operations Director. Tim greeted that news with some glee but I wondered if there would be ramifications for me for of course, Samuels it was, who had convinced me to return to Rank with the promise of progress and rewards to come.

I still felt largely unaffected as more details filtered through. There was barely a muttering amongst the Rank management team and we just got on with the job in hand.

Across the road from us Sherry's was suddenly closed for business and about to embark on a major refit. EMI Dancing was their parent company and we knew if they thought it worthwhile, they would spend big. Sherry's duly re-opened a few weeks later, much the same as before, but boasting a state of the art laser and lighting installation which in truth was quite mind blowing to behold.

Rank's new Operations Director took note and, in the course of determining a strategy for The Kingswest Centre, he decided to move the furniture around.

I was one of the first pawns and was asked to go around the corner to Busby's, a discotheque operation which was doing great business. I certainly wasn't unhappy about it. The schedule there was much more routine. It was basically a four nights a week operation, a straight discotheque every night with hardly any private function business.

There were two good guys there, Graham, the assistant manager, and Farouk, the bars manager and the General Manager was none other than Peter Langley who had been my Number 2 at Busby's back in Redhill. There was no problem for me with the roles being reversed, we had always got on well and Peter probably figured he could have more time off now.

The business seemed to run like clockwork. We enjoyed near capacity crowds on Thursdays, Fridays and Saturdays with a jazz-funk session on Sunday nights. The GAs here were very disciplined and kept an extremely tight door which they prided themselves on. They were all presentable and well-mannered but also had sufficient resources between them to quell any hint of trouble should there be a need.

My role was largely operational and I spent a good deal of time dreaming up 'special events' and themed nights. One had to work at keeping the place fresh and relevant and we were acutely aware that any relaxation would give an opportunity to competitors.

Peter made it easier for me to get away for a couple of days at a time whether it was for nipping up to Kettering to see The Poppies and my folks or taking the long road down to Devon to see the little one who was becoming cuter by the day.

Dorinda and I were still getting along famously but now time was slipping away and her departure was imminent. Whatever happened, there was going to be a big, big vacuum in my life. I didn't know it then but it was going to be bigger than ever I imagined.

I managed to catch quite a few Poppies games that season so ensuring that I got the requisite quota of agony and ecstasy which is all part of the irresistible addiction of non-league football for me. Mum and dad seemed to be enjoying life, their two kids were settled and off their hands and I thought they could look forward to years of planning their own agenda. I knew as far as my father was concerned that work would invariably be his pre-occupation. I had worried that being made redundant a year or two earlier, he would find it hard to get back up again. Instead of that, he was enjoying new beginnings with a new contractor who had come calling for him. They seemed to value him greatly and he really was enjoying a new lease of life in a game he knew so well.

They had just had a holiday in their native Ireland and my father was always on a high after such a trip.

Even though she was soon to depart, Dorinda came up to Kettering with me on one occasion. She finally 'got it' about the town and even indulged me by coming along to the match. I don't think she regarded it as one of her greater experiences in life but she was able to tick it off.

She got on very well with my folks and all in all, it amounted to a nice trip which would make saying 'Farewell' all the harder.

Life at the club was ticking along sweetly, business was good and so was the company. What wasn't there to like about it really then BANG! Something really hit me.....or rather a load of guys hit me!

I had been out in front of the building on the wide expanse of pavement that separated the Kingswest Centre from the seafront road. There had been a lot of banter with the crowds passing by that night and I remembered being engulfed by a large group of girls out on a hen party and intent on letting rip that night.

One moment I was laughing with them and the next I awoke in near pitch darkness. I couldn't see anything and nothing seemed to be moving but I could hear a lot of noise. People were talking and shouting and there was the sound of clanging metal too. I realised I was lying down and gingerly ran my fingers over my body before spreading my arms wider. I could feel fabric and then cold metal. I was lying prone, what had happened to me?

My head was spinning and my body was aching. It was aching so much I wanted to scream but I was scared, I daren't open my mouth. I moved my arms more and then my legs. They felt heavy, but yes, I did seem to be intact. All the time the noise was incessant; was I in bedlam?

My eyes gradually got used to the surroundings and slowly I made out a few shapes. It seemed like I was lying on a trolley amidst a load of clutter, but why? I saw what looked like a mirror on a wall and tried to haul myself up. I felt around for something to hold onto and slowly got to my feet. I felt the sudden cold and realised I had some sort of gown on me.

The mirror was the goal though. I had to take a look at myself. When I did, it shook me. Staring back at me was something resembling a Hallowe'en mask. It scared me witless, but I was relieved at the same time. I could see that I was battered and bloodied but I was alive. I was happy to just crawl back to the trolley and close my eyes.

Suddenly a door opened. The air rushed in, the noise got louder and I seemed to be bathed in light

'Aaaah, you're back with us?'

I blinked my eyes at the sudden brightness then sat up in a start when I realised it was a nurse talking to me.

'What's happening, where am I?', I mumbled, as I tried to fathom out my situation.

I couldn't quite believe her when she told me I was in the Royal Sussex County Hospital and had been for several hours.

Apparently, I had been brought in unconscious after being attacked outside the club. After being checked over, the medics figured I was ok to be left and seen to when I awoke.

Moments later Dorinda appeared and she pieced the sequence of events together. I had, it seemed, denied entrance to a stag party who took umbrage and set about me. Dorinda had arrived on the scene just as the ambulance was about to take me away and she'd been at the hospital for five hours.

It was as if she was talking of someone else, I had no recollection of what had happened and have never been able to recall it since.

The next morning I was discharged, and after a few days off returned to work none the worst for my experience. I knew though, that I had been lucky and if I carried on for much longer in this game, then one day my luck might run out.

As it happened the perpetrators were rounded up and one of them was eventually prosecuted and got locked up for a few weeks. I pursued a claim through the Criminal Injuries Compensation Board and was awarded the princely sum of £800 after being pronounced 2% disabled!

Dorinda and I tried to talk about the future but it was impossible. We knew we had to let Fate take its course and just try to be positive about it all but all the time it seemed like our lives were on hold and looking back we probably both wished for the day to come and go so we could lament in our own way, away from each other.

I drove her up to Heathrow for that final journey along with her friend, Karen, who was finding it hard to contain herself. I gave Dorinda a giant teddy bear as a parting gift which was must have been an unwelcome load for her to carry around the world. It's hard to look at the photos taken that day without feeling the poignancy of the occasion. Then suddenly, she was gone.

Back in Brighton, I duly went through the motions but people were treating me like I had had a death in the family. Life goes on though and I was prepared for the testing time ahead.

We used to call each other once a week but then the gaps would grow longer. She was a great letter writer though and both of us sent long missals to each other which must have seemed very humdrum to the outsider.

Her description of life out there was fascinating and I used to wonder if I could really contemplate it myself. I knew though that I would find it hard, if not impossible, to move so far away from my folks and my daughter. It wasn't going to happen but I couldn't bring myself to say that.

In early December that year I called home one time and my mother mentioned that dad was to see the doctor about a chest complaint he had but there was no concern as such. Dad was however; very depressed about his sister in Ireland who, we had learned, was very seriously ill.

A week later my father was still in a lot of discomfort and had been signed off work which was virtually unheard of him for him. His doctor referred him for a chest X-ray and we hoped that would get to the bottom of it.

I did have some nagging doubts but speaking to them both on the phone, they seemed so upbeat that I quickly put my concerns aside as I got on with work in Busby's.

Everyday there was like a holiday. It seemed like we were the boss venue in town. We could be highly selective in who we let in and consequently we aimed to set the bar as high as possible.

DJ Andy King was doing a fine job and every night he had the place really cooking. Andy was from Nottingham and only got the job by accident after coming down with a mate of his who was being auditioned. I think it was Peter Langley who said to him to get up and have a go himself, he did...and the job was his.

The groove was great in this period with a number of brilliant tunes getting airplay. Phyllis Hyman's *'You Know How To Love Me'* was a very big sound at this time as was Evelyn 'Champagne' King's *'Shame'* and *'Love Come Down'*. Everything George Benson, Luther Vandross and Shalamar were producing always made it to Andy's turntables and his needle would also drop frequently onto the sounds of The O'Jays and Sister Sledge.

When it was really heaving he wouldn't be averse to dropping in The Gap Band's *'Oops Upside Your Head'*. This infernal funk anthem didn't necessarily fit in with the feel of everything being played around it but whenever it was played, everyone immediately sat down on the dancefloor for 'The Boat Song'. The song would have sunk without trace, only initially appearing as a 'B' side were it not for the efforts of an Essex DJ, Nigel Tolley. He had somehow persuaded his audience to sit down in rows with their legs spread either side of the person in front. The crowd would then spread their arms and rhythmically tap the floor in time to the beat. Crazy, but it sure caught on. It then became a staple at Christmas parties, weddings etc. Always fun to watch but many tended to miss the monologue lyrics which contained such gems as;

Jack and Jill went up the hill to have a little fun,
Stupid Jill forgot her pill and now they have a son.

Busby's became the destination of choice for the Brighton and Hove Albion footballers and acts like Bananarama and Lenny Henry made a point of calling in socially when in town. We had a few sports celebrities too as I recall, including the boxer, Alan Minter and the

England cricketer, Alan Lamb, dropped in with the Australians, Dennis Lillee and the moustachioed Mervyn Hughes.

Brighton's football team were playing in the old Division 1 at the time and it was great for business to get them in usually led by their larger than life captain, Steve Foster. Unusually, their manager at the time, Jimmy Melia, was also a party animal and he would often accompany the players in his trademark white suit and spats.

On one memorable occasion, all the team turned up to launch their own record *'The Goldstone Rap'*. The place was packed and the boys were whooping it up big time….the manager as well! It was all a bit surreal as earlier some of the players had been invited to judge the Miss United Kingdom contest taking place next door at The Brighton Centre, so some of those girls came along too.

The record itself was no great shakes, I barely heard it again after that night, but it was a great excuse for a party and those boys always had a great party – no matter how badly they were performing in the league.

Jimmy Melia herded them all away at around midnight. There was a match to be played at Liverpool on Sunday and the team was to be bussed up there just a few hours later.

Eventually the shutters came down and the night came to a close at 2am. If we could cash up quickly and get all the staff away in their taxis, it was possible that we could be out and locked up by 2.30am.

We were on course to do just that when we heard the front door take a ferocious battering. Was there a fight? Was it the police? Graham, Farouk and I jumped out of our skins and proceeded to stealthily climb up the stairs together. Though we held baseball bats, we sincerely hoped we didn't have to use them.

The battering got more urgent along with a few shouts. Then I heard my name…'oh heck'. Who was coming for me at that time of the morning?

'About f***ing time too!', one of them said as we loomed into view. There gasping at the door were those two fine physical specimens; Brighton and Hove Albion's Jimmy Case and Tony Grealish.

'Drink, drink', they shouted. Father Jack on Craggy Island was more restrained than the two of them but I had to humour them. So back down to the bar we went and the three of sat there talking shite until the cleaners turned up at 6.30am.

I offered to get the boys a taxi home and asked where was it to go.

'Straight to the Goldstone', Jimmy answered, 'we daren't miss the bus to Liverpool'.

I'm sure Alan Hansen, Kenny Dalglish, Ian Rush and Graeme Souness didn't prepare for this game in the same way but the tanked-up twosome sobered up enough to face them all at Anfield on Sunday. In front of 44,868 fans, Brighton won 2-1 and of course Mr Case scored the decider!!

In the real world at this time, the press and TV were full of news about the Argentinian invasion of The Falkland Islands. Peter Langley and I would have the TV on in his office every lunchtime for the latest updates and we wondered how it would all pan out.

Young Graham, the assistant manager was innocence personified. He was not worldly wise and he really didn't know what was going on in the wider world nor did he seem to care. He passed through the office one day whilst the news was on and seeing us both engrossed asked why we bothered to keep watching the news; he reckoned it was the same every day.

'He hasn't got a clue that lad', Peter observed.

'He soon will', I said, 'he'll be watching it from now on.

'Eh?', Peter queried me and then split his sides laughing when I made a little proposal.

The next morning Peter and I rehearsed our approach and as soon as Graham arrived for work, we called him into the office. I didn't think we could pull it off but we turned out to be two fine actors.

'Graham, can you come in here for a minute', Peter called out in his best sombre tone.

'What is it boss?', Graham cheerily asked but when he saw our solemn demeanour, he felt distinctly uneasy.

'There's no point in you staying Graham, you may as well go home now'.

'What!!?', Graham was stunned, 'are you sacking me?'

'No', Peter said, 'not at all, your job will still be here when you come back'.

'What do you mean, where am I going?'

'It'll be all right', I said, 'I'm sure you'll manage' I tried to reassure him.

'Manage what? Where am I being sent?'

'You're going to Catterick', Peter beamed, 'you're being conscripted. I think you might enjoy it actually'.

I nodded my head in total agreement, 'You'll love it!'.

'Where's Catterick? Is there a club there? What's this conscription thing?'

'Oh', Peter continued, 'you haven't heard about the conscription. Maybe you'd like to call your mum'.

By now, Graham was beside himself. 'What's conscription? What are you on about?'

'It's when the government haven't got enough troops'; I tried to gently explain, 'when that happens they call up members of the public. We heard today that you'll be getting the call, I expect it'll be on the telly today'.

Graham was steaming. 'What do I have to do, where do I have to go? Why aren't you going?'

Peter said that we'd have loved to have got the call up, it would be an honour to serve the country but sadly, we were too old. They were only calling up 18-24-year olds at this stage. He stood up, looked straight into Graham's eyes and in his best Churchillian manner, waved his finger and softly said;

'This is YOUR moment Graham; your country needs YOU!'

It was as much as we could do to stop ourselves completely corpsing with laughter as Graham turned on his heels and stormed out of the room muttering and swearing. We had to try and quickly compose ourselves when he came back again thirty seconds later.

'What happens now? How do I get to Catterick?'

We patiently told him that he would doubtless be getting his call up papers in the post and once again asked if he'd like to take the rest of the day off.

'Yes, I think I will. I can't quite believe it'.

'Don't worry', I said, 'just take one day at a time. I think you'll enjoy the experience'.

'Yes', said Peter, 'try not to worry about it and rest assured that if you come back, your job will still be here'.

'WHAT!' Graham screamed, 'what do you mean, IF I come back?!'

'Oh, no, no, no. I meant WHEN you come back again', Peter quickly retracted and quickly ushered Graham out of the office because this time he knew our laughter would be totally out of control.

Graham tuned into the news that night but nothing was said. There were of course no reports in the press either and when the letter hadn't arrived after a couple of days, the penny slowly dropped for Graham.

To his credit he saw the funny side of it and Peter and I were mighty relieved because we had felt a tad guilty.

But only a tad!

Chapter 19

'Young Guns Go For It'

The calls to Australia were becoming less frequent now, mainly because I got caught using the office phone and we couldn't have that appearing on the bills! Dorinda and I resorted to sending each other quite extraordinary missals about each other's life and times. I didn't quite tell her everything and later I found there was a lot she didn't reveal to me either.

I didn't feel guilty when I eventually went out with a couple of girls. I missed her undoubtedly but it felt like we were both moving on. Every day when Graham, Farouk and I would go to the National Westminster Bank to deposit the previous day's takings, we'd inevitably have a little banter with the girls there. They were all very nice but I didn't expect the place to become something of a dating agency for me.

We'd give the girls complimentary tickets and occasionally a group of them would come out socially. It's often a little funny to see people out of the environment you've got to know them in but the bank girls were certainly capable of providing a few shocks.

Sedate, polite and efficient by day, some of these girls metamorphosed into real party animals after dark. They drank, they danced, they laughed and some wanted to make love and be loved. Whatever they did, they were transformed back to normal by the morning. But they were fun and when one took a notion, I found myself being targeted by the biggest vamp of the lot.

I was probably fortunate that this particular Fun Girl had no aspirations for commitment and undying devotion from her man, or if she did, she hid it well. A couple of weeks later another group from the bank were in and I got talking to one girl who was particularly quiet and shy. She was the complete opposite to the vamp and I found her altogether far more engaging. I saw her for a few weeks but somehow it all fizzled out; I can't quite recall why but I'm sure she did herself a favour by moving on from me.

The club seemed to be doing spectacularly well and the new Sherry's operation left us completely unscathed. People seemed to notice the little things we did that made us stand out just that little bit. One measure we took was ridiculously simple, yet people still remember it decades later. The normal attire for the doormen or bouncers back then was a simple black suit, white shirt and black bow tie. Quite simple and unpretentious of course but a little bit boring and of course they were indistinguishable from the waiters working in The Grand Hotel just a few yards away. On a whim, we thought we'd ask our guys to wear black shirts and white bow ties. It was no big deal at all but it proved to be a real eye catcher. The boys themselves felt quite elevated by all the attention they were attracting but years later it is hard to appreciate just how such a minor adjustment could be viewed as being almost revolutionary.

Running a nightclub isn't rocket science but neither is it entirely straightforward and one always needed to deploy a certain amount of lateral thinking and occasionally, speed of thought and movement as well. January is always the quietest month on the calendar when the punters are low on funds after Christmas and often it's just too cold and bleak to venture out; but venture out they will if you've got something good or interesting to offer. The question was always; 'What?'.

On Monday 4th January, Peter Langley summonsed his management team plus Lorraine Best, our promotions secretary, for a routine promotion meeting in his office. As always, we were looking for ways to stimulate the business and fresh ideas were especially welcome.

These meetings often proved difficult because hadn't we tried everything at some stage? On the other hand, suggestions would be made which were often so ridiculous that the meetings would descend into helpless laughter.

This particular meeting was to produce all this but to the extent that it will be remembered evermore by all present.

The helpless laughter was provoked by the innocent contribution of the hapless Graham, the erstwhile Falklands hero.

Peter, noticing that Burns Night fell in January, wondered if we might do a promotion around it. 'Any ideas?' he asked.

'We could do a Scotch whisky promotion', said Farouk.

'OK, do it', said Peter, 'get onto the suppliers and blag them….any other ideas?'

'Er….how about free admission if they dress up in kilts and stuff', suggested Lorraine trying to justify her role.

'OK, let's do that too', said Peter but his tone and the long drag he gave on his cigarette betrayed his boredom. It was all so banal and unexciting. He turned to Graham who hadn't said a word so far, 'have you got any ideas, what can we do for Burns Night?'

'Can't we just try and get him down for a personal appearance?'

Cue a stunned silence in the room before Peter sought clarification, not daring to assume his first thought.

'Get who Graham?', he inquired very, very quietly for effect.

'This Burns guy'.

'Are you meaning Rabbie Burns himself?' asked Peter, who, like the rest of us was possibly in a mild state of shock.

'Yes, whatever his name is, do you think he'd cost much?'

Peter was speechless and it was left to me to tell Graham that 'Mr Burns' had died in 1796.

'Oh!' said Graham and smiled as the rest of once again near choked with laughter on account of poor Graham's blissful ignorance.

It took some time before we could get the meeting up and running again but Peter composed himself sufficiently to say that with the weather outlook and seasonal trends as they were, January could prove disastrous for us unless we thought of something.

'How about this?' I asked, waving a copy of The Daily Mirror that I had picked up on the way into work; 'we can't get Rabbie Burns but we might be able to get this lady!'

Splashed across the front page of The Daily Mirror was a picture of one Erika Roe who had achieved her 15 minutes of fame when she ran topless across Twickenham during the England v Australia rugby international a couple of days before. There had been plenty of streakers before Erika and plenty after but none had bared all with such chutzpah as Erika and to do so on the hallowed turf at Twickenham ensured her immortality. The TV and press were full of the story, we had to try and get her.

'Oh Yes!!!!', said Peter, 'make some phone calls Lorraine'.

Lorraine shot back to her office and called Barbara Kelly. Barbara was a well-known face on TV in her own right at the time but she also ran her own agency. If anyone could get Erika, Barbara could.

Barbara had only just got back from an overseas trip and had missed all the fuss over Erika, but she promised Lorraine she would track her down that afternoon. She was as good as her word and just a couple of hours later we got the news that Erika Roe would be appearing at Busby's – just 2 days later. She was to cost us £150….but she was worth every penny!

Two days is not long enough to promote an event but it's plenty of time when you've got the most notorious figure in the land coming to your venue. We hit the phones to the TV, the radio and the press and they all ran with the story giving us blanket coverage for our Wednesday night session when we would be lucky to attract 70-80 customers ordinarily.

Courage the brewers were tapped up to do a Fosters promotion. In exchange for a couple of free kegs we'd get them a shot of Erika holding a pint of the stuff. For good measure, we also got the other Foster, i.e. Brighton & Hove Albion's captain, Steve.

On Wednesday evening the weather was as foul as could be imagined. With it raining hard and bitter cold winds blowing in from the Channel, I feared the weather was going to put a dampener on proceedings but I need not have feared. On opening the door that night the venue was full to capacity within minutes. The crowd just swarmed in to see the woman who had bared her breasts to the nation a few days previously.

In all honesty, Erika's appearance was a bit of an anti-climax. I'm not sure what people were expecting. She couldn't sing, she couldn't dance and she certainly wasn't going to be revealing those famous 40" assets of hers from under the chunky polo neck black sweater she turned up in. She agreed to pose with a pint but refused point blank to be pictured in a Fosters tee-shirt. But the objective was achieved and how?

Two days previously we had wondered how badly our business would be hit. Now we found we had smashed our monthly target in just one night thanks to the public's love of a great British eccentric.

The booking of Erika Roe was certainly a coup, but it was not the only coup we had that year. Unfortunately, we didn't realise the other one at the time!

Because the club was seen to be an influential venue, we enjoyed very good relationships with all the major record companies. They would court our DJs with advance copy promotional discs and occasionally they would ask to send down an act to do a PA. i.e. a personal appearance where the act would sing over the backing track of a record they were trying to promote.

The acts could be very good, very bad or totally indifferent. As they usually only played one or two tracks it didn't make too much difference but their spots tended to break the evening up a little bit and if the artistes were good, then we were seen as offering a little 'added value'. We always tended to stage them on Thursday nights when they could expect to get the enthusiastic support (or otherwise) of the birthday and hen parties who usually appeared on that night.

One afternoon I had an agent begging me to allow a PA from an act she was managing. She had sent me a publicity photo of these two guys which served only to put me off them. They looked to me to be a run of the mill white pop act and very little else.

'Haven't you got anyone soulful?', I asked and then I remembered someone who was on her books. 'How about Alton Edwards? Can you send him again?' Alton had produced a stunning performance a couple of months earlier and I had hoped he'd go on to have a successful career.

'Nah, he's got nothing out', came the reply, 'but I tell you what, I promise, 100%, that I'll get him down again IF you take the boys'.

'Oh, go on then', I said, I felt sorry for the lady who sounded a little bit desperate.

In June, her protégées finally turned up. Two smiley white guys with too much fake tan but they looked harmless enough and were very grateful that we'd allowed them to do their thing. There were two girls with them, who I assumed to be their girlfriends, they were to appear as backing singers. I remember thinking that the £10 fee wouldn't be going very far for them.

At the appointed hour, DJ Andy 'shake your thing' King announced these aspiring pop legends and slipped on the backing track.

The two guys commenced an energetic and enthusiastic dance routine which didn't really seem to synch with the beat of the track they were performing. The girls behind them improvised their moves and gave it all they got. At least they looked pretty good. One of the guys led the vocals and the sound that emerged was much as I anticipated, a white pop act trying to sound soulful.

They weren't too bad, but they weren't particularly good either. I was indifferent to them as was the audience who I noticed treated them as a backdrop whilst they all chatted away.

Job done, they retreated to the dressing room and I told the singer, George, that I'd have his money as soon as he was ready. I had been chatting to the Sherry's DJ, Kelly, who'd just popped in for a drink. He asked if the act might do another PA across the road for his crowd. 'Yeah, I'm sure they will….I'll go and ask them before they change. You'll have to give them a few bob though Kelly'.

'Ask if they'll take a fiver'.

'OK mate' and off I went to see the turn. George agreed straightaway and told the others.

'I've got you a fiver as well', I told George…and that seemed to make his night!

I shook hands with the guys and wished them well, but George turned back again and gave me a little hug. 'Thanks very much my friend', and that was the last I saw of George Michael.

The record they were promoting that night was *'Wham Rap'*. It sunk without trace, not helped by having been banned by the BBC for lyrics perceived to be containing profanities. Three months later, they were promoting their next single, *'Young Guns Go For It'*, when their manager got a call asking the band to step in for a Top of The Pops appearance at the last minute. Their careers took off overnight. *'Young Guns'* went to No 1 and so did *'Wham Rap'* which was subsequently re-released. The two girls also went off to enjoy a little success themselves as Pepsi and Shirley. They became famed for their puffball dresses and Shirley ended up marrying the actor and Spandau Ballet member, Martin Kemp.

Life was never too complicated at Busby's though. We had a very simple offering for customers; just a DJ playing records really, all we had to do was to embellish it slightly…over and over again.

In the 80s this tended to lead to us finding any number of ways to get girls into a state of undress. Not content with a swim-suited pageant like 'Miss Busby's, we'd have a Miss Wet T-Shirt contest or famously Miss In-String; which ended up being syndicated to most of the company's clubs around the country.

The 1980s was also a time when disco-dancing was very much in vogue and those competitions were quite easy to arrange too. We also allowed a local troupe, Cool Breeze, to demonstrate their routines. Very good they were too and some of their members went on to perform on TV and in the West End. Perhaps we used to use them too often though, I thought as much when I heard one punter saying; 'Oh no, not warm wind again!'

If we were really stuck for ideas, we weren't too proud to roll out the old chestnuts like the '999 Ball'. Such nights were guaranteed to generate the numbers. Aimed at attracting the emergency services; flyers and posters would be circulated to hospitals, police stations, fire stations etc., and sometimes free admission would be offered to those turning up in uniform. We'd occasionally get a wag claiming the same concession because he as a plumber, gas fitter or rat catcher was an equally important emergency service. I'd let them in; figuring I might need them one day.

There would be various versions of the same theme including 'Bankers' Ball', 'Publicans' Ball' etc., any sliver of an excuse would suffice.

By now I was more than settled in Brighton and decided that I should be thinking of putting some roots down in the city. I had taken lodgings in a house in John Street, Brighton which was a handy 20 minutes' walk to work every day along the bracing seafront.

The house was owned by a girl who was the friend of our cashier. The arrangement was entirely above board - well mostly - and my rent helped the girl with her mortgage. It was a very nice maisonette which in true 70s style was very orange with a lot of artex! Orange walls, orange curtains, orange cushions and orange carpets; the sort of décor that was omnipresent in soft porn films of that era.

After only a couple of months, the girl decided that she wanted to go to live and work in Spain. I could carry on renting the place or I could buy it, so I did. Within a few weeks, I'd raised the agreed price of £23,500 and I was the proud owner of my orange heaven.

Maybe it was a mistake to have Andy 'shake your thing' King as my lodger. No problem with Andy, a great bloke who was as good as gold, but it meant we got precious little sleep. Invariably we would all want to wind down after the night's work and that usually meant going for a 3am breakfast at The Market Diner in Circus Street. The Market Diner and later The Aqua in the Old Steine were the mecca for all in Brighton's night time economy. There we would congregate with other managers, bouncers, bar staff etc. from the city's many clubs, bars, hotels and restaurants. Into the mix would come taxi drivers, a few street girls and the late club crowd. With the jukebox hammering away it was pretty full on in there all night. Around 4am we would encounter the workers and traders from the Fruit Market opposite who were having their breakfasts at the right end of the day. At least they could burn their calories off.

One could always guarantee an assortment of weird and wonderful eccentric characters would congregate at The Market Diner and my personal favourite was Sid, 'The Flower Man'. Sid was a lovely, jovial character who had evidently led an active and varied life but when I came across him he was a very lonely old soul. He loved the company of young people and thrived on the lively atmosphere generated by the human allsorts the café attracted. You'd see him offering tea and sympathy to young people who might be struggling with their demons. A relationship may have gone wrong or there could be darker problems like drug issues or homelessness. Sid could somehow lift that individual and most nights he could lift the whole place. He'd change the atmosphere in a flash by turning on the jukebox and finding a tune to lift all present. He had a penchant for Sting's *'Every Breath I Take'*, for which he developed his own bizarre dance routine. This often ended with him stripped to his underpants swinging from the ceiling beams. Not an edifying sight maybe but you'd cast your problems aside for a few moments to gaze in wonderment at the spectacle of it all.

I always suspected Sid was more comfortable than he let on but he got by selling roses in pubs, clubs and restaurants. There were always ready takers and Sid had a gift for making people feel that little bit better for meeting him.

One summer's night, I was making arrangements to meet a crowd on Brighton Beach the following afternoon when we knew the town would be packed with Bank Holiday trippers. When Sid heard me making these arrangements he insisted that we go to Brighton Beach there and then. I should have dismissed him there and then but some of the bouncers with me thought that was a great idea and so we duly found ourselves down on the beach at 3.30 in the morning.

Sid immediately stripped off down to those famous underpants which we all knew so well. It mattered not that he was no Adonis, he looked more like Albert Steptoe, the septuagenarian rag and bone man from TV comedy fame. We laughed as he toddled uncertainly on the pebbled beach before disappearing into the sea. Sid was happily frolicking away in the sea where we could easily pick him out in the bright moonlight when he suddenly screamed in some distress.

'What's up Sid?' someone shouted as we prepared to mount a rescue for Brighton's legendary flower seller.

'They're gone, I've lost them', we could hear him say as he shouted in despair.

Our fears soon gave way to helpless laughter as Sid emerged from the sea *without* his underpants.

Very, very funny of course but we couldn't have banked on the sequel that was to follow.

The next day, along with the same gang, I was back on the same spot on Brighton Beach, only this time we were joined by literally hundreds of holidaymakers. Sid turned up too and we teased him about the previous night's performance telling him not to give us a repeat.

'Oh, no, no, I'm prepared this time' before dropping his kecks and revealing a pair of splendid candy-striped swimming trucks which his grandfather had probably bequeathed him. Once again Sid toddled off into the sea whilst I tried to settle down to read *'The Guardian'* in peace.

I managed that for about ten minutes before I pricked up my ears on hearing my name being shouted.

'Paddy, Paddy, over here'

I didn't take too much notice until one of the lads said I was wanted.

'Paddy, Padd-ay!', the shouting became more urgent and soon all around were looking out to sea.

'Padd-ay, Padd-ay – look over here'. My eyes scanned the beach, before they locked on one of the most ridiculous sights I have ever witnessed in life.

Sid was coming out of the sea furiously waving something over his head.

'Padd-ay, look, look – I've found them! Yes, you've guessed it. Sid had been reunited with his (not so) long lost underpants! Truly, quite miraculous don't you think?

Chapter 20

'The Pain Gets A Little Deeper'

Meanwhile back in Brighton's clubland, Sherry's fantastic laser and lighting enhancement had proved to be a short-term fix and the numbers were dropping rapidly for them again. The place had long had a bit of a stigma about it. Although much loved by many, the perception was that it didn't attract a very 'classy' crowd. One could expect trouble breaking out sporadically and underage drinking was also something of a problem.

In fact, the management and door staff worked hard to stamp out the under age issues and to keep a lid on trouble but once a perception is established, it is mighty hard to shift. In Sherry's case, the perception had evolved over generations. Their new owners, First Leisure, decided that they could not afford to let the place drift. Brighton was a major centre of entertainment and leisure and their venue was located on a prime site within it. There had to be root and branch changes. So the venue which had been Sherry's since 1919 closed…..and we wondered what would emerge.

First Leisure's operational directors started to take a close look at the Brighton club scene and to their credit they did so openly and announced themselves. The main man, Mike Payne, told me that they used to visit clubs incognito but had come unstuck at a club in Stockton-On-Tees. He had arranged to meet some of his colleagues at a club up there to check what the opposition was doing and they all went along booted and suited with the plan being to meet inside at the bar. They all got in ok but found they stuck out like sore thumbs at the underage teens disco session taking place there that night!

They started to come in very regularly in the course of monitoring the work taking place across the road. They would usually end up in a session with Peter Langley at the bar where they were occasionally joined by some of the other managers within the Kingswest Complex.

It became very clear from what Peter was hearing that they were planning a radical departure from the Sherry's offering. First Leisure had been set up by Lord Delfont, brother of the TV and theatre impresarios, Lew and Leslie Grade. Delfont secured financing in the

City which allowed First Leisure to take over all the old EMI Dancing venues. Their portfolio also included all three of Blackpool's piers as well as Blackpool Tower itself. The Empire Ballroom in Leicester Square was another jewel in their crown.

We knew they wouldn't mess about now. They would make the necessary investment and they would recruit the best talent in the business to run their operations. It was no surprise that they looked to Rank Leisure's management staff to fill key positions.

There was no room for sentiment and soon we heard that Sherry's was no more. Even though Sherry's had been a fixture of Brighton nightlife since 1919, First Leisure decided that there were too many negative connotations and it just didn't chime with the brave new world they were planning. When we learned of the venue's new identity though, there was a sharp intake of breath. 'Surely not, you're kidding?' was the kind of reaction that seemed to be registering with just about everyone; 'The Pink Coconut?.....noooo!'

At first, we thought it was a working title and even the contractors working there thought that was possibly the case. However, seeing the palm trees being delivered and the pink neon signs being installed outside soon confirmed that the fantasy was in fact the reality.

The reaction around the town was very much the same and so as their opening night loomed, the curiosity of people was cranking up into a fever pitch of anticipation.

Naturally, all of us Rank boys had to pay an early visit and we, like everyone else, couldn't help being impressed by the extent and scale of the transformation. The end result epitomised the décor and style of the 80s; it was a temple of chrome and glass kitsch. Everything was framed in tivoli lighting and pink neons. Everything too, was pink it seemed, including the staff uniforms. The shame for me was that the refurbishment meant the obliteration of some of the building's better architectural features but this was the age of Thatcherism when greed was good and style and image was the be all and end all and you were liable to get it right in your face. The Harry Enfield character, Stavros, was bellowing 'Loadsamoney' every week on TV and maybe The Pink Coconut was his kind of club. I couldn't see it lasting for generations like the old Sherry's but it was right for the moment and we could see that the old image and associations had been well and truly dumped.

Over in Busby's we knew we now had real competition but we knew we also had a very good product. Provided we could sustain that and work hard, very hard...we could still hold our own.

Everything was now cranked up considerably. A successful Tuesday night session, 'Solitaire', was launched for the Singles market. It was unheard of to have a busy Tuesday session but we managed it. On Sunday nights we had a Jazz-Funk session with Paul Clark and Mick Fuller attracting a very discerning niche crowd. The quest to get people signed up as Members gave us a database to mine with invitations for people on their birthdays. This was supplemented with the work of an outsourced company who mined the electoral roll and sent out invitations to people coming up to their 18th and 21st birthdays. We knew if we could attract business on the 'off peak' nights, then the Fridays and Saturdays would take care of themselves.

Instead of our business tailing off in the wake of The Pink Coconut competition, we were seeing it improve spectacularly. At the same time, we were strict on dress standards and did all we could to eliminate the 'under age' problem. Occasionally we would even invite a uniformed police officer or two to come in and poke their head around the door. Theirs was a reassuring presence for customers who had previously only associated the police in nightclubs as a sign of trouble.

Although The Pink Coconut looked impressive and had got off to a great start we sensed that they were having trouble sustaining it. The punters who had tried it complained of the music being too 'poppy', the doormen being very impersonal and worst of all the atmosphere being a bit bland. We also noticed that they had done nothing to establish midweek sessions and instead hoped to rent out the venue for private hire. Having met Mike Payne and company, we knew they wouldn't let the place stagnate after the investment that had been made. But what would they do?

Peter Langley provided the answer for us. He was going over there.

We shouldn't have been too surprised. For weeks before the opening Peter had spent many nights in the company of the First Leisure executives and had been a regular visitor over there since it opened. He had been delegating more and more to me at Busby's which suited me and everyone else really. The relationship was easy and relaxed and all the Busby's management team were happy to help and cover each other.

Peter broke the news to me first adding that he also proposed to bring Andy King, the DJ with him. Andy had a good following and I knew he would be a good fit for the Coconut. It would be a blow for Busby's undoubtedly but I figured we could get by and indeed a change of a resident DJ might even refresh the offering we had.

Peter told me that he had recommended that I should take over from him and the job was mine if I wanted it. I was happy with that. There was a good team in situ and I knew I could depend upon them all. There was nothing broken to be fixed but I reasoned to myself that we couldn't relax for a moment from hereon in.

It was all to happen in a couple of months' time. With my own home, the prospect of being a Number One again, well I was in a real good place. What could possibly go wrong?

That evening I called home to break the good news to my mother. She was delighted for me but when I asked to speak to my father she said he was in bed with a chest complaint and was to go to hospital the next day for an x-ray. I was a little taken aback as my father never ever took a day off work and would work Sundays even whenever possible. I finished the call promising to ring again the following night to see how he had got on. Mum said there was some good news though as my sister, Maureen, was pregnant with her first child. Fantastic news, we were all on a roll.

Instead of calling back the following day, I thought I'd take a run up to Kettering the next day. I called Maureen in the morning to congratulate her but she was a little apprehensive about her condition and hoped everything would go to plan. I thought her over cautious as she often tends to be, but I just hoped that she would soon start to look forward to her little bundle of joy.

When I got to Kettering my folks were in their usual good form and delighted to see me but I could see that my father was feeling pained and looking in some discomfort. He said he felt ok and just wanted to get back to work but the doctor told him he needed to take it very easy for a while. He was more concerned with the news from Ireland that his sister, Ann, was very seriously ill and the outlook was very bleak.

I hit the road back again the next morning telling mum and dad that I'd be back up again on Christmas Day which was only a couple of weeks away.

There was plenty to get stuck into at work as there always was at that time of years but this time I was tackling it with a renewed kind of vigour. Soon, I'd be in charge and I had ideas I wanted to implement to improve and grow the business. After all the ups and downs, I felt I was back on track now and within the company that Rank Leisure was then, I figured I could carve out a solid, progressive career. A career which would allow me to provide for the people that mattered and a career which matched the ambitions I had for myself.

I kept thinking about my father though. He had always been this constant in life, always ready to support and encourage me. Now, he might be able to relax a bit more if he thought I was 'getting on'. I hoped once I was established in the new role that he and my mother would be able to come and stay in my new home and enjoy themselves in Brighton, a town that neither had yet seen. He just needed to get over this problem he was having though.

Christmas Eve can be a very exhausting night in clubland but it usually meant an opportunity to have a few days off. I planned to zoom home on Christmas Day, see the Poppies on Boxing Day and then shoot down to Torquay laden with Christmas and Birthday presents.

Driving home on Christmas Day, I was in such good form and just eager to catch up with everyone but as soon as I walked through the door I sensed things were very much amiss.

My mother tried to be her usual buoyant self, flapping around to make sure we were all comfortable before she got on with the dinner. Dad, though, was in great discomfort. He had failed markedly in just a couple of weeks. His face looked sunken and gaunt and he sat listlessly by the fire devoid of any of the sparkle that people knew and loved him for.

He tried his best to engage with me but it became a one-sided conversation as he was too tired to speak very much himself. Usually he'd want to talk about anything and everything whether it be religion, politics or football. We disagreed about many issues but tended to steer in the same direction over the things that mattered most.

I knew that he was worried about my sister whose pregnancy was now causing some concern. She hadn't been able to join us for Christmas and that made the house seem lonelier too. Above all, he was bracing himself for news of the passing of his sister Ann in Ireland. I had been in such breezy form on the way up but now I felt consumed with guilt for being so unaware of the sadness and despair that had descended upon our family.

After Christmas dinner, we sat around the TV and watched *'The Lavender Hill Mob',* one of the old Ealing comedies which tended to get an outing at that time of the year. Dad always enjoyed them and suddenly he burst into laughter at one of Peter Sellers's escapades. It was pure magic to see Dad laugh so heartily and I hoped against hope that I'd see him do so again.

The news came through the next morning that Ann had passed away overnight. She had suffered for so long that knowing she was now at peace was something of a relief but it didn't alleviate the hurt my father was feeling. He asked if I might go out and arrange for some flowers to be sent and as I was setting off, he came to the front door with me.

'I might be with her soon enough PJ'. I knew he didn't want me to talk freely so I just nodded. He and I knew the situation was ominous but my mother didn't and he didn't want to cause her concern.

I did go to the Poppies that day but my mind was not on the match. Our cosy, tight family who always managed to cope so easily and freely with life was now sailing through turbulence and I knew we'd be lucky to emerge intact.

The following day saw further emotional turmoil as I headed down to the West Country. My visits there by this time tended to be a mixture of eager anticipation, anxiety and a whole lot of angst and guilt. How I wished I could do more for Carrie and Emmeline and how I knew I was incapable of delivering for them because of the circumstances we found ourselves in.

This time my heart was heavy after seeing how my father was. I told Carrie and she was great, it was such a relief to unburden myself. She had met my father and understood just how devastated I was.

Once I got back to Brighton I found it hard to fully function with all that was going on in the background but work is probably the best therapy of all in many ways. I tried to immerse myself in it completely just taking time out every evening to check on how everyone was.

Unfortunately, there was never any good news. Dad was back in for yet more tests before he was finally admitted to hospital. On the same day, I received the sad news that my sister had lost the baby she was carrying. I could only imagine the pain she was suffering.

A new routine of phone calling then developed whereby every day I would call first the hospital, then my sister and then my mother. Each one would invariably answer that 'all was fine' and I would wonder how truthful they were all being. Sophie was the nursing sister taking care of my father, she was married to a friend of mine and she knew all our family very well. For a few days, she was very bullish in her outlook and took delight in telling me how cheerful Dad always was. I didn't doubt that, my father would always be laughing and joking as long as he had breath, but one morning her bulletin was a little more uncertain than it had been.

I pressed her to tell me what she knew but when she said I'd need to talk to the consultant I knew we'd reached an ominous stage.

'Is it cancer?' I asked.

She didn't answer as she struggled to find the right words.

'Don't worry Sophie; I'll take a drive up there'. I could tell she was really struggling to hold back the tears now but what can anyone say or do?

Three hours later I was at Kettering General Hospital and was surprised to find dad's bed was empty but my mother was chatting to some other patients nearby.

She shot up from her chair in surprise when I walked in telling me dad was downstairs having yet more x-rays. I made out I'd just taken the day off and travelled up on a whim. Her behaviour was as it always seemed to be. She just wondered what dad's problem really was and hoped it wouldn't be long before it was all cleared up.

She was totally unprepared a few moments later when the consultant called us into his office. He didn't beat about the bush.

'I'm very, very sorry but there's nothing more we can do for your husband'.

My mother was frozen in shock. 'What do you mean? Is he going to die?'

'Yes, I'm afraid so'.

To hear such a pronouncement about your nearest and dearest is unbearable for the hardest of hearts. The effect on my mother was to virtually sentence the end of her own life. Without him, life really wasn't worth living for her.

Out of such despondency though, stoicism is born and somehow the two of us gathered ourselves together and prepared to go in to see dad who was by now back in the ward.

He was contentment personified which made the situation even harder to comprehend. He was chatting away merrily, about the nurses, other patients in there, the football etc. He looked puzzled to see me though.

'What are you doing here? Don't you do any work?

I figured his bravado was surely to humour my mother. I knew the extent of his medication and the consultant had confided to me that he wasn't expected to last the month. I think that he knew as much too when I said that people were asking for him and wanted to visit.

'Sure, send them all in. I love the company'

That night I was on the phone to his sisters and brother in Ireland, Scotland and Chicago. They all dropped everything and prepared to come and bid that last 'goodbye'. The Irish diaspora in Kettering meant there was a full attendance at the hospital from that night onwards. So much so that the hospital had to find him a room of his own to avoid troubling other patients.

It was during this period that I realised just how well the Irish do death. At the saddest time in life it really is uplifting. Here we were, faced with the calamitous prospect of losing the man we adored, yet there was so much laughter all around. People came to visit him from near and far. In the evenings, many would call around to our house and some would congregate in The Baker's Arms. It had long been the rendezvous for any of the Irish landing up in Kettering and it was at The Baker's Arms where the men would find work; many of them ending up in my father's 'gang'. Some of the shelves in our home were crammed with the trophies dad had won playing for the pub's darts teams. He was pretty good too and had captained the side for years.

Some find such circumstances awkward and unsettling but I found there was nothing better than hearing people telling stories about my father. I learned of another side of the man, one that was rarely revealed at home.

Dad knew well he was on the way out but though it's ridiculous to even suggest as much, he seemed to be enjoying it. As one old face after another arrived he would be thrilled to see them but it became harder as his sisters arrived. They had a difficult job containing their emotions and equally it was harder for him to make light of the situation.

In between times I would sit there alone with him. There would be no need to even talk. All the time he would be thanking me; but all the time I'd been thinking how inadequate I was as a son. I resolved that the next day I would finally tell him about my Big Secret – his grandchild.

That night I took his brother, Eddie from Chicago, to see him and we found he had a few visitors with him already. Maybe dad was getting a bit tired when he asked me;

'Why don't you take them all over to The Globe?'

I thought that was as good an idea as any so we said goodnight to him and I led the gang the six miles over to Wellingborough where my aunt's pub was.

The Globe was a real throwback of a pub. Its interior had remained virtually untouched since the 1950s and it was to its credit that it had avoided the design disasters of the 70s and 80s. It still had a few inglenooks within the bar and lounge areas and towards the rear it had one of the old skittle tables of the type I've only ever encountered in Northamptonshire pubs.

In keeping with its appearance from a bygone era, the pub made a feature of its old fashioned tills. My uncle had taken umbrage at the introduction of decimalisation in 1971 and had resolved never to conform with it. Idiosyncratic of course, but he ended up being something of an expert on the conversion rates. Thus, if one's bill came to say £3.67, he would go to the till and instantly ring up £3/13s/4d which equated to £3 13shillings and 4pence of the old money.

It was also remarkable for the makeup of its clientele. Irish in one bar and West Indian in the other but everyone was welcome and few dared to entertain trouble with Big Pat Murphy!

There was a decent crowd in on this occasion and when people realised who I was, one after another would come over with best wishes for my father. One who came over was Luke, the guy with the golden tonsils I had last seen in Redhill five years before. His was a voice that my father rated highly and I asked Luke if he'd give a song.

With tears streaming down his face he threw his head back and proceeded to give a spine-tingling rendition of 'Danny Boy' which stunned the room into silence. By the end of it, we were all in helpless tears.

The following morning, we were awoken by a call from the hospital to say that my father's condition had deteriorated. I arrived alone at his bedside to find him falling in and out of consciousness. He was fading away and I cursed myself for not having shared the news with him that I had concealed for so long.

'Talk to him', a voice from behind me urged. A nurse had walked into his room and it was as if she could read my mind.

'Talk to him, he can still hear you. It's the last sense to go'.

I hoped she was right but I feared it was too late.

I started talking anyhow. The nurse closed the door and I started to unburden myself. All the guilty secrets poured out. This was therapy for me as much as anything else but that wasn't the point, I wanted him to know. I wanted to be at peace with him.

I found myself saying sorry, over and over again, and then I took his hand in mine. I wasn't sure at first when he seemed to squeeze my hand. Then he did it again and I realised he had been listening, he had heard my confession. I felt that he was granting absolution to me and within my grief I found a terrible joy.

I called my mother and we alerted a few more including our parish priest, Father Bailey, who I asked to administer the last rites.

Father Bailey said he would be up shortly but some time later he told me that my father had received the last rites a fortnight earlier at his own request. So, he had known his fate all along.

Dad finally passed away the morning after. I felt so privileged to be there when the moment I dreaded finally came.

It's you, it's you must go and I must bide.

The whole process of preparing for a funeral is cathartic in the extreme. Whilst emotions are heightened in the aftermath of tragedy I was quite elated and very proud to find just how highly regarded the man had been. I embraced every moment of the process and by the day of the funeral I was ready for the proper celebration of his life which we really did enjoy.

Life had to go on though for all our family and whilst I had a lot to be looking forward to I knew my mother and sister might struggle to cope with the pain and emptiness of their losses.

My pending promotion was now only weeks away and I set about immersing myself in work to prepare for the role and really to exorcise the grief that would take me so long to come to terms with.

I told myself that I couldn't be feeling too sorry for myself, things could be a lot, lot worse. There were 3.2 million people unemployed for a start, the worst since the Depression of the 1930s. Wasn't I a young man at the top of his game in a nice town like Brighton happy to be driving home to my new house listening to Michael Jackson's *'Thriller'* booming out of the sound system in my snazzy new Mk IV Ford Cortina?

There was more good news to from my best friends back home with the arrival of their first born….and they were asking me to be The Godfather! Now, that was a role that appealed too.

The night before the christening happened to be Peter Langley's very last night at Busby's and I knew he would be in celebratory form. I couldn't allow myself to take any drink as I planned to drive up to Kettering straight after the session and grab a few hours of sleep before the ceremony.

Peter left early that evening, as was his usual practice, leaving me to cash up and lock the premises. I was joined by the DJ that night, Chris Barnes, who was trying to persuade me to go to The Market Diner afterwards. Much as I enjoyed going there, it had to be a non-starter that night with the journey I was due to undertake.

With the cashing up done and all the monies locked in the safe, the two of us prepared to leave the building when the phone suddenly rang. An unusual event at that time of the morning but it was The Vamp from the bank asking if I was coming to her party. 'Oh Gawd!' She had invited me when I was in the bank earlier during the week, I said I would but I'd forgotten all about it. I didn't want to snub her, so I said I would pop in for one drink.

Chris was delighted but I said I'd better bring a bottle if we were going. I opened the safe again to get the keys to the spirit cupboard. I duly took a bottle of dodgy white French table wine and signed the stock book saying I'd taken it. The practise was that one could take a bottle of wine as and when one needed it but it always had to be signed for and replaced by a bottle of spirits. The retail value of say, a bottle of vodka, was considerably more than wine so it suited Farouk, the bars manager, as it helped him to achieve a surplus stock report. I duly returned the keys to the safe and then set off for the party with Chris.

The party, such as it was, was all but over when we arrived but The Vamp was pleased to see us making me feel pleased that we'd at least made the effort for her. I was absolutely whacked and didn't fancy the prospect of the long drive ahead. The Vamp could see this so I was tempted by her offer to stay there the night but I knew I needed to get cracking and I didn't want to be compromised by her offer, however well meaning it was.

It was past 6am when I finally flopped into my old four poster bed in Kettering which was the only bed I'd ever slept in at home since graduating from my cot. I left a note for my mother to not awaken me until 1pm which I figured would just about give me enough time to get ready for my role as The Godfather that afternoon.

The afternoon passed off very well and it was nice to catch up with so many familiar faces again but when it was over I just looked forward to a good long sleep before heading back to Brighton the following morning. Once again though, the best laid plans were to be well and truly dashed.

My mother was waiting anxiously when I got home and I could see that she was working herself into a state of sheer panic. 'What now?' I wondered.

'The police have been here', she spluttered, 'they want you to get in touch as soon as possible'.

'What's happened?' I asked, thinking there must have been some sort of an accident.

'There's been a robbery at the club and they need to talk to you'.

When that news had sunk in, I tried to figure what kind of robbery this could be. It was impossible to get to the safe which was contained in an office within an office. One had to get into the building as well first. So, three keys were needed to get that far.

I couldn't see how anyone would have been able to get in through the front doors which opened onto Brighton's main seafront road. I could only think that entry must have been made through a rear fire entrance but even that was implausible as the fire doors were secured with padlocked chains.

Although I was reeling at the news I wasn't too apprehensive before I contacted Brighton police. I was expecting to hear of an act of vandalism perhaps or an attempted burglary which yielded nothing or very little. However, on getting through the officer assigned to the case, my outlook soon changed.

'Where are you? When can you get here?'

'Oh, if I leave now, I'll be there at about 10 o'clock. Are you going to tell me what's happened?'

'The place has been robbed. All the money has gone'.

My heart just sank. I'd done nothing wrong, I didn't have the money. I'd locked up. It wasn't me! I'd done everything right – or had I?

On the drive back down to Brighton, I just knew there was going to be no happy ending to this breaking story. Over and over in my mind I tried to re-run the sequence of events the night before. Doing the cashing up, locking the money in the safe, opening it up again to get the keys for the spirit cupboard, taking the wine, signing for it, returning the keys to the safe, locking the inner office and leaving the premises and locking the door behind me. What's more, I had a witness. Chris was with me every step of the way.

There were two sets of keys. The other was with another manager who had left before me. Had he come back? I dismissed that thought instantly, one of my friends wouldn't do anything so bold…..surely not? But how? What had happened? There had to be a simple explanation.

I can remember nothing of that journey back to Brighton. It was as if I was lost in bewildering thought and the car had driven itself there. I pulled up outside my home intending to drop my bags off before reporting to John Street police station less than a quarter of a mile away; but I found a reception committee awaiting me!

As I got out of my car, I was immediately confronted by two plain clothes police officers who asked me to accompany them. We've all seen the TV police dramas but if you've led a blameless life then nothing can prepare you for the harsh realities of realising that you have been arrested and indeed are being regarded as the prime suspect for a pretty serious crime.

Back in those days I knew many of the officers and detectives at Brighton Police. They were always dropping in for a drink and I had helped them on numerous occasions. I'd hoped they'd be mindful of that but the two dealing with me now were less familiar with me and wouldn't be taking the previous good relationship I'd enjoyed with the police into consideration.

I was not asked for a formal statement and they decided I did not require a solicitor present. Instead they wanted me to talk through the events of the night before and then they would search my home.

They told me that the theft had been discovered by our cleaning staff. When they went into the office they found the door to the inner office open and the safe door wide open. After contacting Peter

Langley, they estimated that over £5,000 had been stolen. No forced entry was evident in any part of the premises.

Their conclusion was that it was an 'inside job' and as I had one of the set of keys then the finger of suspicion was pointing firmly at me.

I knew myself that I was innocent though and reassured myself that this nightmare would soon be over. I couldn't contemplate the other manager being behind the heist but given the details emerging, I couldn't think of any other explanation either.

During the grilling, I explained that I was to take over as General Manager of the club that very week with a significant salary increase. I asked them why would I be putting all that in jeopardy and how would I ever have got away with it?

They suggested that I had had every opportunity to hide the money between Brighton and Kettering and that I possibly had a willing accomplice in Chris Barnes. Chris was known to the police for some minor transgressions in his youth but he had nothing to do with this and I was 100% certain that he would never do anything to cause trouble for me. Chris had been arrested earlier in the day and they were continuing to question him nearby.

After an hour or so of their intense scrutiny I sensed that my interrogators did believe me, but like myself could find no explanation. Their manner softened somewhat and did so even more when we returned to my house where they sought to exhaustively search the premises.

One of the officers was searching in a cupboard below the stairs when he produced a box and asked;

'What's this?'

'I don't know', I replied and I genuinely didn't. I had only just bought the place complete with furniture and some of the previous owner's property which she had asked me to junk if I didn't want any of it.

He opened the box and pulled out a wedding dress!

'Is this yours?'

My former landlady had told me she'd broken off a long-term relationship which had left her feeling pretty distraught and indeed led to her deciding to move to Spain. Seeing the dress, I thought it represented how her hopes and dreams must have been so agonisingly dashed.

'No sir, it isn't', and thankfully they accepted my account as to how it got there.

The police eventually left saying they would be in touch. They actually shook hands with me wishing me well. I knew though, that there was a reckoning ahead, and unless an explanation could be found quickly then the company would be looking for someone to be accountable.

The next morning it did feel that the buck had stopped with me. On arriving at work, I was immediately asked to leave the premises and told that I was being suspended on full pay pending inquiries.

All the other members of the management team were present and going about their normal routines….including that other key holder

For the next few days I led the life of a complete zombie. On the first day, I found myself getting up, getting dressed and heading off for work before realising halfway there that I didn't have a job to go to any more. I'd return to the house and get immersed in 'Good Morning Britain'. Roland Rat and Fred the Weatherman were the only ones I wanted to listen to for a little while.

One morning I ventured as far as St James' Street to buy a card for a friend's birthday. I then popped into the post office and joined a long queue to buy a stamp for it. As I walked away from the counter, I heard the next customer asking the assistant;

'What did that man want?'

Did he mean me? He surely did as I turned around to see him point at me before showing his police ID card to the clerk. He didn't seem too fazed when she told him I'd only bought a stamp. Instead he just looked at me directly and walked on.

Chris had heard I'd been suspended and he called up to see how I was coping, but no one else did from the club. Guilty, until proven innocent seemed to me to be the view that people were forming. But I knew I was innocent, as did the real thief who I now became certain had to be someone I knew very well. He, I couldn't imagine it was a she, was obviously fronting this one out and in time I believed he could enjoy his ill-gotten gains. The police were no longer interested and neither were the company as far as I could see. They weren't really bothered about catching the perpetrator and letting justice take its course when they had found someone to blame. Besides, they were insured for the loss anyhow.

Chris, to his eternal credit, was livid to hear of the treatment meted out to me. He himself had had fingers pointed at him; he wasn't bothered because he understood human nature and he was hearing wild speculation. It was being said that I took the money because I was strapped after buying the house. The girls in the bank had heard that the police had arrested me at a party. Some said it wasn't five thousand pounds, but ten, maybe twenty.

I was just glad that my father wasn't alive to hear what had become of me. How was I to honour his faith in me now?

Shortly after a letter arrived from the company inviting me to attend a disciplinary hearing?

I thought this would be the chance to set the record straight. I had NOT stolen the money and there was absolutely no evidence to suggest that I had. Surely, based on the information I was giving them they'd open an investigation and try to find this thief who I was convinced was still in their midst?

On arriving at the appointed hour, I was pleased to see that a couple of the Rank managers, who knew me well, would be sitting in as observers though they wouldn't be allowed to speak.

It was supposed to be a 'hearing' but sadly it was nothing of the sort. It was a pronouncement, a passing of judgement.

Sentence was delivered upon me by a lady sent down from Rank Leisure's Personnel Division based at their headquarters in Godstone.

She read from a pre-prepared statement saying that my indiscretion amounted to a serious dereliction of duty which could be construed as grievous misconduct. In acknowledgement of my performance and good record, I could resign and receive my full entitlements along with a good reference from the company or I could be summarily dismissed. I had no right of appeal in accordance with Rank Leisure's disciplinary code of practise.

Once her words had sunk in I tried to protest.

'Why?', I haven't done anything. I didn't take the money. There is no evidence that I had anything to do with it'.

'You breached company policy by taking the bottle of wine'.

'But we all do that, it's the practise. I signed for it and we always replace what we've taken. Isn't that right gents?' I looked to the two managers for a nod of agreement at least. But none was forthcoming. The bastards.

I stared at one of them, a man who had spent his entire career with the company but a man I knew to be a serial embezzler from it. What else would you call a man who installed his own cash till to take admission money on student nights? A man who was also happy to dip into the petty cash to fund his gambling habit at Sergeant Yorke's Casino and the Ladbroke's betting shop across the road. Sitting alongside him was the man who thought it ok to pocket any money proffered by customers arriving after he had shut the admission desk. He would buy the silence of the bouncers by bunging them occasionally.

Yet the two of them sat motionless whilst judgment was pronounced upon me. Was it to save their own bacon which would be easier now that there was a fall guy?

Who knows?

Chapter 21

'Feel So Real'

From being on top of my game, I found myself seemingly dumped on the scrapheap all in one fell swoop. 'What do I do now?' 'Who will have me?' 'What will people be thinking?' Over and over I'd ask myself those questions and over and over again I'd draw a complete blank whilst the news filtering through suggested that I was indeed the prime suspect and only a lack of evidence was preventing me from being charged and subsequently 'banged up'. No matter how ridiculous the latter suggestion was; the lack of support from those I'd worked alongside was conspicuous by its absence. Their silence was thunderous. Some of them knew the truth of the matter so I just assumed they didn't want the association.

Others though were magnificent especially Martin, my then lodger, and my old mate, Clive. I also received wonderful support from the Iranian doormen who I'd helped with their asylum and legal issues. Those guys taught me the meaning of honour. They were steadfast and true and defended me throughout. At the beginning, I feared for my very sanity and the thought of the ultimate option repeatedly crossed my mind. Ironically, it was the actions of a friend who did just that which helped me to snap myself back together.

Martin had received a desperate call from his friend, Paul, a popular local hairdresser and well known 'face' at Busby's. The guy spoke of ending it all when his relationship with his girlfriend soured. It could have been any chap feeling depressed at the turn of events and the emptiness he was feeling but Martin realised it was far more serious than that. He had tried to reason with him but Paul was adamant, he had reached the point of no return. Not sure how to react, Martin phoned the Samaritans for guidance who said they would call his friend. A few minutes later they reported back to Martin that there was no reply. Martin just knew he had to get there pronto so jumped in his car and shot across town. There was no answer when he arrived at the flat so a forced entry was needed.....but it was too late. Martin found his friend had hanged himself.

It was an awful tragedy all round. The waste of a good young life of course but what agony for those left behind, his family and friends and of course the girl at the centre of it all? It was senseless and futile and maybe just a little bit selfish. But how can anyone appreciate the depths of depression the poor chap had sunk to?

My troubles were as nothing compared to this and I chided myself for even letting the thoughts cross my mind. I knew I'd pull myself together sooner or later and eventually move on. The support of Martin, Clive, Chris and the Persian boys was a tremendous help. So too were the surprise visits of some of my old staff; people who had only a tenuous connection with me outside of work. Their thoughtfulness was life enhancing for me and slowly I realised that I didn't have to regard myself as a pariah. I even started to venture out again and why not? I had done nothing wrong and I could look others in the eye who I knew, actually had.

Getting one's self-respect back can be a mighty, mighty long haul and I resolved that the best way would be to get back into work as soon as possible. I combed the pages of *'The Hotel and Caterer'* and *'The Stage'* to see what openings might be out there. There were very few but I was greatly encouraged when I was asked to attend an interview with a brewery who wanted an Area Manager for their managed house estate. The job appealed enormously, more money, a nice car and I could escape the nightclub treadmill which I had been on for far too long. The first interview went well and at the end of the second interview in Watford I was overjoyed to be offered the position, subject to confirmation.

I was on Cloud 9 as I drove back to Brighton. I could see myself in the new role driving the shiny new Vauxhall Cavalier I would be getting. Happy days were here again and I marvelled how The Big Man worked in such mysterious ways.

After a couple of days, no letter had arrived so I gently pursued it with their personnel department. The matter was in hand I was assured but still no letter appeared on the third day, or the fourth. On day five I vaulted down the stairs when I heard something plop through the letterbox. I could see the company's insignia on the letter before I opened what was surely confirmation of my redemption; my passport back to the living world. But no….it was anything but.

The letter explained that 'unfortunately, the position was no longer available'. I could have accepted that and got over my disappointment had it not been for the fact that the position was advertised again the following week. I suspected, and I found out later, that Rank had reneged on their agreement to supply a good reference.

I received at least two subsequent offers for other positions I applied for which were later rescinded and I realised that they had adopted a position which would be near impossible for me to resolve. I did try to tackle Rank Leisure on the matter but they just played a straight bat saying that they were not at liberty to divulge the content of references. I knew there was nothing I could do whether the references were good, bad or indifferent. My only recourse was if they had been factually incorrect, but of course they made sure there were no facts to question other than the bald statement of the dates of my employment with them.

I was now getting a little desperate. My funds were running short and my overheads were bearing down on me. Martin's rent was all that was keeping me going so I had to get some income, any sort of income.

Clive had also sailed into stormy waters and found himself unemployed, so now we found we were both reporting at the dole office looking for scraps. The pair of us ended up ferrying vehicles across the country for a dispatcher in Burgess Hill. I liked being on the open road whether driving transits, low loader wagons or even the odd Porsche. The only problem was that the vehicle only took you one way; to get back we had to stick out our thumbs and hitch it. It sure ain't no fun to be standing in a downpour on the side of the road at the Walsall interchange at 3 o'clock in the morning with your bed 185 miles away!

These shillings kept the wolves from the door though, and we even had a lot of fun for the most part. Slowly, I was getting on with life and slowly my bitterness began to ease. One day in town I ran into Johnny Holland who owned the thriving Escape Club in Brighton. Johnny was just about to get married and hoped to get away for a fortnight's honeymoon.

'Could you possibly look after the club for me for a couple of weeks?' he asked and I was more than happy to. I'd always regarded Johnny as one of the good guys and I knew the experience would get me back in the groove again.

The Escape was a cracking little operation and John had assembled a great group of staff who respected him immensely. He knew they wouldn't take liberties and so it proved. That little interlude at The

Escape did me a power of good and suddenly doors began to open again.

A Brighton pub group made overtures to me and then Glendola Leisure came calling. They had me running Night Fever and Swifts in Brighton before dispatching me to Southampton, Greenford and Plymouth which was where I found myself when the news came through that one of my Soul heroes, Marvin Gaye, had been shot and killed by his father.

I was staying in the Continental Hotel in Plymouth at the time, the last time I had been there was after seeing Marvin himself performing in Bournemouth seven years previously.

I was once again the nightclub nomad it seemed – have dicky bow, will travel – but where once I had been tired of the treadmill, now I had renewed vigour. I was just glad to be back in the game and glad to be proving that those who had passed judgment on me had not succeeded in defeating me.

I was out for a drink in the town one night when I thought I'd call in at The Pink Coconut. I had heard Andy McGuinness had been appointed as the new manager and I wanted to go and wish him well. Andy was another graduate of the Rank Charm School and I had last seen him when I was in Northampton and he was managing Peaches in nearby Bletchley.

Andy was delighted to see me and still being the 'bon viveur' I remembered so well, we immediately headed to the bar for a few shants and to catch up on each other's news. Of course, he wanted to get the inside track on my troubles particularly as he knew all the protagonists involved. He was very sympathetic and could see that my world had been turned upside down but there was plenty else for us to talk about and after about four hours I headed for home feeling less of an outcast than at any time since my day of disaster.

The following day, a Saturday afternoon, I was doing my ironing and watching the racing on TV when the phone rang.

'Wanna job?'

'Eh?', I queried, not knowing who I was talking to.

'Do you want a job? Here, with me!'

This was worth turning away from proceedings at Haydock Park but the voice still hadn't quite registered with me.

'Course you do, we'll have a great time...hee hee hee'. Only Andy McGuinness had a machine gun cackle like that. 'Come down tonight and we'll sort it out....see ya!'

When Andy was in full flow it was always hard to get a word in and when he asked a question, he'd invariably answer it himself. So any hesitation on my part would be deemed agreement as far as Andy was concerned.

I was quite taken aback but oh so hugely relieved. 'Thank you, thank you Big Man', I thought and sank to my knees in silent prayer. In truth, the job was not exactly 'big time' but where I was at, at that moment in time, it was bigger than anything I could have hoped for.

We met that night and over another couple of bevvies, we sealed the deal. We both knew we would gel and for Andy it meant he could shed a considerable part of the load he was bearing.

I had watched the evolution of The Pink Coconut over the previous couple of years from across the road and for some time I could see that they had firmly grabbed the middle ground in the Brighton nightlife scene. The regular weekend sessions were getting very healthy attendances and with a gay night on Sundays and regular private functions there was a very solid base to build upon.

Andy did have considerable issues though with some of the staff which he had been fighting alone. It meant he wasn't winning any popularity contests but he never minded about that. He figured with a like-minded ally beside him he could implement the changes he wanted. But we didn't anticipate the drastic turn of events just around the corner for us.

Any experienced manager taking over a venue will invariably rely on the tried and trusted methods and practices which have stood him in good stead in the past. From time to time though he may encounter resistance from staff members who find certain of the changes proposed to be unwelcome or uncomfortable. Invariably, it is the most trivial issues that provide the trigger for confrontation and so it proved for Andy and I on one of the busiest nights on our calendar; New Year's Eve.

A full house was expected and we knew it wouldn't be too long before the staff would be working flat out. With that in mind, as Andy and I stood on the front door with all the doormen, we discussed getting the staff breaks out the way early. I was just about to arrange this with the bar supervisors when Andy turned to Amir, the head doorman, and asked him to start the breaks for the doormen.

'No'. Amir simply replied and turned to look out the door. The calm bluntness Amir displayed didn't augur well. I caught my breath at the sheer insolence of the man and I could see the rest of the doormen shifting in silent uneasiness.

'Can you organise the breaks now Amir', said Andy quietly but with firm resolve and everyone knew that Amir's next response would determine if we'd be starting the New Year, happily or otherwise.

Without turning his head, Amir waited a moment before declaring;

'I decide when they take a break'.

The music from the disco was just kicking in, there were crowds massing outside and all the usual hurly burly of Brighton nightlife was all around us but for what seemed an age this group of men were trapped in a bubble of silence.

Andy popped the bubble when he took a step forward, opened the front door and gestured to Amir;

'Goodnight'.

Would Amir walk? Or maybe he was inclined to punch him?

'If I go, they all go', he confidently asserted.

'Goodnight', Andy repeated with equally confident assertion.

Amir walked through the door and looked back at his colleagues.

Andy held the door open and simply asked them all;

'Well?'

They all walked meekly out and Andy shut the door after them just as a half-hearted trickle of abuse was being hurled back at him.

We watched the assembly of bow-tied bravados now gathered on the pavement outside. All dressed up with nowhere to go. Many of them needed the money they earned from the job but they had felt obliged to follow their leader. It was a little sad in a way.

'Oh heck', said Andy, 'what do we do now?' I just looked at him and we both burst out laughing. Strictly speaking we shouldn't have remained open that night as we were now in breach of our license but the pair of us felt quite liberated and it certainly sealed our working relationship.

As it happened, we called in the passing police inspector patrolling West Street that night and explained the situation to him. We'd always had a good relationship with the police and that night it sure paid dividends. It was arranged that we'd cater for all the police patrolling the area that night by providing them with drinks and refreshment throughout the evening. It saved the police from going back to their station a couple of miles away and we had their reassuring presence in the building all night.

Thankfully, the night passed without incident and at the end of it we stood a drink for all the staff that night. We knew, and it felt like they did too, that a turning point had been reached and there was no going back now.

If you are going to have a massive upheaval of personnel in your nightclub business then the first couple of weeks of January is probably the best time of year to have it. Customers tend to hibernate for a few weeks and St Valentine's is usually the date when the social calendar really gets going again.

Our priority now was to recruit an entirely new team of doormen and as we were starting from scratch we saw it as an opportunity to set our own template. We didn't want to take on experienced 'old hands' who were likely to adopt a similar approach to those just departed. There were plenty of applications from just such characters but we were intent on avoiding the easy options. We were looking for attitude and presentation above all else and within a week the new team of virgin soldiers was assembled. Amongst the ranks was a bricklayer, a paramedic, a cosmetics salesman and one character we just couldn't be sure of but he made us laugh so much we thought he was worth taking a chance on.

The new door team all gelled very quickly and the reception from the patrons was hugely encouraging. The guys did exactly what was asked of them and once we realised they could be relied upon for their attitude and trustworthiness then we felt we could relax a little in that area at least.

Just before Christmas the company had allowed us to engage a couple of assistant managers, Judith and Steve, who were primarily concerned with the bars and catering operation. The two of them were sufficiently experienced enough to make a quick impression upon their charges so for Andy and I, the day to day issues were now greatly alleviated and we could concentrate on just developing the business.

Although, soul and disco music still provided the bulk of the Pink Coconut soundtrack, other influences were filtering through on a nightly basis. The New Romantic movement had had a modest impact on the playlist but much more evident was the plethora of hi-nrg (energy) sounds that were being increasingly accepted by our patrons with artists such as Bronski Beat, Miquel Brown and Sylvester featuring particularly prominently. Nothing but hi-nrg was played at 'Bolts', the gay session we staged on Sunday nights but now it was clear a much wider audience was happy to embrace it. Another reason for its sudden popularity was the fact that it was championed over the road in 'Coasters', a new addition to the Brighton nightlife scene. This was largely due to the efforts of the outrageous Rory Steele, Coasters' larger than life gay DJ. Decades later Rory's influence is still recalled with affection by the many who saw him perform. In an age where it was still difficult to be openly gay with a straight audience, even in Brighton, Rory stood there loud and proud. To describe the man as 'flamboyant' would be a serious understatement. Rory knew no bounds and Gloria Gaynor's anthem; *'I am what I am',* summed him up perfectly. He dressed how he felt, didn't spare the make-up and when he took his weekly trip to the hairdressers he would bring along his two toy poodles. Often, they would emerge with the same pink, purple or blue rinse that Rory had decided upon for that week.

Ironically, one act whose records seemed to be featured constantly at this period was Wham! It had been barely 18 months since we had dismissed them as being quite inept when they had appeared at Busby's. Indeed, I had done well to secure that extra fiver for them when they came over the road to appear in Sherry's; the Pink Coconut's previous incarnation. In just a few months they had emerged as probably the biggest act in the land.

With some stability finally back in my life again; I was able to resume trips down to Devon to see Emmeline and Carrie on a regular basis. The little one was fairly shooting up now and becoming quite the little lady. The two of them seemed more like sisters than mother and daughter and I could see that theirs was a very, very special bond which would withstand any pressure; particularly that applied by any man.

With some trepidation, I even started to think about a return to the dating game but I needn't have feared. It was all a process in returning to normal service but I was relieved to abandon the straitjacket that it felt like I had been wearing for far too long. I was a regular guy once again. I tried not to dwell on the injustices I felt I had been subjected to. People do talk about Karma and it did start to feel that if you do the right thing you will eventually get the right outcome.

It's always tricky conducting any sort of relationship with your staff but I knew I was quite taken with one girl who had applied for a bar staff position. She looked pleasant enough and presented a quite outstanding CV; probably the best I'd ever seen. Yet she was quiet and unassuming and that as much as anything endeared me to her. I gave her the job and she duly proved to be very diligent and hardworking. I should have been grateful just to have a trusty and dependable member of staff but of course my heart ruled my head and soon I found I was taking too much of an interest.

The drinks company, Pernod, came to me with news of an interesting promotion they were running which appealed to me greatly for its novelty value. That year, Halley's Comet was due to circle the earth again as it did every 76 years. In exchange for running a number of promotions of their brand they would be happy to allow me to take a party of 20 or so on a VIP chartered flight to get a once in a lifetime view of the comet. We duly ran the promotions and I had 18 delighted patrons looking forward to a jolly day out. As I needed someone to help me look after them, I thought I'd ask Rosie, my bright-eyed, clever barmaid, if she'd like to come along for the ride.

She did and we both set out on the trip which was to change our lives.

The jaunt went well, Rosie and I went for a drink afterwards and after a few more hook-ups we were seemingly an item!

We both thought it best to keep our liaison to ourselves. We weren't to know how things would pan out and it was just too awkward to conduct a courtship in full view of all our colleagues. Besides, how sure were either of us that this was anything more than a fleeting association?

That was a question I was asking myself less than two weeks later when Donna came calling. Donna was a truly stunning lady as far as I was concerned. Always immaculate in manner and presentation, Donna was frequently engaged to conduct promotional work for the local paper and other organisations. She was both very pleasant and very modest but so striking was her appearance that one noticed people taking a sharp intake of breath on first sight of her. I was no exception but I was surprised when she called into the club one Monday afternoon asking to see me.

What she said left me frozen in disbelief and even now I find it hard to believe it happened. Closing the door behind her as she stepped into my office, she looked at me and smiled saying;

'My mother thinks we'd make a nice couple!'

I wasn't going to disagree with her mother and when Donna wondered if we may go for a drink together, I found myself nodding my head and arranging to pick her up that same night. She gave me an enigmatic smile not unlike Mona Lisa's and just said 'See you later!'

I was in something of a state of shock whilst I reflected on our brief meeting and then I remembered Rosie. 'Oh heck', I thought. Almost on cue, the phone rang and it was Rosie inadvertently helping me to figure out what to do next. She had been invited to spend some time with a friend near Maidstone and she had decided that she would go the following day for a week.

I liked Rosie, an awful lot, but Donna, she really was a bit special wasn't she? It's only been a couple of weeks with Rosie I thought; if I was going to be thinking like this, surely, it's better that I end it quickly. I didn't think she'd be that fussed anyhow. On the other hand what if there was no 'spark' between Donna and I. Oh, what a mess….but a nice mess in a way. I just had to make sure no one got hurt or upset.

I picked up Donna that evening and immediately told her my situation. I had to be straight with her and she seemed to appreciate that; so we thought we'd take it one step at a time. It felt that we'd 'clicked'; there definitely was a spark and I realised I liked her….. a lot. I suppose I was a tad smitten. All the time though my mind was on Rosie; I would have to let her down gently.

Donna and I had a lovely evening and we made arrangements to meet again in a couple of days. The next morning Rosie called when I was at home. She said she was missing me and I found myself saying the same. I used to love the sound of her voice and suddenly the certainty I had the night before completely dissolved. I began to think she might be very hurt indeed if I dumped her and was that really what I wanted to do?

'I'm just a two-timing cad, aren't I?', I was telling myself. This wasn't fun and I had to bring it to a stop….but it sure wasn't easy.

I met Donna again the following night and again she had the same effect on me though it seemed we both felt compelled to behave with total propriety. My mind was in a total turmoil. One of these girls seemed to be the key to my destiny but I just couldn't make my mind up.

The company had scheduled me to go on a 3 day course up in Blackburn and I thought that would give me the opportunity to clear my head. I told Donna I would meet her on my return and one way or another I had to do the right thing by both of them. She agreed but added one tantalising offer. She had a promotions assignment in Birmingham whilst I was up North and would be staying in a hotel just off the M6. I could drop by, she suggested, on my way back from the North.

I thought the break would give me some respite but if anything, I felt more muddled than ever. It was said that when Winston Churchill found himself in such a quandary trying to make a decision, that he resolved it by simply drawing up two columns on a blank sheet of paper. A column for pros and a column for cons. I tried the very same method but both girls scored equally highly on the pros and were devoid of cons. Gut feeling was going to have to be the determinant.

I drove back down the M6 that evening and as I neared the Walsall interchange, where a few months earlier I had stood in the pouring rail forlornly trying to hitch a lift, I realised my future would be determined by whether or not I decided to turn off there. I knew that a few minutes away there was a lovely lady who awaited me, a lady with whom I could surely be very, very happy and contented with. I decided I had to see her, I was aching to. I indicated to turn off the M6 but my head was pounding. I just couldn't do it……..so I drove on.

My eyes were moist but I thought to do otherwise was to abuse the trust that Rosie had placed in me. I'd already acted the cad. I just felt I had to do the right thing and at the time I felt I was doing that. I did meet Donna briefly a couple of days later and apologised for the outcome but she was great and we genuinely parted on the best of terms. She probably had a lucky escape!

Back in Brighton normal service was resumed. Rosie returned and Life was sweet. Of course, I was feeling guilty and remorseful and the selfish man in me still wondered if my choice was right but I also knew that I was with a 'good un' and enjoying life in a way that I couldn't have contemplated just a few short months earlier.

By this time, I had spent a decade in the business and as I used to look out at the crowds every night, I realised that whilst the basics remained the same – there had been some extraordinary changes. I had started at a time when ballroom dancing was still a feature of the weekly entertainment offering and rock and roll was not quite dead (at least in Plymouth). Sound and lighting needed only to be adequate enough to set the mood and there was little need to be anything but predictable about the music being played to the punters. Let's not forget the resident house bands in some of the establishments I worked in which had to be foisted upon the customers whether they liked them or not.

Now the resident live bands seemed a total anachronism. We needed to be able to respond to consumer tastes instantly and the pop charts weren't necessarily the best barometer to gauge public tastes. In the large, mass market venues such as The Pink Coconut, that task was even harder as one needed to find DJs capable of keeping most of the people happy most of the time. I did despair of the diet of Lionel Ritchie, Whitney Houston etc., but these were strange times with many British 'pop' acts like Culture Club, The Thompson Twins, New Order and the 2-Tone bands getting regular plays alongside the disco fodder. It was now necessary to have a stonking sound system and a state of the art lighting rig to generate the right 'experience' on such a night. Fashions were changing fast too and the work suit was no longer the fallback outfit of choice for many of the guys as it had once been. 'No jeans, no trainers' was still the mantra on the front door but one wondered for how long?

From the perspective of looking back in time, the Pink Coconut era did seem to reflect something of the ethos of Thatcherism. The 'greed is good' culture was anathema to me but it is strange to recall how people, even young people were swept up with the clamour to get hold of the share issues being made available to the public when the public utilities were privatised. House prices were the number one dinner time conversation piece for seemingly everyone and you just had to get on the ladder!

They were fun times alright but for me there was something of a loss of the age of innocence. Where once we set out to entertain, now the primary considerations were becoming 'the margin yield' and of course the return of investment for the not inconsiderable capital sums the likes of First Leisure were laying out. The company came under regular scrutiny in the financial press and one knew that shareholder satisfaction and the views of the City were the main concerns for the board.

They were a dynamic outfit though and there were opportunities aplenty as the company grew their estate and extended into other areas such as resorts, health clubs and theatres. They were also prepared to pay well too for the right talent and if I wanted to play the game and was flexible enough; the opportunities certainly appeared to be there for me too. The question was, did I want that?

I had fought hard to get back on track and having done so, I certainly was enjoying the life. I found it fun and I found it fascinating. It was the perfect career for the social animal I saw myself as but life was moving on and I wasn't the young 'greenhorn' who had been so enthralled with clubland a decade or so previously.

I had indeed seen it all and done it all. To carry on would mean repeating the old tricks and maybe this Old Dog wouldn't be capable of learning all the new tricks that would be required. All the time I had been in clubland, I had always wondered about some of the 'old guys' in the business. Sure, I respected the knowledge and skills they had picked up and was grateful for what they taught me. But did they have another life at all? Some were married and had families, I used to wonder how this environment could be conducive to those relationships. Indeed, it seemed it wasn't for many and they stumbled on from town to town after broken marriages and relationships like the proverbial drifters of the wild west. I just couldn't see myself welcoming the children of my past punters or warming to the music of future generations and what sort of establishments would the nightclubs themselves be in the years ahead?

With Rosie and I getting closer, I had to think of the future I could offer her and yes there was still Emmeline. How could I truly be a role model for her? It would be hard enough to demonstrate I was a father who truly cared despite being so absent in her life.

For the next few months I determined to explore possible exit routes, but what? Although educated to a pretty good level I hardly had a CV that stood up to a lot of scrutiny in the world of commerce unless of course it was related to the field I was already engaged in.

I couldn't tell anyone what was going through my mind, not even Rosie. Andy and his seniors thought I was relatively happy and occasionally I was asked if I had a notion for General Manager roles that were coming up in various parts of the country. I didn't. It wasn't a question of money now but I knew these were not challenges I would welcome. I wasn't looking to conquer the world but I wanted a suitable role to stimulate me and one I could be proud of as a potential husband and father. The solution came, as it usually tended to for me, right out of the blue and rather closer to home than I imagined. For that, I always owe a certain gratitude to the cast of 'EastEnders'!

Chapter 22

'Respectable'

Andy and I were always looking for an angle to exploit and if it was topical and relevant then all the better. I had done it to great effect when securing the services of Erika Roe after her bare-chested trot on to the pitch at Twickenham so what could we do now?

The answer came as we both got ready for work one evening.

In 1984, the BBC had launched their own soap series *'Eastenders'* to vie for ratings that ITV enjoyed with *'Coronation Street'*. It had started during my wilderness period when I had little choice but to watch the telly every night. The series was an instant success and soon the names of the characters, Dirty Den, Nasty Nick Cotton, Angie Watts, Dot Cotton etc were on everyone's lips. The tabloids couldn't get enough of them and Andy and I realised if we could get hold of them it would be box office gold, no matter what night of the week it was.

The stars themselves were little known before the start of the series and we soon found they were ready to capitalise on their period in the spotlight. Unlike the Coronation Street actors who were prevented from making public appearances without the programme's approval; no such restrictions applied to the Eastenders cast.

We duly tracked down their agents and soon we had a procession of them all delivering bumper business. 'Angie Watts', the landlady of the Queen Vic was the first and she was soon followed by 'Nick Cotton' (John Altman) and 'Wicksy' (Nick Berry) as well as several more. We only had to say they were coming and a full house was guaranteed. Nick Berry actually appeared when his first record, *'Every Loser Wins'* was sitting at No 1 in the charts.

At £1,000 a time the costs were easily covered but we approached the Courage Brewery to ask if they'd be interested in the association. They agreed to donate 4 free kegs for every appearance and the revenue from 352 pints sold would largely cover the outlay.

Would that business could always be so simple but you have to ride the waves when they come in like this.

The activity was drawing new customers to the club for the first time and we could see the benefits knocking on to all the sessions.

We also started tapping into other popular shows and were delighted to secure the services of Jason Connery who was starring in *'Robin of Sherwood'* at the time.

He was an instantly recognisable figure at the time – but not to our doormen who had stopped him on the door for not being dressed to the standard we desired!

Perhaps though the lady who really left her mark was Linda Lusardi, famous at the time for being Britain's most popular Page 3 girl. Every few weeks her ample bosom appeared in *'The Sun'* and a large portion of the populace were entranced.

For the second time in my career I was securing the services of a girl made famous for baring her breasts. It's odd what will strike a chord with the great British public – now of course, it's hardly politically correct but people really loved that girl.

We wondered what to do with her ahead of her visit but inspiration came via another very popular TV show that had just caught the public imagination. *'Blind Date'*.

I envisaged Linda in the role of Cilla Black. I'd find the contestants, prepare the silly questions and we'd stage The Big Reveal.

'How are you going to do that?' Andy asked, for we couldn't put a sliding screen on the stage.

'Don't you worry my friend, all will be revealed on the night'.

Andy was sceptical to say the least but he just let me get on with it figuring that just having Linda there was all that we needed.

Eventually, the great lady arrived and she introduced us to her partner, Terry. A very nice guy but he really was built like a brick outhouse.

Linda Lusardi was a delightful lady in every respect. She had been leading a quiet life in Wood Green when she was catapulted to fame after her first appearance in The Sun at the age of 18. She was very modest and amenable and happy to go along with anything we asked of her.

She was even happy to visit the local Royal Alexandra Children's Hospital before her appearance where she displayed a wonderful empathy with the children and all the staff she came across. The press coverage we got from it was a great help of course but it was just so nice to see the girl appreciate the difference she could make just by being there.

That night I gave Linda her brief and whether she had any trepidation about it, I don't know if she had, but she just went for it anyhow. Cilla herself would have had a job to match her. She, like Andy though, couldn't figure out how we were going to stage it all without the famous sliding screen.

'It'll be alright on the night', I tried to assure her but she didn't look convinced.

I rustled up some likely competitors and took them off to a backstage area to brief them. Andy, the DJ, then halted the music and introduced 'our Linda' to a capacity crowd who were fully tuned in to see one of the most famous faces in Britain at that time, renowned more, of course, for her famous chest.

Andy conducted a quick interview with Linda before bringing her over to the Blind Date set where an attractive young lady from the Halifax Building Society was sitting in anticipation of meeting her 'date'. I knew her as a regular and had asked her earlier in the evening if she'd go along with it all.

Linda interviewed her in Cilla style and then it was time to bring on her three options.

'Bring the boys on', cried Linda then watched as three characters with sheets covering their heads took to the stage to helpless laughter from the audience. We had cut eyeholes in the sheets for them with another slit for their mouths but as they perched on their stools they looked more like outriders for the Klu Klux Klan.

It took Linda a moment to compose herself but she went through the format that everyone was so used to seeing every Saturday evening on the telly.

Once the questions were answered it was up to the Halifax Girl to make her choice. There was a daytrip to Dieppe on offer for the Blind Date couple to get to know each other and at the time, that little hop across the channel seemed quite an exotic prize.

The choice was made and then it was time for The Big Reveal. Linda called the two losers forward and whipped off their sheets before inviting Halifax Girl to remove the sheet from her chosen Blind Date. She did it with a real flourish but the underwhelming response from each of them said it all. So much so that we didn't have to fork out for the Dieppe jaunt.

A couple of days later I was in the office when I got a call from Thames Television. It caught me on the hop at first as it was someone claiming to represent the producers of the actual Blind Date programme. They mumbled something about breaching copyright and I thought for a moment we were in for a censure which might cause some problems. Instead, they said they'd heard of our efforts and just wondered if I could arrange some auditions down in Brighton and select a few people to appear adding that I could nominate myself if I wished.

I didn't really fancy going on national television but Martin, my lodger, certainly did and begged to go on the audition. I was happy to put him forward and he made the cut for the national TV show. Not only that, he was the 'chosen one' when he appeared, meaning he got a nice little jolly to the races in Deauville and appeared again a week later.

It was then that we really found out how powerful the medium of popular television really is. Wherever he went for the next few months he was instantly recognised and for years after he continued to be recognised and remembered from taking part in it. He had only expected 15 minutes of fame but it seems now, even his grandchildren will become very aware of the time the old fella was on national television.

When there were no TV formats to milk nor celebrities to make a personal appearance, Andy McGuinness and I would look at every conceivable way we could add a little spice to the lives of our patrons. The discos were great of course but we wanted them talking about the place at work, out of work, everywhere. It had to be the 'go to' venue of choice for the mass market in Brighton where they knew they had to dress to impress to be part of the 1980's In Crowd.

If in doubt we'd resort to the tried and trusted beauty contests. We staged Miss Brighton and Miss Pink Coconut – and the beauty pageants with a twist, i.e. Miss In-String, Miss Lovely Lingerie etc.

Inevitably, a lot of the same girls would enter all of them. There was an amazing camaraderie that was built up amongst them all when one might have expected a few petty jealousies. One night though, a new competitor turned up who made them all stop in their tracks. She also made everyone else present take a look at themselves and their own prejudices.

The procedures for all the beauty pageants were by now firmly established and we'd follow a routine familiar to contestants and the audience alike. On this particular night, we didn't expect anything other than a routine show. There were around 18 contestants and most of them were well versed in the drill.

We would usually check the girls in, show them to the dressing rooms before preparing 'the cards' which contained the essential details of each of the contestants. Usually, this just consisted of their names, where they were from and perhaps details of their job and interests. The DJ or presenter would use the cards when commenting as the girls paraded individually around the dancefloor.

DJ Andy would usually pop his head in to say 'Hi' to the ladies, tell them how he'd be conducting proceedings etc., then he'd take the cards and go off before I would signal for him to start the contest.

On this occasion when he arrived at the dressing room door, I was about to introduce a new contestant to the other girls so I asked Andy if he'd leave us alone for a few minutes. Andy seemed surprised at my brusqueness but he hadn't got wind of the surprise the girls had just encountered.

The new contestant had arrived later than all the rest and I knew when she presented herself that she was uncertain and afraid but I soon learned that she had the guts to overcome her inner turmoil.

'Lynette' as she introduced herself was transgender and known to her friends as 'Steve' until just a few months earlier. It was apparent too that 'Steve' hadn't been totally eradicated from her appearance. I think she was probably aware that I was taken aback a little, no doubt she had grown used to such a reaction but she simply said to me that taking part in the contest was something she had to do.

I took her in to meet the other girls who by now had changed into their swimsuits and were ready to parade. Some of the girls thought at first that this was just a very bad taste joke that I was playing on them and started to say as much but thankfully a few others read the situation straightaway and kindly showed 'Lynette' to the changing area.

When Andy came knocking I feared his reaction might not be so instantly understanding and that he might give vent to his own feelings. If that happened, I thought Lynette would be destroyed if she felt the subject of ridicule but I was conscious too that it may be a whole lot worse once she stepped out in front of the Friday crowd with a few bevvies down them.

'I'll be with you in a couple of minutes Andy; just give us a moment'.

'What's the matter? What's the matter?' he insisted, he sensed something was very much amiss.

I hustled him out of the dressing room making out one of the girls was upset about something; which was not being untruthful.

'I'll call you back in a tick but check these in the meantime' I said giving him the cards which I figured would buy a little time.

'Ok', he said but he remained unconvinced.

By the time I got back to the dressing room Lynette was ready and so were all the other girls. The girls seemed to be accepting of the cuckoo who had landed in their nest but all of us wondered how the crowd would react. We wouldn't have to wait long to find out now.

I called one of the bouncers over and asked him to start clearing the floor in readiness for the parade about to start. Andy bounded down from the stage saying to me, 'I'll see the girls now'.

'Nah', I said 'we're running too late, just go straight into it.

He was quite narked and irritated as he liked to keep to his routines but I had the first girl about to take to the floor and he had little choice but to go along with it.

Once the first couple were out, Andy soon settled down into his usual silver-tongued patter. He'd use the cards to get started with, then add a few little ad-libs as he saw fit. Often, he'd be so wrapped up in his own little jests that he'd fail to look up and see the girls themselves.

That's exactly what happened when he got to the final contestant who I had deliberately scheduled to come out last.

'And finally, we have our last contestant; Lynette from Woodingdean….'

Andy didn't pick up on the sharp intake of breath from what seemed the whole audience as Lynette tottered into view.

'Lynette is 22 years old and works in a veterinary prac….prac…practise….' and his voice just tailed off to a murmur.

Andy had noticed that the audience had gone very quiet and he glanced over his prompt card to see Lynette making her way uncertainly around the dancefloor.

His jaw dropped, he tried to speak but was momentarily paralysed.

Just then a lone voice wailed.

'It's a geezer!'

The silence gave way to uproar. Laughing, shouting, whistling. Lynette's effect on them all was mesmerising.

Andy looked over at me and glared.

'You've set me up', he mouthed at me but I just shrugged from the edge of the dancefloor and I could see that he could see the funny side of it all. But was there a funny side to it?

Lynette had strode out with quite unbelievable courage. In effect, she was saying; *'I Am What I Am'*.

Andy composed himself sufficiently to conduct a short interview with Lynette. In those few minutes, it was as if the audience was taking stock of itself. Yes, it was a shock, yes, it was a bit funny but yes too, this person had shown phenomenal courage in putting themselves out there.

Lynette was never going to win the contest that night but as she tottered off there was a ripple of applause followed by a great wave of clapping. She had encountered people with ingrained attitudes so commonplace at the time but she also succeeded in challenging the outlook of many of them in a way that few had ever witnessed. I never saw Lynette again but I can never forget her.

All these nights were now being shared with Rosie. The staff eventually learned that we were an item and it didn't prove as awkward as we first feared.

The only question that remained was what future path would we be taking and would it be together or apart?

After Donna, I found it easier to be faithful and I appreciated the qualities and talents of Rosie who was a quiet and very appealing girl and so it got to the stage when I thought she was one I was happy to devote myself too and I hoped she felt the same way.

Just after a year since I'd met her I decided to propose to her but not before telling Carrie down in Plymouth to whom I was still getting down to as often as possible. She wished me well and I thanked her for that though with a sense of enormous guilt. I felt I was making a platform in life whilst she was still in something of a predicament that was largely down to me. I had hoped and prayed down the years that somehow things could have been so different and much better, if only for her, but that hadn't come to pass and we were both just getting on with Life even though we still had that unbreakable tie to each other.

Rosie and I got engaged on her 23rd birthday just before Christmas that year. My path was set fair, all that remained now was to pursue that exit route that I had decided I must seek.

Because of the Eastenders tie-up, I had established a very good working relationship with senior managers from the Courage Brewery who were now frequent visitors to the club both on business and socially.

In the autumn, they had introduced me to the local representative, a very quiet chap called Peter Charlesworth. He had seemed a nice guy but it struck me that he was at odds with the lifestyle of someone in that job. Just after Christmas, when his boss Jack Clark visited, I asked how Peter was assuming he might be on holiday.

Jack told me that he had resigned as he found he was physically and mentally unable to do the job. His confidence was so lacking that he found himself unable to go in and talk business with his customers. He had fought the condition for a long time but with his results indicating a problem, Jack had had to investigate.

It was a terrible personal tragedy for the man and his wife and young family. It was evidently acute depression that he was suffering from but it soon became clear that the situation was not easily resolved. I later learned that Peter and his family emigrated to Australia in the hope of making a new start.

I asked Jack if they had anybody lined up and he said they would be recruiting shortly for someone to cover Sussex.

My heart skipped a beat and I found myself asking would it be worth me applying?

Jack gave me encouragement straightaway. I would have to formally apply but he promised he would endorse me to the Sales Director, Sid Liddiard, who I had met on a few occasions.

I went home that night thinking could Life really have improved so much for me that I could now be contemplating a 'proper job'; one with real prospects and likely status. Not only that but it would be one which I'd be starting married life with?

There was a long way to go though, Jack had warned me there would be a lot of applicants and I knew too that the demands of The Pink Coconut would not be lessening in the coming weeks.

The next two or three weeks were times of great uncertainty. Whilst I was preparing for interviews with Courage, I was repeatedly being asked if I fancied this position or that with First Leisure. They were a growing company offering some excellent opportunities to those they had regard for but if there was no enthusiasm being shown then it was certain that those people would be passed over in future.

At first, it wasn't too hard to say that a position was too far away or in a sector that didn't appeal but when plum jobs became available closer to home people began to wonder why I didn't throw my hat in the ring. I'd say I was having too much fun with Andy or I liked being beside the seaside but I really needed Courage to make up their mind soon.

Eventually, for these very reasons, I felt compelled to force the issue with Courage. There was also the small matter that I was now getting married.

So much was going on in Life at that time that it was a wonder I could concentrate at all sometimes. I had also sold my house and recently purchased a new place in the Preston Park area of town though I realised that doing that would make it hard to be flexible with First Leisure, should Courage fail to make an offer to me.

Eventually, I got word from Courage. Jack Clark broke the news to me and he seemed as delighted as I was. We quickly sorted a starting date and agreed when I should serve notice on First Leisure. Ironically, I would now be looking after all their outlets in Sussex.

I'd like to think Andy McGuinness was a little disappointed when I handed in my notice. We had worked very well together and I was indebted to him for the break he gave me which in truth got my life back on track.

It was hard to think I'd no longer have to face disputes on front doors, have to do any more tedious stock controls or have to dream up ever more ridiculous stunts or promotion nights. I wouldn't be too bothered now about what was in vogue musically or whether we had DJs capable of delivering to the punters.

As for those punters, well no longer would I be giving the ladies amongst them, an admiring glance, would I?

I'd given eleven good years to that life. There had been some enormous highs and some desperately depressing lows. I'd met superstars and super slobs, Prime Ministers and prime losers.

My whole time in that industry was a changing social tableau. I'd seen huge changes in music tastes, fashion tastes and phenomenal changes in social attitudes. One couldn't imagine a Gay Night being staged in Plymouth in 1976; indeed, it was rare to see an openly gay person in public. By the time I exited a decade later all the barriers were coming down with Lynette's appearance in the beauty contest leaving a particularly lasting impression.

Whilst attitudes regarding sexual orientation had changed considerably, issues regarding race and religion were more nuanced. In Plymouth, every minority seemed worthy of suspicion be it blacks, Jews, Muslims etc. I'd even encountered The Plymouth Brethren who found me, a Catholic, as potentially untrustworthy. Thankfully the Brethren were not seen to be prominent in clubland.

I remembered that Rank House Note (an internal memo) imploring managers to tell their DJs at one outlet not to play reggae or Soul Music because it only encouraged black customers who would put off their more desirable clientele. Sad, but very true as was the attitude of some establishments in liberal and very hip Brighton who would ensure that only a certain quota of 'ragheads' (Iranians) be allowed in.

Ironically those 'ragheads' over the following years became part of the established order themselves in Brighton. They started to control a large element of the security operation in the city before running many of the bars, restaurants and clubs themselves. I have never seen them systematically discriminate against any minority.

Along the way I'd seen the best of people and the worst of people. Maybe that happens in every walk of life but I haven't encountered anything since in life where the best and the worst are presented in such sharp contrast so frequently. It was a highly addictive way of life which I couldn't get enough of at times but which I couldn't wait to get away from in the end.

In truth though, the nightclub era of which I have spoken of is of a bygone age. Between 2005 and 2015, late night dancing venues in Britain dropped from 3,144 to 1,733. It had been in decline before 2005 and it has reduced further since 2015. There is little chance, it would seem, of there ever being a significant renaissance.

Legislation such as late licensing for bars and the smoking bans account for a large part of the early decline in particular; but social attitudes have also played a big part not to mention technological advancement.

Of course, the internet, You Tube etc were unimaginable concepts back then and sourcing your music by downloading would have been hard to envisage.

Ironically, my beloved Northern Soul scene has been reinvigorated by embracing technology. Once the preserve of the seediest and most basic venues, the internet has spread the word for that scene in a way that had never seemed possible. The music is now easily accessible and suddenly Over 50s and 60s are keeping the faith with a new younger demographic in some quite fabulous venues which would once have been thought an anathema and in such numbers, that would once have staggered belief.

That's the exception though and certainly not the rule. I'm just glad it all happened for me when it did and at a time when thanks to John Travolta and company, disco, became such a magic word and a magic way of life.